Damian Platt was born in 1972 in
up in London, he studied modern
University. He subsequently spent
with Redemptorist Catholic missionaries in Tocantins, in the
northern interior of Brazil. There followed eight years at the
International Secretariat of Amnesty International in London. In
2005, he relocated to Rio de Janeiro to work for AfroReggae, a
favela-based youth and culture organisation, which he described
in his book *Culture is Your Weapon*, co-authored with Patrick
Neate. Later he teamed up with TED prizewinning French artist
JR to work on his *Women are Heroes* project in Rio. In 2019, he
mobilised a team of local and international volunteers to build
a world-class skate park in the Maré favela complex. In 2011,
he completed a Master of Studies in International Relations at
Cambridge University – the same year in which he was awarded
an MBE by the Foreign Office of the British Government, for
"services to community development and human rights" in Rio
de Janeiro. He is a qualified teacher in the UK, since completing
the Teach First leadership programme in 2018.

NOTHING BY ACCIDENT

BRAZIL ON THE EDGE

NOTHING BY ACCIDENT

BRAZIL ON THE EDGE

DAMIAN PLATT

Copyright © Damian Platt, 2020

1 3 5 7 9 10 8 6 4 2

Typeset in Adobe Garamond by mexington.co.uk

Printed and bound by KDP

The moral right of the author has been asserted.

All rights reserved. Without limiting the rights under copyright reserved above, no part of this publication may be reproduced, stored or introduced into a retrieval system, or transmitted, in any form or by any means (electronic, mechanical, photocopying, recording or otherwise), without the prior written permission of both the copyright owner and the publisher of this book.

A CIP catalogue record for this book is available from the British Library.

ISBN 978-1-83853-485-1
eISBN 978-1-83853-486-8

IMAGE CREDITS

Map by João Vitor Menezes using icons by Yorlmar Campos, Focus Lab, Gregor Cresnar and Valter Bispo under Creative Commons license from the Noun Project.

All photos by the author except for "Women are Heroes, Providência" used by kind permission of JR.

The use of Marielle Franco's image is authorised by the "Instituto Marielle Franco" www.institutomariellefranco.org.

PREVIOUS PUBLICATIONS

Culture is Our Weapon: Making Music and Changing Lives in Rio de Janeiro
(Penguin 2010)

Cultura é a Nossa Arma: AfroReggae nas Favelas do Rio (Editora Record 2008)

Culture is Our Weapon: AfroReggae in the Favelas of Rio (Latin America Bureau 2006)

COVER PHOTO

A poster in central Rio de Janeiro asks who ordered the killing of Marielle Franco.

For Pinga, Rousseau and all their friends.

in memoriam
Gabriel Rodrigues, Marielle Franco
and Fr. Matt Ryan C.Ss.R

CONTENTS

Preface 1
   Key Characters 5
   Some Key Events 9
Introduction: Homicidal Times 13

Part One: Chaos

1. Poor and Admirable Favela! 27
2. Waging War: A Way of Life in Rio de Janeiro 50
3. Peace lost: The Failure of Pacification 66

Part Two: The Greatest Show

4. Cocaine: White Gold 91
5. The Animal Game: Misrule of Law 104
6. Beija-Flor: Samba is Power 122
7. The Shining Star of Brazilian Communication . 141
8. Xangô's Curse 153
9. The Parade 164

Part Three: Truth and Lies

10. Truth   181
11. Molotov   196

Part Four: The Hornet's Nest

12. Marielle   227
13. Barra Villas   239
14. The Hornet's Nest   247
15. Because the Show Will Go On   256

Afterword   262
Further Reading   265
Selected Bibliography   267
Endnotes   270

Baixada Fluminense

NILÓPOLIS

IRAJÁ

BANGU

REALENGO

MADUREIRA

Rio de Janeiro City

WEST ZONE

CITY OF GOD

JACAREPAGUÁ

RIO DAS PEDRAS

VARGEM PEQUENA

VARGEM GRANDE

BARRA DA TIJUCA

BARRA VILLAS

RECREIO DOS BANDEIRANTES

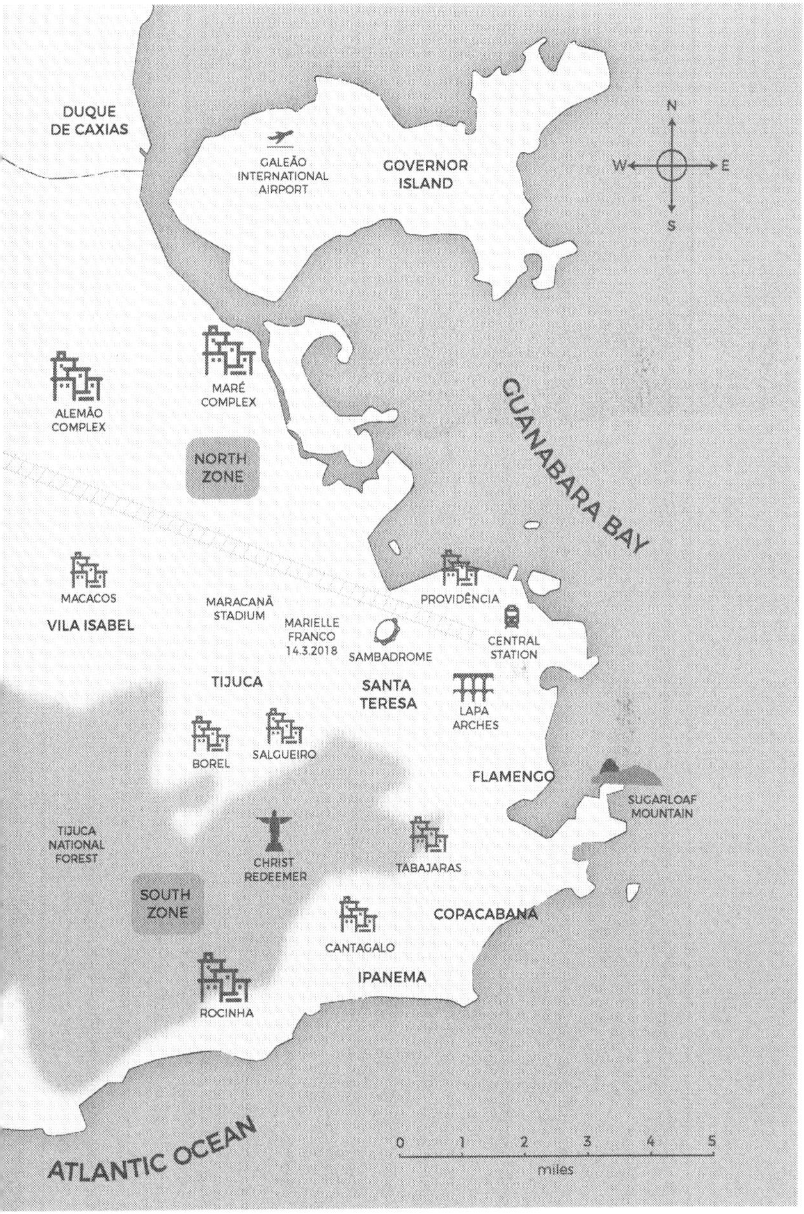

DUQUE DE CAXIAS
GALEÃO INTERNATIONAL AIRPORT
GOVERNOR ISLAND
N
W
E
S
MARÉ COMPLEX
ALEMÃO COMPLEX
NORTH ZONE
GUANABARA BAY
PROVIDÊNCIA
MACACOS
VILA ISABEL
MARACANÃ STADIUM
MARIELLE FRANCO 14.3.2018
SAMBADROME
CENTRAL STATION
TIJUCA
SANTA TERESA
LAPA ARCHES
BOREL
SALGUEIRO
FLAMENGO
SUGARLOAF MOUNTAIN
TIJUCA NATIONAL FOREST
CHRIST REDEEMER
TABAJARAS
SOUTH ZONE
COPACABANA
CANTAGALO
IPANEMA
ROCINHA
ATLANTIC OCEAN
0 1 2 3 4 5
miles

"Our most terrible heritage is to always carry with us
the torturer's scar branded on our soul,
ready to explode in racist and classist brutality."

– Darcy Ribeiro,
The Brazilian People

PREFACE

THIS BOOK IS BASED ON MY experiences living and working in Rio de Janeiro over the past fifteen years. I focus on what I have learnt about the operation of violence in the city and how it intersects with organised crime, corruption and politics. Recent years in Brazil have been fast-moving and tumultuous; I do not attempt to describe or include everything that has taken place. The impeachment of Dilma Rousseff, the imprisonment of former president Lula and the "Car Wash" corruption scandal all contributed to the rise of Jair Bolsonaro and will doubtless be well addressed in other works.

My personal involvement with Brazil began at the age of 21 in 1994, when I arrived alone as a backpacker in Rio de Janeiro. I quickly found myself the target of an extortion scam conducted by police. Following this, I spent several days without money. I passed much time in conversation with a street-dweller (not exactly a "kid", he had my age) called Getúlio. One day, when I had not eaten, and had no funds for an evening meal, he frogmarched me across the road and paid for my dinner. The experience marked me. I decided to return to Brazil to investigate the dynamics underpinning this topsy-turvy situation. I also hoped to repay Getúlio's kindness, if not to him in person, to the Brazilian people, many of whom I got on well with.

In 1996 and 1997, I spent eighteen months living and working with Redemptorists, Catholic missionaries working with liberation theology in Tocantins, a large rural state in the interior of Brazil, about 12 hours bus ride north of Brasília, the federal capital. Essentially, liberation theology came about during Latin America's Cold War dictatorships as a strategy employed by progressive sectors of the Catholic Church to raise political consciousness and create nuclei of education and resistance. Following the return to democracy in 1988, this form of politicised Catholicism fell out of favour in Brazil. However, many individual priests, nuns and churches continue to apply its principles in their work. Marielle Franco, raised in a strongly Catholic family, was a catechist during her teens in the Maré favela complex. She personified the benefits of this approach.

With the Redemptorists, I made many visits to isolated rural communities. These encounters enabled me to better understand the lives of the many migrants who populate Rio and São Paulo favelas. During this time, I was lucky to come under the tutelage of Matt Ryan, a gentle Irish missionary from a Tipperary farming background. I learnt many lessons on how to behave as a foreigner in Brazil from Matt, who sadly died in 2019.

I subsequently spent eight years, five of them working on Brazil, employed at the Americas Research programme at the International Secretariat of Amnesty International. During this period I made numerous trips across the country, investigating and reporting on matters such as conditions of detention, lethal state violence, torture and violence against rural or indigenous populations. During multiple visits to Rio, I began to build networks of friends and to develop an affinity and feeling for the city. I eventually left Amnesty International and relocated to Rio to work for AfroReggae, a favela-based youth and culture organisation. This experience is described in the book called *Culture is Our Weapon* (Penguin 2010), which I co-authored with British novelist Patrick Neate.

Following AfroReggae, I joined forces with the French artist JR and Rio photographer Maurício Hora to work on the Brazilian leg of JR's international "Women are Heroes" project. JR and Maurício subsequently founded a cultural centre, the Casa Amarela, at the top of Providência, the first urban community in Brazil to be called *favela*. Maurício and the Casa Amarela led

Saturday morning at Maré Favela Skatepark, August 2019.

the local response to the COVID-19 pandemic, distributing food packages and installing washbasins across the community.

In 2019, I fundraised for and mobilised a team of local and international volunteers, together with a project called Make Life Skate Life, to build a world-class skate park in the Maré favela complex, one of many flashpoints for armed violence in Rio. Skateboarding is a fantastic tool for promoting social mobility, physical and mental health, creativity and resilience – all fundamental for young people growing up in a conflict zone.

I hope readers will understand that Rio de Janeiro is not always the tragedy described in these pages. It is also a fantastic, exhilarating, culturally exuberant city that is home to an inspiring, imaginative and welcoming population.

Key Characters

Beltrame, José Mariano. Public Security Secretary for Rio de Janeiro (2007–2016). Responsible for reforms to policing and public safety in the city in the run-up to the 2014 FIFA World Cup and 2016 Olympic Games. A driving force behind the UPP (*Unidade de Polícia Pacificadora*) favela "pacification" policing programme.

Bolsonaro, Carlos. City councillor in Rio since 2001. Jair Bolsonaro's second son.

Bolsonaro, Eduardo. Elected to federal congress in 2018 with 1.843.735 votes, the most ever for a federal congressman. Jair Bolsonaro's third son.

Bolsonaro, Flávio. Member of Rio state parliament, 2003–2018. Elected federal senator in 2018 with more than 4 million votes. Jair Bolsonaro's eldest son.

Bolsonaro, Jair. Former army captain and politician. Elected President of Brazil in 2018.

Boni (José Bonifácio de Oliveira Sobrinho). Director of programming and vice-president of the Globo network (1967–1997).

Brizola, Leonel (1922–2004). Politician. Governor of Rio de Janeiro for two mandates in the 1980s and 1990s.

Cabral, Sérgio. Governor of Rio (2007–2014). Imprisoned on corruption charges in 2018 with sentences totalling more than 280 years. More than $40 million of gold, jewels and cash was repatriated to Brazil from personal accounts he held in Switzerland.

David, Anísio Abrãao. Founder member of LIESA (*Liga Independente das Escolas de Samba do Rio de Janeiro*), samba schools organisation, and *cúpula* of the *jogo do bicho* (the illegal animal game lottery). Patron of Beija-Flor samba school.

da Nóbrega, Adriano (Killed by police in 2020). Former policeman. Suspected assassin, militiaman and founder member of The Crime Office. Linked to the Garcia family and Flávio Bolsonaro.

de Andrade, Castor (1926–1997). Flamboyant founder member of LIESA and *cúpula* of the *jogo do bicho*. Patron of Mocidade Independente samba school.

de Andrade, Rogério. Nephew of Castor de Andrade. Patron of Mocidade Independente samba school.

de Queiroz, Élcio. Former policeman. Accused of driving the car from which a gunman fired the shots that killed Marielle Franco.

Drummond, Baron (1825–1897). Property developer, entrepreneur and creator of the *jogo do bicho*.

Franco, Marielle (1979–2018). Human rights defender, politician and feminist. Assassinated 14 March 2018.

Freixo, Marcelo. Teacher, human rights defender and politician. Elected member of Rio de Janeiro state parliament (2007–2018). Elected to Federal congress 2018. Worked closely with Marielle Franco and presided a 2008 parliamentary investigation into militias that led to charges against 226 individuals, including 7 elected politicians.

Garcia, Bid (Killed 2020). Brother of Maninho Garcia.

Garcia, Maninho (Killed 2004 age 42). *Jogo do bicho* banker, son of Miro Garcia.

Garcia, Mirinho (Killed 2017 aged 27). Son of Maninho Garcia, grandson of Miro Garcia.

Garcia, Miro (Died natural causes 2004 age 77). *Jogo do bicho* banker, *cúpula* member and patron of Salgueiro samba school.

Garcia, Shanna. Daughter of Maninho Garcia, twin sister of Tamara Garcia. Granddaughter of Miro Garcia.

Garcia, Tamara. Daughter of Maninho Garcia, twin sister of Shanna Garcia. Granddaughter of Miro Garcia.

Guerra, Cláudio. Former police chief. Military regime agent turned evangelical pastor.

Guimarães, Ailton Jorge. Former army captain and alleged torturer. Founder member of LIESA and *cúpula* of the *jogo do bicho*. Patron of Vila Isabel samba school.

Laíla. Carnival director at Beija-Flor samba school between 1995–2018.

Lessa, Ronnie. Retired policeman. Suspected assassin. Accused of firing bullets that killed Marielle Franco.

Lula (Luiz Inácio Lula da Silva). Metalworker and trade unionist. President of Brazil (2003–2010). Imprisoned on corruption charges in 2018, released 2019. His imprisonment prevented him for running for office against Jair Bolsonaro and is understood by many to have been politically motivated.

Malhães, Colonel Paulo (1938–2014). Military regime torturer and assassin. Killed in suspicious circumstances after making extensive statements describing his activities to the 2014 National Truth Commission.

Marinho, Roberto (1904–2003). Owner of Globo group.

Meinel, Valério (1940–1997). Prizewinning investigative journalist.

Paiva, Rubens (1929–1971). Civil engineer and politician killed by the military junta.

Queiroz, Fabrício. Policeman and chief of staff for Flávio Bolsonaro (2007–2018). Accused of managing corruption scheme in Flávio Bolsonaro's office. Close friends with Jair Bolsonaro and Adriano da Nóbrega.

Ribeiro, Darcy (1922–2007). Anthropologist, writer and politician.

Rousseff, Dilma. President of Brazil (2011–2016). Impeached halfway through her second term in circumstances described by many as a "soft coup".

Siciliano, Marcello. Rio de Janeiro politician. Falsely accused of ordering the assassination of Marielle Franco.

Witzel, Wilson. Judge and politician. Elected Governor for the state of Rio de Janeiro in 2018.

Some Key Events

1500 The Portuguese claim Brazil.

1534 Brazil divided into 15 hereditary "captaincies".

1565 Foundation of Rio de Janeiro.

1808 The Portuguese royal family relocate to Rio de Janeiro.

1831 Slave trading forbidden by law.

1888 Slavery abolished in all its forms.

1888 Baron Drummond opens his zoo in Vila Isabel.

1889 Portuguese monarchy overthrown and Republic declared.

1891 First Brazilian constitution.

1892 Baron Drummond invents the *jogo do bicho* lottery to raise funds for his zoo.

1897 Canudos uprising in Bahia.

1925 Irineu Marinho founds O Globo newspaper.

1932 First sponsored competition between samba schools in Rio de Janeiro.

1941 *Jogo do bicho* prohibited by federal decree.

1946 Gambling banned in Brazil.

1960 Brazil's capital relocated from Rio de Janeiro to Brasília.

1964 Military coup.

1965 Roberto Marinho, son of Irineu Marinho, launches TV Globo.

1968 Institutional Act AI-5 suspends constitutional rights for all Brazilians.

1979 Amnesty declaration and subsequent return of political exiles signals softening of military rule.

1984 New sambadrome built in Rio de Janeiro. *Cúpula* of *jogo do bicho* bankers establish themselves as Carnival parade organisers through foundation of LIESA.

1988 New Brazilian constitution.

1989 First direct elections since 1964 coup lead to victory for Fernando Collor.

1992 Congress votes to impeach Collor.

1994 Fernando Henrique Cardoso elected. *Plano Real* introduced to stabilise economy.

1995 Darcy Ribeiro publishes *The Brazilian People*.

1998 Cardoso re-elected.

2002 Lula elected to head first left-wing government in more than 40 years.

2005 Lula's government rocked by corruption allegations.

2006 Lula re-elected.

2010 Dilma Rousseff, Lula's successor, elected as first woman president.

2013 Civil unrest and mass protests sweep Brazil.

2014 Rouseff re-elected. "Car wash" corruption investigation reveals massive corruption network involving politicians, state companies and businesses across country. Brazil hosts World Cup losing 7-1 in the semi-final to Germany. Colonel Paulo Malhães, a former secret service operative, is murdered within weeks of testifying before a Truth Commission documenting military regime abuses.

2016 Rio de Janeiro hosts Olympic Games. In April, congress votes to impeach Dilma Rousseff. Sérgio Cabral, former governor of the state of Rio, receives more than 200 years in prison sentences for corruption.

2018 Marielle Franco is murdered in Rio de Janeiro. Former President Lula, ahead in the polls and due to stand for re-election, is imprisoned on corruption charges understood by many to be politically motivated. His rival, Jair Bolsonaro, is elected President.

2020 During the COVID-19 pandemic, President Jair Bolsonaro supports demonstrations calling for the closure of federal congress and Brazil's supreme court and in favour of a return to military rule. The President also discourages lockdowns, blaming state authorities for economic disruption. Two ministers of health resign. His Minister of Justice resigns, claiming that Bolsonaro attempted to interfere with the federal police force in order to protect his family from corruption investigations.

"Violence has always been and, more than ever,
is the primordial and decisive issue facing Brazilian society."

— Fernando de Barros e Silva,
Piauí magazine, May 2020

Introduction

HOMICIDAL TIMES

RIO, AUGUST 2019. MY PHONE PINGS. After a happy Saturday at the beach I'm waiting at an underground station for a train. Bad news. Pedro, a longstanding, respected human rights activist and the owner of the house where I live, is telling me that Gabriel, the son of our beloved housekeeper, has died a violent death. That the burial will be tomorrow.

Now I remember what I had put out of my mind during my day of sun and sand. As I was preparing to leave that morning, Alessandra had rushed past me out of the gate to get a taxi home. She had just arrived for work, when relatives called to inform her that Gabriel hadn't returned from his usual Friday night shift driving an Uber around Rio's sprawling dormitory suburbs.

My phone pings again with an update from Pedro: "Facts still unknown. He is disappeared."

A story emerges over the next few days. Gabriel's last customer was "Steel Leo" a prominent member of one of the drug dealing gangs, locally known as "factions", that dominate many of Rio's favelas. Leo used to run a big community in the west of the city. But a paramilitary group had violently expelled his crew. Such illegal groups are called *milícia* (militia) in Rio and are primarily made up of off-duty or former police. Since the early 2000s they have grown dramatically both in number and influence. Their power base is Rio's *Zona Oeste* (West Zone), home to several million *cariocas* (Rio residents). Here the militia elect the politicians.

Steel Leo, who was on the run, had not only lost his fiefdom but was also helping to put corrupt police behind bars. In 2017, he testified to making weekly cash payments of US$ 20,000 to members of the BOPE, Rio's feared military police commando unit, in return for protection.

While Steel Leo had many enemies, Gabriel was apparently a victim of circumstance. After collecting Leo on Friday night, he drove the whistle-blower to a rendez-vous with a girlfriend at one of the many short-stay "love" motels found on the edges of Brazilian cities. Upon exiting the motel gunmen ambushed his car, leaving Steel Leo dead in the forecourt. Gabriel disappeared.

Alessandra didn't return to our house for weeks. Instead, members of Pedro's family reversed her daily commute, making long journeys out to her suburb. There they joined neighbours in comforting her as they dealt with journalists, filtering news and gossip for some hope of Gabriel's return. The first days were filled with speculation and false leads. Alessandra travelled by car to visit a West Zone militia leader in a neighbourhood where Gabriel was supposed to have been taken. But no one there knew anything. One night she joined friends and neighbours with torches on a search of wasteland near the motel, where apparently – a body had been spotted. Nothing. Then the stories petered out, leaving Alessandra in a limbo of hope, anguish and despair. Now Gabriel was officially a "disappeared person".

In his early teens, Gabriel sometimes came to work with his mother. Charismatic and engaging, we would sit in the kitchen with him and his mother and engage in the comic banter at which *cariocas* excel. Conversations in the kitchen were both manifestations of, and an antidote to, social inequality. While the employer-servant hierarchy was unquestioned, the informal conviviality of such occasions forged strong bonds. Time spent together was time learning about each other. In the context of the screaming social violence and disparity outside, these moments provided comfort and relief. Our home in the affluent heart of the city, equally – felt Gabriel's disappearance.

Number 472 was more community centre than mere house. An extended social unit of relatives, dogs, cats and friends lived on the premises. These consisted of a main house, a studio, an apartment, a veranda with an extra kitchen and bathrooms and an outhouse where I slept. Tucked into a hillside, virgin tropical rainforest covered the slopes above the property, which looked towards a mesmerising vista of city and sea. A perfect venue for parties and meetings, 472 was also a popular social hub for Rio's human rights activists and peace-seekers.

Alessandra wasn't the only woman who worked at 472. A close friend and neighbour of hers, called Helvia, shared the responsibilities. The pair constituted an impressive tag team. When not working at 472, Helvia also looked after two friends of the household, a couple who had begun a relationship at the house and were later to be married there.

Their wedding had taken place on a warm Saturday afternoon in 2010. Marielle's father led her into the garden past flower arrangements floating on the swimming pool. A leading politician led the ceremony, a samba band the festivities.[1] This was a happy, memorable occasion and when the couple moved into an apartment nearby, Helvia went to work for them on her days off. Marielle and her husband thus joined the extended social network emanating from the kitchen at 472.

Although they separated a few years after their marriage, the couple remained close friends. Marielle was embarking on a political career. Her former husband remained her adviser and confidante. Helvia continued to work for them both.

In 2016, Marielle ran for election as *vereadora* (city councillor), and won, with one of the highest returns in the city. She quickly rose to prominence as defender of the disadvantaged and as a person unafraid to denounce the homicidal violence of Rio's police. Charismatic, quick-witted and tenacious, a formidable career lay ahead of her. She was a life force to be reckoned with. Too strong a force, certain parties decided. On 14th March 2018, as she returned home from an event after dark, a meticulously planned assassination left her, and her driver, dead.

Marielle Franco suddenly became world famous for the most tragic reason. And when an enormous crowd turned out to see her coffin, it was clear this crime would not pass quietly. An anguished community of supporters, which included many Afro-Brazilian women who recognised her leadership and inspiration, took the callous executions as a call to arms. The outcry dominated local and international headlines for days.

---

[1] Samba, both a style of music and a dance, is often described as Brazil's national music.

The network of friends and acquaintances at 472 grieved. Marielle's family weathered the media storm. Her ex-husband stayed quiet and spoke little. He did, however, make one point clear. Marielle had never received death threats. He saw her a few days before the tragedy and spent several hours discussing her plans and worries. She did not once mention fears for her own safety. Marielle's murder was a strike out of darkness.

Such is life and death in Rio. Violence is routine, impacting families and friendship groups the whole time. At 472, two tragedies within little over a year, while affecting the household equally, were to have radically different public repercussions. Gabriel became a statistic, one of many people who "disappear" each day in Rio's suburbs; Marielle, a global icon. What is more, the investigation into her murder eventually led, literally, to Brazilian President Jair Bolsonaro's front door.

THIS BOOK DESCRIBES LIFE IN RIO DE JANEIRO against the backdrop of Brazil's boom and bust years of the early 21st century. From the optimism afforded by socially progressive Cardoso and Lula presidential mandates, dreams of becoming a global power and force for good on the world stage, discovery of huge offshore oil deposits and winning the right to host both the 2014 FIFA World Cup and the 2016 Olympic Games.

Then, the collapse into harsh reality begins. Massive street protests, public disorder and civil disobedience; a humiliating 7-1 World Cup defeat to Germany; failure of the underwater oil reserves to generate revenue; a massive corruption scandal at Petrobras, the state energy giant; with the extension of this corruption scandal into every nook and cranny of the political system. The dubious impeachment of President Dilma Rousseff and imprisonment of Lula with scant material evidence, follow. Finally, the death knell for optimism arrives; the election to President of a formerly obscure politician from the shadows, a champion of torture and military dictatorships; a peddler of hate. How did one of the world's most exuberant and well-resourced countries experience such a spectacular collapse? How could this sympathetic, creative people elect a monster?

Insecurity, state violence and politics complement each other in Brazil. When Jair Bolsonaro publicly championed the killing of criminal suspects ("if a policeman kills 10, 15 or 20 with 30 bullets each he must be decorated, not charged") he deployed traditional populist rhetoric used by hardliner candidates come election time.[1] However, the 2018 election campaign pushed further than usual, with loud public promises to make it easier for more police to kill more people. Despite already frightening numbers of police killings, individual cases of which are rarely scrutinised, Bolsonaro committed to the introduction of new legal mechanisms to protect killer police from investigation. In Rio, Wilson Witzel, an unknown former judge running for the state governorship, used terminology normally reserved for the killing of cattle when pledging to deploy snipers in favelas. João Doria, gubernatorial candidate in São Paulo, offered to pay the legal costs for police investigated after fatal shootings. The homicidal posturing paid off. All three candidates won comfortably. None of them contemplated tackling root causes of violence. They consciously sought to perpetuate them. In Brazil, violence is a *modus operandi*.

Following a last-minute endorsement by the Bolsonaro family (Jair has three sons who also hold political positions) Witzel shot from 1% in early polls to a 41% second round victory. Taking office in January, Rio's new governor did not delay in delivering the promised violence. In a few hours in February 2019, during a single operation in a favela, his police shot and killed 13 suspects. These included nine young men in a house, who, according to witnesses, were trying to give themselves up. During Witzel's first 90 days in office police killed 434 suspects, beating all prior records and accounting for 50% of violent deaths in the state of Rio. By the end of 2019, Witzel's police force had shot and killed 1810 alleged suspects, the highest annual number on record and almost double the 1003 victims of police fatalities for the entire USA that year.[2] Standard practice is to register these killings as deaths in confrontation. However, research has consistently proven that extrajudicial executions are frequently the norm. In 2009, a Rio public prosecutor told Human Rights Watch that "almost all" the resistance killings he investigated were "farces".[3] In 2020 lethal police violence and operations in favelas in Rio continue at full steam; they did even under COVID-19 lockdown.

The instant transformation of Bolsonaro and Witzel's pledges into reality, demonstrates precisely how lethal state violence is deployed to regulate and maintain Brazil's social inequality. Killer cops, drug traffickers and death squads have long terrorised low-income communities across the nation. In rural areas, local police and hired gunmen provide such a service. In cities and their peripheries, absence of the state and lack of regulation in poor neighbourhoods and favelas offer a wealth of illicit opportunity. Whoever provides security in these areas can step in to control the local economy and provision of services. Rio's militias are the latest manifestation of such parastatal despotism. For such groups, public endorsement of the police as a killing machine is an implicit call to arms. Cameroonian political theorist Achille Mbembe calls this process – the political management of vulnerable populations through their exposure to death – "necropolitics". He has identified its implementation and expansion at a global scale.[4]

Nothing by Accident aims to challenge conventional narratives about organised crime in Brazil. The prevailing discourse about law and order in Rio de Janeiro, like many cities in Latin America, is about violent gangs that come out of poor neighbourhoods and threaten society. Because of this, whole communities are stigmatised. This discourse fuels misunderstanding and enables further violence against these communities. In this sense, *Nothing By Accident* also aims to express the impact of insecurity and chronic armed violence upon ordinary people forced to live in abnormal conditions. Digging below the superficial representations of events, I seek to identify and reflect upon elements that bind this disastrous scenario together.

Nothing by Accident is divided into four parts:
The first, "**Chaos**", describes urban warfare in Rio's favelas and the failure of a state "pacification" programme to reduce violence in the city.

"**The Greatest Show**" introduces a little known but enormously powerful branch of Brazilian organised crime, *jogo do bicho*, "the animal game" in English. Illegal in Rio since the end of the 19th Century, the game is extremely popular and run by family clans who control the city's Carnival parade and have tight links to the military dictatorship.

"**Truth and Lies**" focuses on the 2014 Truth Commission (which was intended to reveal facts behind Brazil's 1964–1984 military dictatorship) and the mass street protests of 2013. Both processes highlight fault lines in Brazilian society: when the chief witness of the Truth Commission is murdered in suspicious circumstances, I discover that the trail for his murder leads back to the *jogo do bicho*. Examining the failure of the street protests, I tell the story of Bruno Teles, a young protestor framed in a terrifying episode of staged violence.

"**The Hornet's Nest**" discusses the aftermath of the murder of Marielle Franco in 2018. When a cover-up fails, investigators discover that not only does one of the actual alleged assassins live in the same housing complex as President Bolsonaro, the group also enjoy connections with his family. The gunmen belong to a racketeering death squad formed by ex-police and militiamen with strong connections to *jogo do bicho* clans.

IN 2020, UNDER THE COVER OF THE COVID-19 pandemic (which he dismissed as a "sniffle") Jair Bolsonaro ratcheted up his campaign to undermine democratic institutions with constant attacks on the judiciary, congress, state governments and the traditional media. He made regular appearances to support protestors calling for military intervention, portraying himself as the victim of establishment conspiracies, and although increasingly politically isolated, the President and his sons continued to enjoy solid support from 30% of the Brazilian population.

Gun ownership rocketed by 98% during Bolsonaro's first year as President, confirmation of his intent and ability to arm his supporters. Weapons newly obtainable to the public included the Brazilian-made T4 semi-automatic rifle, previously only available to the army. In April 2020, he revoked decrees that existed to facilitate the tracing and identification of weapons and ammunition. One week later, he tripled the quantity of ammunition available for purchase by civilians, saying on record in a ministerial meeting, that he wanted "everyone" to carry guns.

In the same month, Sérgio Moro, Bolsonaro's minister of justice and the judge responsible for Lula's imprisonment, resigned. Moro claimed that the President had attempted to interfere with the Federal police in Rio in order to protect his sons from corruption investigations.

With more guns and ammunition than ever before available to the general public, more than 2,500 members of the armed forces employed in senior government positions, and strong, vociferous support from the rank and file of the police and armed forces, Jair Bolsonaro and his backers now effectively held Brazilian society to ransom. His political philosophy, wrote Fernando de Barros e Silva, editor of the respected Piauí current affairs magazine, represented "the victory of the militia model of management of Brazilian violence".[5]

The rise of Jair Bolsonaro, and his subsequent onslaught on democratic institutions, represents the greatest setback for social progress in Brazil since the military coup of 1964. Readers of this book will learn about some of the conditions that made his ascendance to power possible, and why his rise is so dangerous; not just for Brazilians – but also for all of us.

A note on policing in Brazil

Brazil is a federal republic with 26 state governments and a federal district. Federal parliament includes a chamber of deputies and senate. The 26 states and federal district each have their own legislative assembly.

Brazil has three principal police forces. Federal police work on issues of national interest such as border control, immigration, drug trafficking and interstate crime, and are subordinate to federal government. The civil and military police forces come under individual state government jurisdiction. Civil police conduct criminal investigations and pass these to the judiciary. Military police are by far the most numerous (425,000 in 2015) and worst remunerated of the three.

Military police are on the front line, with responsibility for patrolling streets, maintaining public order, responding to crimes in progress and arresting suspects caught committing crimes. They are not authorised to conduct investigations. Under the Brazilian constitution, military police are counted as ancillary army reserves. They are prosecuted for infractions in military courts, and therefore generally not accountable to civil institutions, with the notable exception of cases of intentional homicide of civilians. However, Jair Bolsonaro has striven to create legal mechanisms that protect police who kill unlawfully.

Public security in the states is the responsibility of state governments and largely a political football, with federal authorities often blaming state governments for delinquency. "Crime fighting" is also a strong political platform. Bolsonaro's principal support base is serving and retired police and military officials. Large numbers of police joined the Bolsonaro campaign machine in the 2018 elections, especially in Rio de Janeiro with the support of Jair Bolsonaro's eldest son, Flávio. Estimates put numbers of serving and former police in the state at 250,000.[6]

In Rio de Janeiro and across Brazil, most military police work on a shift basis, often with 48 hour breaks between police duties. Consequently, it is standard practice to take second jobs as security guards, as they have the right to carry weapons. Many private security firms are owned by police and staffed by off-duty or former police. Such companies, often unlicensed and therefore illegal, have a vested interest in maintaining levels of crime and insecurity that enable them to sell services.[2]

In 2019, there were more than 41,000 active military police in Rio. Police corruption is common in the city. A high ranking civil policeman told me he believed that the Rio police force was 10% very honest, 10% criminal, and that the 80% in between would act in accordance with the prevailing climate at any moment in time. I have met many upstanding, ethical police officers in the city.

Context on race and violence in Brazil

Brazil is a highly unequal society where disparity runs along racial lines and is reflected in all spheres of life. According to official statistics, 55% of Brazil's population identifies as black. The highest levels of unemployment and illiteracy affect Brazil's black population, who also receive the lowest salaries. In 2019, an annual nationwide report on violence stated that young black Brazilian men are most likely to be homicide victims, victims of lethal police violence and subject to incarceration.[3] According to Human Rights Watch in 2020, 75% of 9,000 people killed by Rio's police in the last decade were black. Black police officers, highly represented among lower ranking officials serving on the "front line", are more commonly exposed to violence and die in higher numbers than non-black colleagues.

---

2 In 2006, the brother of federal congressman and human rights activist Marcelo Freixo was shot dead on his doorstep. He had refused to renew a contract with an illegal private security firm allegedly run by military police officials.

3 The Atlas of Violence 2019, a report published by the Brazilian Forum for Public Security.

PART ONE
CHAOS

*The Brazilian army on patrol in the
Maré favela complex, 2014.*

I

POOR AND ADMIRABLE FAVELA!

THE FAVELA MIRRORS BRAZILIAN SOCIETY TO ITSELF; everything it is, and everything it doesn't want to be. The name *favela* originally belongs to a plant found in Brazil's arid north-eastern interior. The spiky shrub's botanical name is *Cnidoscolus quercifolius*. Tangled with other spindly bushes, *favela* constitutes part of the *caatinga*: huge, rambling expanses of dense, thorny thickets of brambles and branches that can resist the region's heat and lack of water. Many of those Brazilians who populate favelas today once came from these dry, inhospitable lands. Driven from the countryside by drought, hunger and misery, they trickled, poured, and eventually, between the 1960 and 1980s, flooded into the big cities of the south, bringing the word *favela* with them.

I first visited a favela in 1996, when visiting Rio with my English girlfriend. It mostly rained on us. We stayed in a poky, cheap hotel called the Hotel Hispano–Brasileiro. Helen, the hotel manager, was an elderly woman of Russian–Chinese

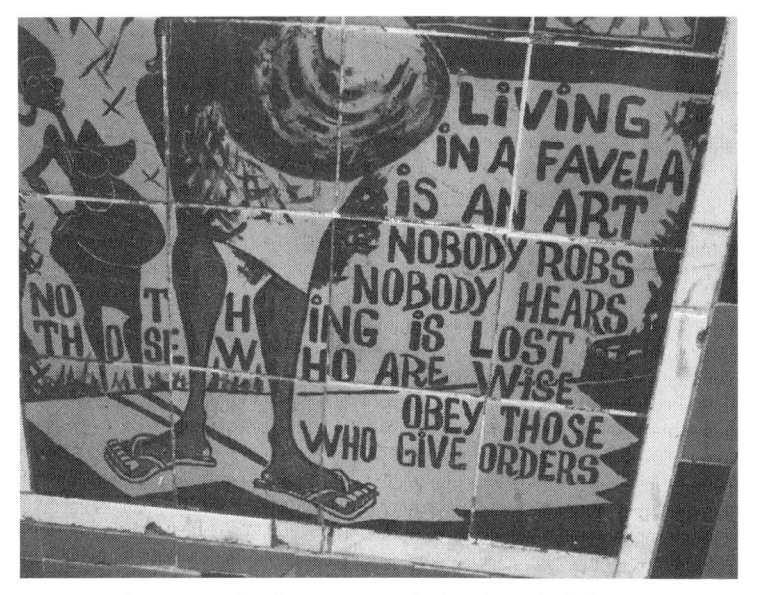

Living in a favela is an art; nobody robs, nobody hears, nothing is lost. Those who are wise obey those who give orders. Part of a mural by Chilean artist Selarón, Rio, 2009.

descent who spoke faultless English. With beautiful otherworldly handwriting, she signed us in to a dusty leather-bound register. During our time there she took a shine to us and even delivered beer to our room. After the evening news, a tiny push-button TV showed grainy erotic films from the 1970s. The only other visible hotel guest was a Canadian who, with his head of fuzzy grey hair and a droopy moustache, could have stepped right out of the kitsch cast of one of these productions.

We got talking at breakfast over soupy coffee, thinly sliced paw-paw and cheap crackers. The Canadian, called Richard, made ends meet by giving private English lessons in Rio. Also, he said, he could take us on a favela tour. He told us his nickname:

1 / POOR AND ADMIRABLE FAVELA!

"SpeakEnglish". When times were tough he survived by scouring Copacabana and Ipanema for wealthy looking gringo tourists. Then he would approach them with a sob story about how he had just been robbed. He always began "Hey man, excuse me, but do you speak English?", before asking them if they could help him out with some cash. SpeakEnglish didn't seem to mind sharing this information. He was disarmingly dishonest and for this reason we trusted him enough to book a favela tour for that morning. It was overcast and drizzling and we had no other plans.

We caught a blue and beige bus to Copacabana where we turned our backs to the sea and walked up a gentle cobbled hill. Apartment buildings eventually gave way to rough orange-brick unplastered houses and alleyways. At the end of the road, called Ladeira dos Tabajaras, Richard pointed across the rooftops of penthouses to a favela called Cabritos. Things were calm for the time being, he said, but when Cabritos and Tabajaras went to war they lit up Copacabana with tracer fire at night. We stopped in a shop at the top of the favela to buy Antarctica Guarana in small green bottles. Richard purposefully left his wallet on the counter when we stepped outside to sip the sticky, sweet fizzy drink through straws. It was a weekday and although there weren't many people about, Richard did point out a beefy guy wearing no top, sweatpants and a gold chain, whispering that he was a killer for the drug traffic. The tough guy nodded at us. Richard said he brought all types of curious foreigners – including writers, criminologists, journalists – up to the favela. He didn't say so, but I was sure he went there to buy drugs as well. When we returned to the shop to give back our empty Guarana bottles, Richard picked up his wallet with a theatrical flourish.

"Look, no one has touched it! Aren't favelas supposed to be full of thieves? Well they aren't! It's just society says that they are."

It was a tacky way to make a point. We continued over the hill and down the other side towards the Botafogo neighbourhood. On our way down, Richard began a detour along a side alley, but stopped short, turning back down the steps towards us, his expression tense.

"I was going to take you guys another way round, but I just remembered there's a lot of heavy weaponry up there."

When we reached the road at the bottom of the favela, an old man leaning against a wall asked Richard for a light. He handed over some matches. As the man struck one against the side of the box, Richard told me in a low voice that he was a lookout for drug dealers and that by asking for a light he was confirming that our tour had ended. I was not sure which part of Richard's story to believe. I was intrigued though by this glimpse of a Brazil I had always wondered about. The houses didn't look all that poor. I wondered how the favela fitted into this society. Why was it run by criminals? And was it really as dangerous as Richard made out?

MY NEXT FAVELA GUIDE was MC Playboy, a work colleague and the first *carioca* to invite me for a night out when I moved to Rio in 2005. He was 40, had a gold tooth, a teenager's desire to party and the temperament of a ten-year-old. Playboy lived in a huge sprawling community in the *Zona Norte* (North Zone) of the city called the Complexo do Alemão. He invited me there one Saturday night. The evening began at one of Rio's famous gang-organised favela parties called *baile funk*. The music was crude and very loud, and the drugs on sale and the guns on display intimidated me. I was relieved at two in the morning when Playboy said we were going to another party. We embarked on a trek through a maze of razor-like alleys, so thin that at times we could only walk through the dark in single file. I felt we were going round in circles, but eventually we arrived at some steep steps where a long queue had formed. At the top, couples whirled at high speed to the sound of *forró*, traditional accordion based music from the north-east of Brazil. In a bar area, a severe-looking bespectacled woman despatched dripping bottles of cold beer over a counter. Playboy introduced me to a well-dressed guy with short black hair. He carried an air of authority and was flanked by two bodyguards armed with Uzis. This was Pezão, one of the bosses of the Complex. We exchanged small talk and a handshake before I begged his leave to brave the riot of the dance floor. Condensed sweat gathered on the ceiling and dripped onto our heads. A balcony looked over the rooftops where a crescent moon hung in the star-specked night above tangled electricity wires and the black outline of hills. Unable to keep up with the speed or skill of the dancers, I hovered near the bar and spoke to a girl with waist length hair called Claudia.

"I'm Playboy's friend," I managed. "Would you like to dance?"

I couldn't dance very well but hung on tightly. The next morning, I woke up on her sofa. A little girl with a wild bouquet of blonde hair was sitting next to me playing with pieces of my mobile phone, which she had disassembled into its component parts. I was to become a friend. Bia had two younger sisters, Rayssa and Bruna. Bia was dark-skinned but because Bruna and Rayssa were blonde people often mistook me for their father. We had fun, which was a necessary distraction from the constant police raids when the Alemão descended into chaos. Shootouts occurred every few days. Claudia lived near an abandoned Catholic church, decorated with bullet holes, in a micro neighbourhood of the favela called Vivi. One day I spoke to her on the phone over the sounds of a gun battle. Commando police had broken their way into the church and were using it to fire rounds at some boys scampering over her rooftop. Operations against drug traffickers were fierce and frequent. Reporters in flak jackets and helmets gave breathless interviews in front of the giant black police armoured car known as "the big skull", while behind them police fired endless rounds at an invisible, implacable enemy. Residents only ever appeared when running for cover, or mourning someone killed. If anyone stood up to speak for the people of the Alemão, the media never found them.

When I wasn't with Claudia and her girls, I hung out at Playboy's. He lived an energetic twenty-minute trek downhill and then uphill in a flat that boasted three bedrooms, a fully tiled kitchen and bathroom, air conditioning, a glass dining table and a widescreen TV. The best feature of his residence was its mock castle-come-roof terrace, decorated with painted turrets, where I found myself alone one Sunday afternoon. It was a hot day and rooftops across the favela were dotted with people flying kites. Some families had set up paddling pools in which children splashed contentedly. The romantic sounds of *pagode* (poppy samba) accompanied the smell of multiple barbecues. As the sun went down, the entire cityscape was bathed in an orange glow, breathing again after the afternoon heat. Christ the Redeemer stood out miles away on the horizon. Laughter drifted across the rooftops and I didn't want to be anywhere other than the Alemão. Then someone below fired off several rounds of tracer fire at the neighbouring enemy favela of Adeus. I dropped my beer on the tiles and lay face down in it.

Sometimes on Friday or Saturday nights, I attended *baile funk* parties with music so loud that conversation was impossible. Recorded voices encouraged girls to gyrate downwards by screaming *chão, chão, chão* (floor, floor, floor) or *senta, senta, senta* (sit, sit, sit) over syncopated beats. The bass was so heavy, so aggressive that it squeezed the breath out of you. Offensive lyrics contaminated the air. I shifted from side to side and observed

Sound system in the Complexo do Alemão, 2014.

bizarre pre-mating rituals where boys in the gang showed off their guns, new clothes and gold chains – while the youngest, prettiest girls vied for their attention. I poured beer into plastic cups, topped up with splashes of Red Bull. I drank quickly before the sticky liquid could warm, so it always went to my head. Soon I would be swaying on the dance floor between kids, dogs and teenagers with guns. I always gave them a wide berth. They held their weapons like small children might wave knives.

Even so, there were always lots of "normal" kids – teenagers not involved with selling drugs or carrying guns. They wore their best outfits: uniforms of hot pants and twinkling halter tops for girls; jeans, T-shirts, running shoes and baseball caps for boys. A small army of mothers and grandmothers stood guard over polystyrene boxes from which they produced Red Bull, beer and Coca Cola. There were hot dog stands and older customers, apparent visitors to the favela. Tiny local urchins mingled and fought between the dancers practicing complex steps; girls dropping to gyrate their hips, thrusting to the floor, boys occasionally breaking out into body-popping routines.

If the *baile* was in the local basketball court no guns were allowed because it was being recorded for a private TV show, watched on DVD by gang bosses in prison. Higher ranking, older traffickers sat in plastic seats on a VIP balcony out of sight of the cameras and above the dancefloor, where they watched projections showing repeat reels of porn spliced with car crashes. At the height of the *baile*, when the music was switched from one system to another, the sound cut out. There were untoward silences as the dancers paused. The chatter of voices, motorbikes and music from the bars outside began to filter through. Then there was a hissing and a whizzing, and from nowhere an explosion and rush of yellow flame as a row of Roman candles atop the giant speakers lit up the inside of the court and for a short moment everyone was visible. As the fireworks fizzled out the speakers emitted recorded gunshots. Gunshots and more gunshots, until the *boom-cha-cha, boom-boom-cha, boom-cha-cha* of the electronic music set the party off again.

Some nights the hypnotic music, light show and enthusiastic throng of dancers sent me into a trance, when I lost myself in the multitude and, for a few minutes, forgot everything apart from the moment itself. And then I might catch sight of a thin, ill-looking child a few steps away, eyes rolling back into his head. I would recoil at the acrid crack smoke wafting across my face. Sometimes a woman's voice would whisper a foul nursery rhyme over and over again: "*Você quer meu cu? Você quer minha buceta? Ou você quer te faça uma punheta?*" (Do you want my arsehole? Or my pussy? Or do you want me to wank you?) I'd try not to notice the boys in the half distance dancing with grenades on their belts. I would glimpse inferno.

I preferred the Alemão on Sunday afternoons. Along the alleyways you might run into children clustered in the dirt around marbles and wooden spinning tops, or playing ping pong with books for bats over home made tables. Families and neighbours would sit outside after lunch and, if the weather was good, boys and men – sometimes girls too – would climb up onto the roof terrace to fly and battle lightweight paper kites. These were decorated in bright designs with soccer colours and super heroes, strings coated and reinforced with crushed glass and glue. I would lie on my back to watch the best kite fliers as they circled over the others, becoming tiny vibrating specks in the depths of the blue. When close-up, top pilots used the crushed glass strings to snick through a lesser navigator's line. While the vanquished kite dropped, the attacker circled decreasingly to wrap his own string around its tail to reel it in, just as if he had thrown a line into the sea to pull out a multicoloured fish. And if he didn't catch it, gangs of children raced after it, pushing, shoving, whooping and falling, then climbing over walls, shimmying up pipes, knocking over washing. Shouting friends would point to where the ownerless and falling kite might land, and the fastest or toughest, or the just luckiest, might catch it and take it back to their big brother, or keep it themselves to cast back into the blue ocean of sky overhead.

Sunday was also birthday party day. I often came across people stepping gingerly across broken paving stones and open sewers, cradling on a tray a delicious cake, big enough to feed many mouths.

Looking over Central Station and the sambadrome from Providência. Christ the Redeemer is on the skyline, 2010.

1 / POOR AND ADMIRABLE FAVELA!

IMAGINE YOU LIVE in a village on the edge of a precipice high above the centre of a city. Your grandparents struggled to build houses here. They built shacks perched on the cliff. If these didn't collapse in the rains, your parents bettered them brick by brick. Now you are a child and your house is safer, but the alleys that criss-cross the hill present a different danger. People are selling and buying drugs and police are trying to catch them. Then the sellers have guns. Sometimes they shoot the police, sometimes they don't. You're more frightened of the police than you are of the drug dealers, because the police beat you and your friends and sometimes they kill innocent people. Now imagine that in the middle of this world, in a tragic accident, your father shoots your mother dead.[7]

All this happened to my friend Maurício. He lives in Providência, a small favela perched on a rocky outcrop in the centre of Rio. Many favelas have breathtaking views, but only Providência lies at the city's heart. To the south it overlooks the business district and beyond, Sugarloaf Mountain and the Atlantic Ocean. Immediately underneath lies Central Station, Rio's principal rail terminal and gateway to the Baixada Fluminense, Rio's dormitory suburbs. The sambadrome and floodlights that illuminate the spectacular Carnival parade four nights a year, lie just beyond the rail tracks and the metro trains that disappear into a tunnel underneath the shadow of high-rise office blocks. Beyond, Christ the Redeemer stands guard above the bohemian Santa Teresa neighbourhood. Further west are the favelas of Turano, Borel and Formiga, clinging impossibly to hills above the middle-class neighbourhoods of Tijuca, Andarai and Grajaú. In the distance there is the Maracanã football stadium and the fairy-tale Penha Church, floating like a Walt

Disney castle above the Complexo do Alemão and Rio's endless northern suburbs. The eastern ridge of the hill sits above the port, with a view over the bridge to Rio's sister city, Niterói, and the container ships, cruisers, tug boats and oil rigs that crowd the Guanabara bay.

Few places in Rio have witnessed as much change as Providência. The favela used to hang over me when I passed by on the raised ring road called the Perimetral, or when I took a train from Central Station. Providência held answers to many of my questions about Rio. Before it was called Providência it was known as *morro da favela* (hill of the favela). In 2008, I found my way into it and on up to the top of the hill. The renowned French artist JR had asked me to help him find a place to paste giant photos of the faces of female inhabitants, as part of his global project called "Women Are Heroes". He planned to put the photos on the walls of houses high in a favela.

We chose Providência for its history. Our first piece of luck was that the drug traffickers – whose permission we had to seek – had liked pictures of a similar project developed by JR in Palestine and thus gave us the go-ahead. Our second bit of luck was the fact that the residents themselves quickly came over to our point of view and did all they could to help. But our big break was Maurício – he was a photographer and he knew what we were after.

Photography is probably the riskiest of projects you can attempt to undertake in a small, volatile location stuffed with gun-toting, drug-selling teenagers and equally violent police. If even one photograph were to find its way into the wrong hands, people's lives can be at risk. Maurício understood this better than any of us. He had been raised in Providência and photography was his life. Largely thanks to Maurício and his preternatural survival instincts, JR safely completed the project.

Subsequently TV helicopters filmed the giant faces covering the hillside. When the images of women's eyes looking out of the favela and over the bay were broadcast back into the houses of residents, JR and Maurício became local celebrities – and JR's own photographs of his installations on the hillside would later introduce them to a much wider world.

From that time I started visiting Providência as much as the Alemão. I made friends, argued, bought presents, attended parties, ducked bullets and ran for cover. I got to know the stevedores who had made their lives working in the docks. I learnt about their love of samba. I discovered that no one was untouched by violence, that if your husband hadn't been in prison or shot, then your son or brother had – that daily survival meant not seeing things you saw, liking people you did not like, saying things you did not believe. It meant knowing hell could break loose from one second to the next – and that when it did, you should stay still – because a moving person is a target. But I am white, and when I ran from shootouts (I always did) I left my black friends sitting where they were. When the gunfire stopped they would always remind me that their skin was the danger, and that if a moving white person might be merely unsafe, a moving black person could quickly become another "dead criminal".

I visited the *Cemitério dos Ingleses* at the bottom of the favela; a tidy, small English-built cemetery where I secretly hoped not to be buried. The orderly, pretty graveyard lies a stone's throw from recently discovered mass graves of thousands of slaves who failed to survive the Atlantic crossing. Rio's cruel, barbaric past lurks all around this part of town.

JR's Women are Heroes project, Providência 2008.

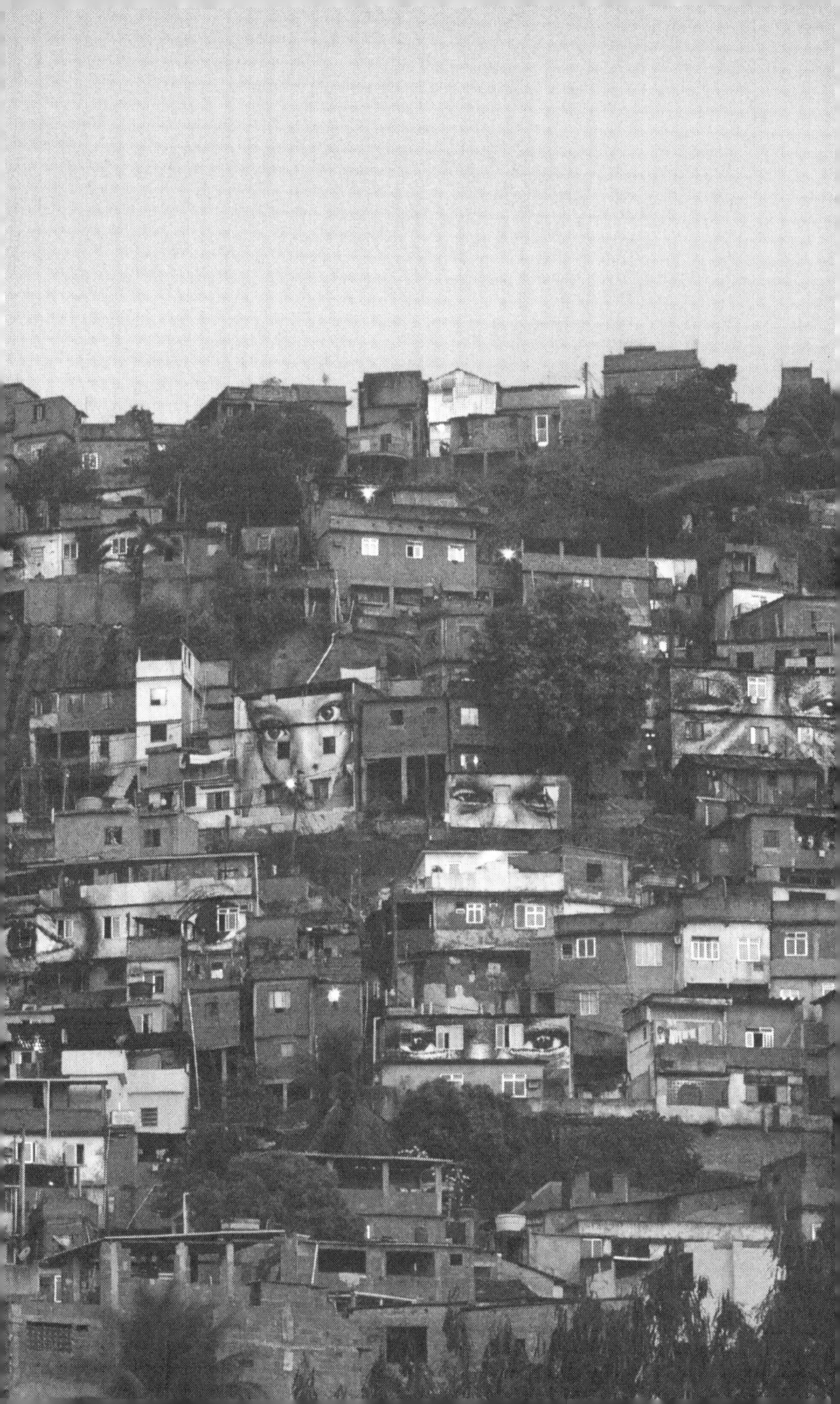

The streets around Providência were empty by night. Down by Central Station, cutthroats, junkies and bag snatchers mingled with prostitutes and drunks after the last commuters had caught the late train or bus out to the suburbs. I often walked down the steps and alleys in the darkness on my way past the *boca* (the drug sales point) with its queue of customers and armed guards – and then down more steps where a mass of crackheads huddled in permanent desperation and comic togetherness, manically negotiating the minutiae of their next score. They resembled chronically confused visitors from another land; lost and babbling in no known language.

If the Alemão is like a city, Providência is the hilltop village where everyone knows each other's business, and where everyone's life stories are interwoven with shared births, marriages, deaths, battles and betrayals. Physically, Providência is a geographical puzzle formed by winding alleys, steep flights of steps, cliff edges and rocky overhangs. One old cobbled road climbs the hill to what used to be the favela's main square. This road and the houses that sit on either side of it used to be considered the city proper, while the actual favela occupation began on the land behind the square. A long flight of slave-built steps leads up to a church and a very old chapel. However, over time the favela crept down by stealth as families occupied abandoned houses and apartment blocks, and the drug dealers moved their *bocas* and guns further down the hill towards Central Station and the port. Meanwhile on the occupied land behind the square and around the chapel, bricks and mortar replaced walls of wood.

Like the Alemão, Providência was also at war. Police raided the favela. Drug traffickers sold drugs and had shootouts with police and each other. In 2008, the army took over the community to facilitate a politician's ambitious housing renovation project (the lawmaker in question was Marcelo Crivella – mayor of Rio in 2020). Young soldiers kidnapped three youths, handing them over to rival drug traffickers in the nearby Mineira favela complex who tortured then killed them, slicing their bodies into pieces. Protesting residents took down the Brazilian flag, hoisted above the favela by the army, and handed it back to the commanding officer before descending into the streets to demonstrate. The scandal led to withdrawal of the troops and the abandonment of the housing project. One morning not long afterwards I ran into Maurício. The strain in his eyes contrasted with the bright, sunny day. We had a coffee in the baker's shop, and while the community went about its business, he spoke to me.

"Some traffickers just came to see me. Somehow – I don't know how – they got hold of two kids from Mineira."

Maurício was usually able to disguise his true feelings, but today his face was different.

"They took them to the top of the hill to a house they have up there, and tortured them."

He called me outside into the square where no one could hear us.

"They recorded what they did on their phones."

He looked over the docks below us, beyond the "city of samba" where the samba schools build their floats for Carnival. The hooting of cargo ships drifted up from the port.

"They just showed me."

He stayed silent for a moment.

"Well, they had one of them. They had cut both his ears off, and they had a long kitchen knife, and they were shoving this into a hole in the side of his head where his ear had been. He was screaming for mercy."

His face screwed up.

"They showed me the film. Then they opened a small metal tin containing two human ears. They said I should be happy now, because now they had avenged the boys we lost."

PROVIDÊNCIA'S VIOLENT HISTORY can be traced back to Canudos, a godforsaken, parched corner of the backlands of Brazil's north-east, where a wandering preacher called Antonio the Counsellor founded a religious settlement at the end of the nineteenth century. The Counsellor was a popular mystic who toured the impoverished, arid interior, repairing churches in the towns and villages forgotten by the church. Deeply pious and charismatic, he attracted a large following of devotees who gathered to hear his sermons and established a community, which then grew into a town called Canudos. In the early 1890s, powerful architects of the new Brazilian Republic grew fearful of Antonio the Counsellor and his following of ruffians, free thinkers, former slaves and peasants. They sent the army to extinguish any possible threat of insurrection. The few photos taken before its subsequent destruction show a ramshackle sprawl of houses and dwellings on a hillside. Canudos looked just like a modern favela.

Antonio's men routed the first three expeditions. They hid in the undergrowth, protected from the spindly thorns and brambles by the heavy-set leather outfits used by *vaqueiros* (cowherds) to ride at speed through the bush. They lured the badly equipped and inexperienced soldiers into ambushes. They dug trenches, carried out night raids and killed the army's horses. The southerners were neither prepared, nor equipped for the boiling temperatures or the harsh terrain, and were soon exhausted and starving, their uniforms in shreds. They underestimated the tenacity of their wily, unseen adversary who vanished into the landscape after each attack.

The failed missions were a public relations disaster for the new government. They responded by sending a final enlarged expedition, which first besieged and then bombarded Canudos into rubble. It was a near total massacre. They beheaded every living man and boy, and took all the women survivors prisoner. Many of these women then accompanied the soldiers when they returned to Rio de Janeiro, where the successful combatants had been promised houses by the government. There they waited and waited, camped out by the Ministry of War in the centre of the city. When the government failed to make good on its promise to provide them with places to live, the soldiers occupied adjacent land on a crag overlooking the Ministry. This crag reminded them of the hill where they had camped out before the final assault on Canudos, a hill called *favela*, and they gave their new home this name. When other clusters of houses began to climb up hillsides all over the city, these too were christened *favela*. In order to distinguish it from the others, residents of the community founded by the former soldiers now called their hill Providência, the name that exists today. But we must not forget: *favela* refers back to Canudos and the shrub with sharp thorns. Thorns which tore at the soldiers' clothes during combat in the *caatinga*, ripping them, cutting their skin, causing deep sores which grew gangrenous with infection. One scratch from *Cnidoscolus quercifolius* could render a man useless for combat.

"The Valley of Death", Canudos battle site 2010.

In 2010, I made a pilgrimage across the northeast to modern Canudos – a third incarnation of the original settlement – the first was reduced to rubble, a second was flooded to make way for a dam. I visited the original *morro da favela* and other battle sites with names like "Valley of Death", where I looked over quiet waters that cover the place where so many had died. The only sound was the tinkling of goat bells and the crunching of our feet. My guide, a portly mototaxi driver called George, told me to look out for coiled rattlesnakes. As well as the *favela* plant, he showed me other hostile-looking shrubs that constitute the *caatinga*, with names like *xique xique*, *macambira*, *unha de gato* (cat's nail) and *palmatória do diabo* (devil's whip). While George pretended not to see, I collected stones and *favela* twigs to take back to Maurício in Rio.

1 / POOR AND ADMIRABLE FAVELA!

A QUARTER OF *CARIOCAS* live in more than a thousand favelas in metropolitan Rio, of which Providência and Complexo do Alemão are the two that I know very well. I write now about violence, not because there are not other stories to tell (there are and they are many) but because heartbreakingly, these tight-knit micro-societies are some of the most violent urban areas in the world. Essentially, endemic violence serves to dominate and subjugate these communities, thus preserving Brazil's unequal and racist social pyramid.

No two favelas in Rio are the same. Each has its own idiosyncratic racial, social, cultural and topographical formation. Although Providência and the Alemão are very different in many ways – Providência is small and village-like with a population of some 4,000; Alemão is giant, with upwards of 70,000 residents – both suffer from exclusion, marginalisation and entrenched violence. Although Brazilians of all colours inhabit them, most residents are mahogany skinned or black. However, Providência is the more mixed; in addition to descendants of slaves and Canudos veterans, many European immigrants came to the hill in the first half of the twentieth century. The population of the Alemão, formed during the post-1960 boom in urban migration, is fundamentally from the north-east.

Social exclusion is the common denominator that binds together their population. As informal, self-built communities, favelas exist outside the regulated city. Services like water and electricity are typically pirated from the main grid and not paid for. A policeman I know calls favelas "post-modern slave quarters" and in many ways they are exactly that. The persistent failure of Brazil to incorporate favelas into official society keeps them vulnerable and condemned to exploitation by criminals, police and politicians, in many cases these working together. Although the drug boom worsened the situation, by entrenching violence and the interests of crime and corruption, it is far from a modern phenomenon. In 1924 Benjamim Costallat, a Paris-educated, avant-garde young Brazilian intellectual, wrote about Providência for a series of chronicles about the city called *Mysteries of Rio*. In a chronicle called "The favela that I saw", Costallat describes the favela as a territory that belongs to no one and everyone. He sees a diverse, autonomous city within the city where no one pays taxes and the law is administered by the strongest and the bravest. He observes that in the favela crime and death were commonplace, these being solutions for all kinds of business, both financial and moral. But while depicting the crime and marginality of favela living, Costallat also recognises its innate beauty, and champions the paradoxical happiness of the favela dweller as a lesson for us all:

The Favela doesn't have electricity. It doesn't have drains. It doesn't have water. It doesn't have hospitals. It doesn't have schools. It doesn't have assistance. It doesn't have anything...

But the Favela is happy, up there in its hideaway, with the marvellous panorama of the city unfolding at its feet.

The Favela that sambas, when it should cry, is a marvellous example for those who have everything and still aren't satisfied...

Poor and admirable Favela!...[8]

During his visit Costallat takes lunch – the "best chicken" he has ever tasted – with Zé da Barra. Big-hearted and the undisputed boss, Zé da Barra "is president of the little Republic of the Favela". He owns the only house with real roof tiles and rules the hill "with courage and strength. And principally a formidable truncheon that crashes like lightening on ruffian's heads". The two men talk of assassination attempts, bullets in the dark and gun battles with police. It sounds just like Providência today.

2

WAGING WAR: A WAY OF LIFE IN RIO DE JANEIRO

IN 2009, RIO BEAT MADRID, CHICAGO AND TOKYO in the contest to host the 2016 Olympics. It seemed too good to be true. While a euphoric crowd cheered and danced on Copacabana Beach, in Denmark, President Lula and Sérgio Cabral[4], then governor of the state of Rio, hugged each other and wept. But on buses and in backstreets, most people just went about their business in quiet surprise. While many *cariocas* are dreamers, years of decline and disappointment have tempered their natural exuberance. Even so, the next day everyone was thinking the same thing; maybe, just maybe, life in the city might improve.

This cautious optimism hung in the air for a few weeks before dissipating one Friday night, when drug faction soldiers invaded the Morro dos Macacos favela. Monkey Hill, as it would

---

4 Cabral was imprisoned in 2016 on a multitude of corruption charges for which he received a total of more then 200 years of sentences. In July 2019 he claimed under oath to have paid $2 million in bribes to secure the Olympics for Rio.

2 / WAGING WAR: A WAY OF LIFE IN RIO DE JANEIRO

To die like a man is the prize of war.
Graffiti in Casa Branca favela, Tijuca, 2011.

be called in English, lies above Vila Isabel, a pretty, middle-class neighbourhood in the north of the city. The initial invasion was slick and well organised. Shortly before midnight raiders drove up the hill in stolen cars and vans. Moving quickly they took over strategic points in the community. Then the plan went awry. The attackers got trapped between police and local traffickers.

Intense gun battles continued for 24 hours. Live TV broadcast images of shoppers taking cover in doorways and behind cars. The black *caveirão* (big skull), a greatly feared police armoured vehicle, bore down on residential streets. Bullets hit a police helicopter, brought down by its pilot only seconds before going up in flames. There were six police inside; three died.

When news of the failed invasion spread, drug bosses allied to the invaders sent minions out in the streets to commandeer and then set fire to buses – a traditional faction tactic for protesting and distracting attention. Alarm and an atmosphere of instability gripped Rio. People cancelled shopping trips, nights out and parties. *Cariocas* stayed at home to watch constant replays of the helicopter circling and churning thick black smoke before exploding on the ground. Residual high spirits about the Olympic victory evaporated before the resulting pyre of blood, torn metal and ash.

José Mariano Beltrame, Rio's laconic Police Chief at the time, later admitted he had prior intelligence about the invasion, but alleged that he lacked the manpower to take preventive action. The body count included three men, described as criminals by police, shot dead in a car. Their families said they were innocent residents caught in the crossfire. Images of the helicopter on fire travelled across the world as the international media questioned Brazil's ability to host a peaceful Olympics.

Now Rio became an international newsroom priority. A hard-nosed BBC journalist reporting on violence in the city hired me as a facilitator. She insisted on visiting Macacos to speak to the families of the innocent men killed during the invasion. No one I knew could connect us to community leaders, so we drove to the bottom of a road leading to the top of the favela and asked locals how to find the residents' association. Someone made a call and asked us to wait. It was late afternoon and there was a sleepy Rio warmth in the buzz of conversation in bars, the to and fro of shoppers and shouted greetings between friends. This corner of Vila Isabel is tucked away between giant rocks and hills. The day-to-day here is less hectic than central and beachside neighbourhoods. We paid for several rounds of beer. Eventually a community street sweeper, called a *gari* in Rio, turned up in his bright orange uniform. He hopped in the car and we drove through a tunnel leading to the other side of the hill. Orange clad *garis* are popular figures in the city and he would ensure our safety.

Grey clouds clogged the skies as our car climbed the trash-strewn cobbled street. When our driver wound down the window, heavy, humid air billowed in. Residents returning from work mingled with locals drinking at kiosk bars. Our guide was keen to show off his pimped ride and greeted friends according to their football team *"fala Vascaíno! e aí Flamengo!"* Despite the bonhomie, caution and fatigue showed on strained faces. Teenagers in baseball caps handling shiny automatic pistols stepped out of the shadows to see who was in the car. The street sweeper leant out and gave a thumbs-up. He told them he was taking some journalists to the association. They waved us on.

Further along we stopped to speak to the cagey president of the favela's residents' association. He kept talk to a minimum and introduced us to someone who could take us to the families. Suited and carrying a briefcase, this man got into the car and guided us further into the favela, up over the top of the hill and down a wide, sweeping road offset by houses, shops and a twinkling dusk panorama of the city. As we navigated a U-bend, he showed us where the three men had died, driving in the same direction as we were, when someone in the road above had opened fire.

We parked and continued on foot. More boys with guns peered at us from the shell of an abandoned bullet-pocked house. We had come full circle around the favela and below us was the point where we had met the *gari* a short time before. We climbed steps and walked in single file along a dusty, unpaved alley that twisted between boulders and unplastered red-brick dwellings hewn into the primordial rockface. A group of women sitting on a doorstep stopped their conversation when we appeared.

The women pointed us to an impossibly steep, narrow set of tiled steps that led into a spacious air-conditioned living room. The walls were sky blue and the neatly corniced ceiling was white. The room was furnished with chairs, sofas and a dining table. Framed family photos sat on shelves by a state-of-the-art widescreen plasma TV. The room opened onto a kitchen, a second room on the left and a corridor to the right. The house was clean, orderly and snug. A heavy white woman with a crumpled face sat on the largest sofa. Maria was the owner of the house and mother to one of the dead. We took our shoes off. Other people came in quietly and sat or leant against the walls.

Maria answered the journalist with sobs.

"Yes, they'd been to a party, because like all young people they have the right to go out and enjoy themselves, and then they heard the shooting start. So they decided to come home and that's when…"

She stood, picked up a photo of her son, a nurse at a private hospital, and circled the room, picture in hand. When she sat down again, another woman put a hand on her shoulder, while a man appeared from the room in the corner. These were the other boys' parents. Out of five in the car, two had survived. They were all close friends. Maria put on a DVD, made at a birthday party on a schooner a few months before. The room was filled with sunny scenes of happy, attractive young people partying underneath Rio's iconic Sugarloaf Mountain.

Standing by the TV Maria touched wrinkled fingers to the image of her son's face, talking about his death and how they would be suing the state, about the personal problems he had shared with her – troubles with his girlfriend. She talked about him in both past and present tenses. The other parents quietly said they believed the invading traffickers had received support from corrupt police, how it might even have been police who killed their children.

Maria showed us her son's bedroom, where ironed clothes were neatly stacked and Flamengo team posters decorated the walls. A collection of model cars gleamed proudly under a TV showing a football match. When she lay down on the bed, we offered our last condolences and departed. Raindrops spattered as we made our way back between the rocks in a silent row. Nearby a walkie-talkie crackled. In the gloom of an empty house, the watching drug soldiers and their guns made murky silhouettes.

RIO HAS ALWAYS BEEN AN EXPLOSIVE CITY. In 1915 the celebrated *carioca* author Lima Barreto wrote: "Rio is like a vast bunker and we live with the constant menace of exploding, as if we were aboard a battleship, or living in a fortress full of terrible explosives."[9]

Today's constant menace, the so-called "war on drugs", is mysterious and multidimensional. Fought out against the backdrop of the city's kaleidoscopic topography of sea, jungle and mountain, this war constantly reinvents itself. Neither crisis nor emergency, it is a modus vivendi constructed on fear and hate. Everything changes, and everything stays the same. The war maintains a tragic status quo, serving entrenched political, social and economic interests. It keeps the city divided; the poor vulnerable and the rich powerful. Favela residents are treated like criminals, or at best, non-people to be ordered around. When the innocent die – and they often do – the authorities usually treat such loss of life as mere collateral damage.

Brazil's war on its own people has deep and multiple roots; colonisation, genocide of the indigenous population, slavery, racism and repression of social movements like Canudos. The "war on drugs", its modern manifestation, was born in the military dictatorship of the 1970s, when common criminals were held together with subversives on the Ilha Grande island prison, a few hours from Rio. According to a widely accepted version of events, the political prisoners influenced kidnappers, bank robbers and drug dealers into organising themselves and creating a chain of command and hierarchy that brought order and discipline to prison life.[10] The founders called their new organisation the *Comando Vermelho* (Red Command), or CV for short. The CV created rules for both inside and outside prison. They looked after offenders' families and pooled resources. Crucially, the CV power structure extended into Rio's favelas, which thus became aligned – in some cases through force – with the new criminal organisation.

At the same time, during the late 1970s and early 1980s, Rio de Janeiro became a hub for the international cocaine business, as demand for the drug increased in Europe and the US. During this boom period spin off local markets, attended by favela-based drug sellers who organised themselves according to CV rules, expanded rapidly. Dealers needed weapons to protect their product and earnings, from theft or attack by rivals and the police. Consequently, a symbiotic and lucrative trade in small arms and light weaponry grew in tandem with the drug businesses. As these dual markets took root in the favelas, they became inextricably linked to the CV, who as the local chiefs now exercised territorial control over communities awash with guns and drugs. Splits and betrayals led to the emergence of rival factions, the *Terceiro Comando* (Third Command) and the *Amigos dos Amigos* (Friends of Friends). A very important note to this latter – the "friends" referred to here were shady police. By the end of the 1990s, what began as a cottage industry run by a handful of entrepreneurs peddling coke and grass with a discrete pistol shoved down their trousers, was now the dominion of highly organised, heavily-armed informal armies who – alongside corrupt lawmakers – disputed the substantial revenues of these illegal markets. The body counts skyrocketed.

Today, Rio's "war on drugs" is both pretext and euphemism for a war on the poor. Not a silent war of economic oppression and the subtle undermining of civil liberties and human rights – but a fire and brimstone, guns blazing, no prisoners taken, armed assault on the city's most vulnerable. Encouraged to obey the rich and abuse the poor, police are the only arm of the state to consistently reach inside the favela. Criminal police acting inside the official structure profit from extortion, arms and drug dealing and kidnapping. Hidden within an institution that penetrates all the favelas in the city, they can act like businessmen, choosing which favelas to make alliances with, and which favelas to attack.

Whether the police raid a favela or not depends on which faction dominates the community. Different factions have different connections. During my first years in Rio, when I was a frequent visitor to Playboy and Claudia, the Complexo do

Alemão was Brazilian society's enemy number one. The complex was *Comando Vermelho* HQ, its top men refusing to pay bribes. In 2002 they had murdered Tim Lopes, a popular investigative journalist, who had been caught secretly filming a *baile funk* party. The consequent media demonisation and constant police raids turned the Alemão into an inferno. But the complex was too big and the police never prolonged their stay. Even the BOPE, the military police's much-feared special ops commandos, could never penetrate very far inside the community.

I first encountered the black-shirted BOPE (pronounced 'boppy') in 2006. They were looking for a CV member known as Shock. After shooting dead a BOPE policeman in a favela called Mangueira, Shock was hiding in the Alemão's labyrinth of alleys.[5] The BOPE did not have the manpower to sweep the whole complex, so they set up roadblocks at various points, including at a square near Claudia's house where they put snipers at the top of the bullet-riddled Catholic church. But after initial confrontations, the drug traffickers simply disappeared. The impotent police blamed residents. They cut off electricity and water supplies and when that failed they tortured local youths. They plundered shops for food and drink and threatened girls with rape. They wanted to provoke the CV into combat, or into handing over Shock, but the traffickers didn't respond. So for several days and nights they vented their spleen on the innocent. Eventually a visit by NGOs and the public defender's office forced them into withdrawing without finding their man.

Not long afterwards in 2007, shortly before Rio hosted the Pan American Games and in what bore the hallmarks of a

---

[5] Mangueira favela is home to the samba school of the same name.

publicity stunt, hundreds of law enforcers from different police institutions united for what was then the biggest combined police operation in the city's history. They flooded the Alemão and executed 19 supposed drug dealers, many of them in an alley near Claudia's house. After this operation, federal troops were deployed to keep watch over the complex. They set up sentry boxes at all access points. They patrolled the streets around the perimeter. But they never went into the favela where drug dealers and criminals continued to circulate freely, doing business and throwing parties. There were guns outside the Alemão, guns inside the Alemão. Stuck in the middle were 70,000 residents, normal people with abnormal lives like Claudia and her children. The situation was absurd; a siege without an objective, military occupation with no action. MC Playboy called his community the "world's largest open plan prison". Later in the year, I helped organise a research visit to the Alemão by Philip Alston, UN Special Rapporteur on Extrajudicial Executions. Alston stated that the police had given no plausible explanation for the operation, which he believed was politically motivated and a failure in crime-fighting terms.

The hero of the 2007 killing mission was a drugs squad inspector called Leonardo Torres. Rio's media adulated the photogenic cop, nicknamed "Thunder", who wore combat goggles, military fatigues and after operations smoked thick Cuban cigars. The day after the invasion, Rio's establishment broadsheet *O Globo* hailed it as a resounding success and published two photos of Torres on its front page; one of him in an alley in the Alemão, smoking his traditional cigar; another in a downtown bar with a beer, once again puffing on his cigar. In the accompanying interview, Torres, man of the moment, used the limelight to declare he was a "warrior by nature" whose dream was to go to Iraq.

In 2010, Torres took part in another massive invasion of the Alemão. This time, internal police investigators were tapping his phone. Torres was subsequently arrested and unmasked as a key player among Rio's corrupt police. He was charged with selling tip-offs to drug traffickers in Rocinha, one of Rio's largest favelas (run by the *Amigos dos Amigos*), as well as reselling drugs and weapons confiscated in the Alemão. This time there was no mention of Iraq, or photos of cigars, as *O Globo* conveniently forgot Torres' recent celebrity status. Before his demise, the flamboyant Torres participated in *Dancing with the Devil*, a 2009 documentary about Rio's drug war. During a particularly eloquent moment, whilst out drinking whisky with fellow cops, the inspired, table-banging, cigar-waving Torres waxed lyrical:

> *I am Inspector Torres Galvão, son of the storm. I was born in filthy weather. I was born for combat, for the bad times. I want evil to fuck itself and I will always fuck evil. And whoever is with the bad guy is fucked. We don't look for confrontation [...] but once the first shot is fired, we hope it never ends. That is the warrior's vocation. Then, you forget you are a policeman. You are at war.*[11]

Both hero and villain, Torres epitomises the schizophrenic absurdity of a police force deeply and inextricably involved in the very criminal activity it is mandated to suppress. Vinícius George, a civil police chief with more than 25 years of experience, once told me that a "code of dishonour" maintains the illegal arms trade in Brazil. In Rio, Vinícius said, there was not a single weapon in a favela that state officials could not trace if they wanted to. In November 2014, police discovered a stash of ten automatic rifles, two machine guns, two submachine guns, nine pistols and more than twenty thousand bullets in the West Zone garage of a 42-year-old navy sergeant.[12] Theft and "losses" of registered police, military and private security arms are routine. A 2011 state legislative enquiry into weapons found that 8,912 guns were "lost" or stolen from police stocks between 2000–2010.[6] A 2016 follow-up enquiry learnt from federal police that 17.662 weapons (30 per cent of these companies' total supply) were "lost" or stolen from Rio's private security firms between 2005–2015. The same federal police statement reported that 95 per cent of these private security businesses were owned by active and retired police and military personnel.[13]

A VIOLENT CITY IS A FRIGHTENING CITY. A frightening city is an insecure city, which means money for the bullies; money for the private security companies owned by high-ranking police; money for the weapons and munitions industry; money for corrupt officials who supply drugs and guns; and money for dealers who buy and distribute these within voiceless communities. The war keeps the poor on their knees. Like a slave, the favela continues to provide the city with cheap, pliant and endless labour. Despite its innate strength and resilience, war renders the favela traumatised, supplicant and deferential; an easy target for cheap drugs and alcohol, corrupt

---

6 Investigation of such incidents is next to non-existent. Out of 1,870 enquiries opened by the state prosecutor during a five-year period, only 42 were concluded. *Relator diz que CPI das Armas no RJ tem encontrado 'coisas absurdas'*, G1 website, 26 May 2016.

politicians, consumer goods, junk food, junk TV and feel-good religious quick fixes. *Fé em Deus*, the drug traffickers say. In God We Trust. And you had better trust in God because here there is no rule of law.

Since 2005, illegal paramilitary groups, known locally simply as *milícia* (militia) and formed by off-duty or former police, firefighters, prison guards and members of the armed forces, have scaled up the war of oppression, flushing out drug traffickers from communities and taking control. Once installed, the militia establishes itself as local security provider, charging all residents and businesses a "tax"'. Militia leaders include city councillors and elected representatives in the state parliament. Because of their close ties to officialdom, police raids on militia areas, and consequent gun battles are rare. However, militia members torture and kill innocent residents in order to spread fear in the communities they dominate. While drug traffickers avoid unnecessary violence – they need to keep the community on their side – the militias have no such qualms. Residents, who are a source of income, must be frightened into paying.

Militias dominate Rio's West Zone, which includes the opulent, aseptic Barra neighbourhood, home to the 2016 Olympic Park[7]. The West Zone, where more than one in three of the city's voters live, is a political power base. In 2008, a then-obscure Rio politician, Jair Bolsonaro, defended militias in a BBC interview, claiming they provided security, order and discipline for poor communities.[14] Their modus operandi suggested otherwise; in the West Zone favela of Barbante in

---

[7] The neighbourhood's full name is Barra da Tijuca, but to avoid confusion with the North Zone Tijuca district I refer to it as Barra, as *cariocas* usually do.

2008, hooded militia gunmen belonging to a group called "The League of Justice" executed seven residents at random, with the apparent aim of terrorising residents into voting for a particular candidate. But it is not just the poor and defenceless who risk their lives; in 2011 rogue police killed Patricia Acioli, a judge who had issued more than 60 arrest warrants to police suspected of militia and death squad activity.

There is nothing accidental about the status quo. It works very well for certain parties. In *Drugs and Democracy in Rio de Janeiro*, a formidable analysis of this toxic web of interests, political scientist Enrique Desmond Arias argues that crime and criminality are integral components of politics in Rio. He identifies the formation of illegal networks between residents' associations (the only form of quasi-authority that exists in favelas), police, politicians and criminals that sustain the conflict by creating a configuration of local "governance" that reinforces illegal activity. The formal state exercises violence by proxy through the drug traffic or the militia. Criminals dominating a given community act as local muscle; armed bullies who sustain a social order. To speak out or question their motives is to risk one's life. Residents must see, hear and speak no evil. Such malleable passivity is highly useful to politicians seeking votes, or wishing to do business with crime. Police corruption is normalised and integral to the process, to the extent that it can be easier for police to engage in illegal activity than to fight crime. Arias acutely observes that:

> *...police not on the take will face criminals who have intelligence about their activities from other police. Police who would normally not take bribes may start to take bribes*

out of a sense of hopelessness because it is less risky than actually trying to enforce the law when other police actively work with criminals, or because pervasive corruption renders corrupt activity one of the few ways of moving up the career ladder. This progressively undermines the rule of law, leads to higher levels of human rights abuse, and can pose profound challenges to democracy.[15]

The rot goes to the top. Early in September 2014, following a tip-off, a military policeman was arrested while escorting a 400-kilo marijuana consignment into Rio. The drugs were hidden in a lorry full of frozen chickens. The story (and the policeman) promptly disappeared from the news. Two weeks later, security secretariat intelligence officials arrested 24 military police officials. The arrested policemen included the number three in the entire state military police force at the time – Colonel Alexandre Fontenelle, commander in chief of the feared BOPE and the state riot police, called the CHOQUE. Fontenelle was charged with masterminding a massive militia scheme to extort protection money from vans, taxis and bus companies operating transport services in the West Zone. As if that was not enough, a military policeman-turned-informer said that every single one of the 41 battalions in the state made illegal monthly cash payments of $6,000 to the *Estado Maior*, the military police supreme command.[16]

RIO'S TRAGEDY is symptomatic of Brazil's entrenched violence. According to the Brazilian Forum for Public Security, there were 65.602 violent killings in the country during 2017. This total is higher than 58,220, the official number of US military fatalities resulting from the Vietnam War. In 2018 killings by police in Brazil stood at 6220 – in Rio alone that year, police registered the killing of 1538 alleged suspects in "confrontations". In the light of such depressing statistics, it is hard to think positively of the future. In the meantime Rio's futile, endless war will continue to pit white against black, black against black, black against white, rich against poor, poor against poor, poor against rich, police against thieves, favela against favela, the top of the favela against the bottom of the favela, good police against bad police, bad police against other bad police, faction against faction, militia against faction, haves against have-nots and all against all. Eye for tooth, tooth for eye. Neighbour against neighbour. Like going to the beach, or dancing samba, waging war is a way of life in Rio de Janeiro.

3

PEACE LOST: THE FAILURE OF PACIFICATION

EARLY IN 2011, I WALKED INTO the Hotel Turístico in Rio's Gloria neighbourhood where I stayed on my first ever visit to Brazil in 1994. Inside, little had changed. The hotel lobby, with its faded beige paintwork and row of pleather easy chairs lined against the wall, was as I remembered. A dumpy, uninterested receptionist sat behind a bulletproof window underneath declarations about cockroaches and child protection legislation. I asked to see a room on the top floor and she shoved a key at me. Passing an open door on the way up, I glimpsed backpackers getting ready to leave. I opened room 116 and sat on the bed. Out of nowhere I remembered the sharp, stabbing loneliness I'd felt on reaching Rio all those years ago, a feeling now long forgotten.

Within weeks of my revisit the Turístico closed for renovation. Radical change had arrived in this small corner of the city. Eike Batista, at the time Brazil's richest man (and according to Forbes, then seventh richest in the world), playboy and energy entrepreneur, had purchased the grand Hotel Glória. Favoured by businesspeople and presidents, the Hotel Glória was second in the city only to the Copacabana Palace and lay a short walk from the Turístico. Eike (as he was known in Rio) had snapped up my grubby hotel to be an annex for his ambitious renovation project. All local street dwellers were relocated under a FIFA-standard zero-tolerance policy now sweeping the city.

Change had not come to Glória alone. Rio was beginning to look like one gigantic construction site. Work was underway on a metro extension, a massive revamping of the port area and road building for cross-city high-speed bus services. The city was enjoying a self-confident, ebullient moment thanks to its recently discovered offshore oil reserves, a stable economy and the status of a World Cup final host. In order to make Rio feel and look safer, military police had begun permanent occupation of key favelas near beaches, the town centre and the Maracanã football stadium. Eike Batista put up R$20 million a year towards the project.[8] The official name for the favela occupation process was "pacification". But where the state governor claimed to promote peace and citizenship, sceptics saw the gentrification and militarisation of poor communities. I was uncomfortable with the terminology from the outset. "Pacification" made the favela population sound like dangerous savages in need of taming or hordes to be controlled. Imperial Portuguese authorities had even employed the same nomenclature in Rio at the end of the eighteenth century.

---

[8] I have converted Brazilian Reais into dollars. At the end of 2014, the exchange rate was US$ 1 – Brazil R$ 2.68. In March 2020, US$1 – Brazil R$ 5.19. Eike Batista went bust in 2013. In 2018 he was sentenced to 30 years in prison for bribing state officials.

My first direct experience of pacification came in 2009 when I was working with a British TV journalist on a piece about walls around favelas. The international media choked at the emotive notion that Rio's dastardly authorities were going to wall off the poor. In fairness, they mainly wanted to limit further unregulated expansion and destruction of the rainforest. We met Captain Priscilla, the woman in charge of the first pacification unit – UPP for short – in Dona Marta favela in the Botafogo neighbourhood, where the proposed walls were to be built.[9] Dona Marta is famous for a video made there by Michael Jackson – there is even a statue and a miniature "plaza" named after him on the roof of a resident's house. As we chatted to Priscilla in her new base at the top of the hill, children played around us. The informal atmosphere was more that of a crèche than a military police HQ. Priscilla explained that the first step of the process involved the retaking of territory, and that the second foresaw the arrival of decent public services – sanitation, electricity, water – and eventually the provision of full citizenship for residents. For the first time in the city's history, favelas would no longer be off-limits to outsiders. Illegal guns would be off the streets and drug dealers would have to run their business in secret, as they do elsewhere in the world. Pacification provided a chance of peace and, although it had the wrong name, I wished it would work.

The black-shirted BOPE spearheaded pacification by occupying communities before the arrival of the UPP. They frighten me. They always have done. Their institutional symbol is a white skull on a black flag – a pair of pistols lying underneath

---

9   UPP stands for *Unidade de Polícia Pacificadora* in Portuguese.

3 / PEACE LOST: THE FAILURE OF PACIFICATION

resembles the cross-bones from a "Jolly Roger" pirate flag. A long dagger cleaves the skull through the cranium from the top and out under the chin. According to BOPE propaganda this symbol reflects intelligence, knowledge and the will to overcome fear of death. For many it means murder. Nevertheless, the BOPE undertook the first phase of pacification, retaking the territory for the state. Because their occupation of different favelas was always pre-announced, local drug traffickers left well in advance. There was never any resistance to pre-UPP operations. The BOPE simply walked in and set up shop, proving that peaceful policing of favelas is entirely possible, when given the necessary backing from government and society.

We visited their hilltop HQ in the Laranjeiras neighbourhood to talk about our "walls around favelas" work, that had now morphed into a wider ranging piece about the pacification process. A number of their bullet-damaged armoured vehicles sat in the car park. Inside, their affable public relations officer Captain Gripp (appropriately named for a no-nonsense policeman) invited us to accompany a patrol of the newly occupied Cantagalo, an old community that crawls up a steep escarpment separating Copacabana from Ipanema.[10] I knew Cantagalo well and often used to walk up the hill on Fridays after midnight for a *baile funk*. One New Year's Eve, I'd left the fireworks and celebrations on the beach to do so. At the bottom of the favela I had waded through a throng of crackheads, bombed out of their minds on the year's inaugural high. After dark, Cantagalo used to be that sort of place.

---

10 Captain Gripp, a popular and respected policeman, was killed in an alleged shootout in September 2013. The circumstances of his death – in a remote area at dawn, no witnesses, no follow-up operation – seemed strange to me.

Unlike the amiable Captain Gripp, the BOPE officers on patrol were sullen and un-talkative. Keen to be rid of us as soon as possible, they prowled Cantagalo's alleys, part helter-skelter, part maze, guns pointed at anyone and everyone. They performed random searches for the camera and stopped a man carrying a black plastic bag. They insisted on reviewing its contents – *kangas* (sarongs) for sale at the beach. Carefully and slowly, the vendor removed his pieces one by one until the bag was empty, the multicoloured *kangas* balanced in a neat pile on the ground. As we walked away, one of the policemen clumsily knocked them into a puddle. While the man kneeled to pick up his spoilt merchandise, we continued down the favela.

In 2010, pacification arrived in Providência. The UPP programme only sent new recruits to favelas. Sitting on a kerb next to some 11-year-olds, I observed young police on one of their first patrols, creeping around the favela's alleys, nervous and scared. Providência's kids are raised on shootouts, drug dealing, arms dealing, police operations, corruption and murder. They know well how police might extort money from gang members one day only to return to try and kill them a week later. Comparatively, favela children are war veterans, and for them, the fresh-faced new UPP recruits were funny to watch. Everyone knew they didn't need to patrol the favela with guns drawn. Once pacification was on its way, Providência's drug traffickers had long since fled to the Complexo do Alemão, leaving behind a few discreet pairs of eyes and ears.

It was a relief not to worry about the shooting that used to break out so often. But because Providência occupies prime real estate overlooking the port, powerful parties were keen to occupy the land. The surrounding area was due for a massive

3 / PEACE LOST: THE FAILURE OF PACIFICATION

Protest against favela removals, Providência 2011.

pre-Olympic facelift. There was talk of building a luxury hotel at the top of the favela. Now pacification brought another form of instability to the community – the threat of forced removals. Without prior notice, City Hall staff roamed the hilltop equipped with spray cans. Like official vandals they marked houses due for demolition with "SMH", an acronym for the municipal housing authority.

Maurício and I got involved in subsequent protest activity. We photographed residents at risk of removal and over several days they wheat-pasted their magnified portraits on the outside of houses for an outdoor exhibition that covered the authorities' Orwellian scrawl with human faces.[11] Beside legal activity, NGO efforts and a visit by the UN Special Rapporteur for Housing, the exhibition was successful, and the planned removals were postponed. All the same, some residents accepted the meagre compensation offered by the government and moved elsewhere. When they did so, the municipality quickly demolished the empty house, leaving craters where homes once stood. The authorities aimed to wear people down. Each house demolished inflicted a psychological blow on the neighbours. Who likes living next to a gaping hole?

But not everyone in the police was happy about pacification. In Providência, cancerous forces worked to sabotage the process from the outset. One night during the new UPP's first year, men wearing balaclavas roamed unchallenged around the favela for several hours. They gave out severe beatings and informed victims to spread the information that they planned to set up a militia

---

[11] JR's team supplied us with the prints as part of his global "Inside Out" art intervention.

3 / PEACE LOST: THE FAILURE OF PACIFICATION

in the favela. People were terrified and sought out Maurício. Through friends we arranged a private meeting to talk about the incident with Colonel Robson, the policeman in overall charge of the pacification programme. With authorities I was always aware of my gringo status, so I kept quiet while Robson listened carefully to Maurício and promised to take action. He said he would find out which police were on duty that night.

After our meeting the men with balaclavas did not appear again, but now their message and purpose was well known, not just to us and everyone else in the favela, but also to the police top brass. The men, probably corrupt police, aimed to undermine any advances achieved by the process so far, by spreading fear in the favela. They succeeded. Meanwhile, at numerous UPP inaugurations now coming thick and fast around the city, governor Sérgio Cabral gave speeches on restoration, liberty and legitimacy. Police Chief Beltrame, pacification's principal architect, spoke about reversing the established state practice of violent policing and substituting it with saving lives. He urged society and the rest of government to support the process by bringing long-term social improvements to favelas. Buglers, not always in tune, heralded the raising of the Brazilian and Rio de Janeiro state flags above their heads. A highly expensive publicity machine churned out pro-pacification propaganda. Cabral was up for re-election as state governor and pacification was his flagship project.

I HELD MISGIVINGS about the long-term viability of pacification. Many favela residents complained that it was just another form of occupation. Critics thought the programme was based on Cabral's short-term political objectives and the upcoming mega-events. They said that, statistically speaking, it would be impossible in the long term to place so many police in all favelas across the city. Despite such concerns, I applied for work at UPP Social, a mayoral programme organised in partnership with UN Habitat, that aimed to inform and connect authorities and service providers with pacified communities and vice versa,

Borel, 2011.

3 / PEACE LOST: THE FAILURE OF PACIFICATION

to facilitate the favela–city integration part of the UPP process. But I didn't hear back for weeks, and had all but given up when one of the coordinators asked to meet me. I was well qualified, he said, but as a foreigner they had reservations. They didn't know what public officials in local government would think of a gringo working in the UPP programme. Nor did I. But they could offer me an assistant role, he said. I took the job. If I doubted the lasting potential of the initiative, at least I could try and support the process. The fatigued city deserved better. Violence was decreasing. When would we get another chance to bring peace to Rio?

My colleagues were psychologists, social scientists, social activists and Masters and PhD students. We were keen to get to work and after receiving a standard issue pencil case I felt all the excitement of starting at a new school. My team was assigned to three UPPs in northern Rio's Tijuca neighbourhood; Borel, Andaraí and Formiga. The hills behind Tijuca are lush and green, not unlike Swiss chocolate-box photographs. Favelas are not dens of deprivation, especially when a community is built next to a rich neighbourhood like Tijuca. Favelas hide bustling internal economies; clothes shops, bars, restaurants, supermarkets and dozens of tiny grocery stores. They have their own transport services, not to mention residents' associations, cultural organisations and dozens of churches. Tijucan favelas were built and populated by neighbourhood service providers; washerwomen and domestic servants married to carpenters, labourers and porters whose children now painted nails, drove buses, swept streets and manned cash tills at supermarkets. This symbiotic socio-geographic formula, of a middle-class neighbourhood serviced by an adjacent favela, reproduces itself ad infinitum across Rio.

Work in Borel began with a tense meeting about parties. In the past, the drug traffic operators were in charge. The music was as loud as they wanted. The party ended when they wanted. Now, under the UPP, there were no more *baile funk*. Residents who now tried to put on their own events complained that police approval was arbitrary and erratic. They only had to have a birthday gathering for police to appear and close it down. No one knew the rules any more.

Amaral, the UPP Captain, sat with his face scrunched up, his eyes focused on no one. He looked like he was about to explode. People complained that while someone called Bruno was allowed to put on parties, when they asked, the police refused permission. Everyone talked over each other. Colonel Robson got up as if to leave. The meeting was on the edge. But eventually there was a moment of lucidity. Robson talked about the beginning of a cathartic process. The president of the residents' association, a fiery woman called Roberta, vented one last burst of frustration, saying that the association was disrespected, that no one valued their work, and that they

A photo opportunity I couldn't resist; a poodle wears a combat vest. Borel, 2011.

weren't even asked to help out for the UPP's first birthday. But when she said that despite everything she liked Captain Amaral, he smiled. People laughed. For a moment you could feel real hope in the air. Colonel Robson, speaking slowly and sincerely, closed the meeting with an apology for past violence on behalf of the police. The room became very still and quiet as residents digested his words.

On quiet weekdays, when most of the population was at work, I patrolled the alleys of the communities and sub-favelas that constituted the territory with my colleagues Ebenézer and Monique. We took impassable roads, where, until recently, rival gang members took pot shots at each other day and night. We traversed the frontier between Borel and neighbouring Casa Branca where a vicious war was famous for illuminating the Tijucan night with tracer fire. I got on well with my colleagues, except for the occasional faux pas. Sometimes I took one too many photos; of the view, of crooked alleys and the tangled wire spaghetti created by pirate electricity supplies. I took photos of children, old people, cars, walls, cats and dogs. One afternoon Monique tut-tutted and Ebénezer winked and nudged her. "He thinks it's exotic", he said. I pretended not to notice, but I was troubled by his comment. Maybe I did find favelas exotic, but the important thing was to get the job done. We wanted the process to work as well as it could. We wanted to stop the violence and we were full of enthusiasm and a fair amount of hope.

Captain de Souza however, the Commander of Andaraí and a neighbouring UPP, comprehensively demolished our hope. He spouted convoluted sociological argument to camouflage his love of war and disdain for the favela and its inhabitants. With gleaming eyes, he recounted the good old days when he used to

3 / PEACE LOST: THE FAILURE OF PACIFICATION

lean out of a patrol car window to exchange gunfire with drug traffickers on the footbridge above the road that passes Borel. It was "very good", he said with a sigh. He talked cheerfully about night-time operations to break up *baile funk* where they would drive the *caveirão* straight through the dancefloor and into and over the sound system. He added that, at the end of such operations, they would "*fazer o serviço*" – or do the job. Arresting people? I asked. The captain looked me straight in the eye. There's no point, he said. Arresting them solves nothing. His euphemism "to do the job", meant executing suspects on the spot.

Even if the psychopathic affability of this captain was not going to dampen our enthusiasm for the UPP project, many locals had little faith. A vocal community leader believed pacification would never work because once the illegal money – funds raised from bribes and extortion – stopped coming in, the ubiquitous corrupt Major in each local military police battalion would no longer have the means to sustain his over-inflated, high-maintenance lifestyle; the extra maid, his daughter's society wedding, private school for his lover's child. This was funny but it was also true; corruption breeds extravagance. Pacification was always going to set police against each other. Deep-rooted practices undermined its chances of success. The unregulated favela economy and income from drugs generates serious money and much of it goes to the police. The war also produces a parallel economy of licit and illicit weapons supplies. And there were policemen like the captain in Andaraí who simply enjoy violence. For such men, war is a way of life. For the UPP to succeed, serious, honest officials like Colonel Robson would have to outnumber the war-loving and corrupt police. It was never going to be simple.

By 2013, the pacification we hoped for – peaceful integration of the favela into the city – began to unravel. The traffickers slowly returned and rearmed. Corruption schemes were uncovered. Police Chief Beltrame continued to declare that pacification would not work without full engagement from all sectors of state and society; the favelas needed inclusion, decent public services and citizenship. His appeals fell on deaf ears. Rio society embraced the new found sense of safety that pacification provided, but not the favelas. By reducing the ability of criminals to circulate, pacification had reduced crime and violence in middle-class areas. However, although many Rio residents did feel safer, their goodwill did not extend to the wider favela population and the communities themselves. For their part, the latter had hoped pacification might work. They were exhausted by gunfights, exhausted by *baile funk* that went on all hours and the sale and consumption of drugs on their doorstep. When pacification came and the shooting stopped, most people hoped the process would bring peace. Then, bit-by-bit, the drug traffickers and their guns reappeared. The shooting restarted and the police began to take bribes again – or not, you never know who is on the take and who is not. A schizoid routine took over. Once more, you lived with the permanent threat of a gun battle on your doorstep. Rio had changed again, in order for everything to stay the same.

Eventually, the UPP Social programme went no further than box ticking and map-making. It had no teeth and the promised deluge of social investment failed to materialise. The coordinator was first to leave. Then the military police high command rewarded Colonel Robson, and his honesty and dedication, with removal from his post. He was promoted to a

3 / PEACE LOST: THE FAILURE OF PACIFICATION

desk job. "Kicked upstairs," he said. The eager staff that joined the UPP Social at the beginning, myself included, drifted away. Despite this, pacification continued to be centre of global media attention on the city. Reporters breathlessly accompanied huge theatrical invasions of strategic beachside favelas like Vidigal and Rocinha. In the run-up to the World Cup, pacification became an international media event. There was truth in the fact that the state was retaking territory, but no one outside Brazil bothered to tell the story of what happened next. Now residents lived with two sets of rules and two sets of armed groups, as gun-toting drug traffickers and police now circulated in the same spaces, often only a winding alley away from each other.

IN 2013 A BRITISH TV COMPANY that had won awards for a documentary on India hired me. They had found men who sieved sewers in Bombay's jewellers' district to survive by finding gold in shit. They expected to find parallel stories in Rio. Looking for such drama, but finding none, I explored lesser-known favela complexes like Caju and Lins in the days before their pacification. In Caju – a community sandwiched between main roads, the port and a cemetery, just days before the police were due to occupy the community – a teenage drug trafficker stood in front of our car, waving his automatic pistol at me. He wanted to know what we were doing. Nothing special, I explained. Just making a film about pacification.

At the same time, in the gigantic Rocinha, pacification revealed its true nature, hitherto hidden to the world, when UPP police took a 43-year-old local bricklayer called Amarildo de Souza into their base for questioning. No one ever saw him again. Security cameras recorded the moment when he was detained and witnesses heard his screams. The case hit the headlines but was met with a wall of silence. Four BOPE vehicles were recorded entering and leaving the UPP base that night. When investigators tried to trace one of them, which they believed might have been carrying a corpse, they learnt that the vehicle's GPS system had been switched off. Major Santos, a former BOPE officer and commander of the Rocinha UPP at the time, initially tried to blame Amarildo's disappearance on drug traffickers.

Santos based his argument on the false testimony of a resident who, it was later revealed, had been bribed. When the lies collapsed, prosecutors charged Major Santos and 24 police with torture, conspiracy, fraud and concealing a body. Despite the eventual conviction and imprisonment of Santos and 12 others, Amarildo's "disappearance" and the bungled cover-up was fatal to the credibility of the UPP project. His body has never been located. BOPE involvement in the scandal is highly likely but is, as yet, unproven.

Even when I was busy with work in Providência, my UPP Social duties or hunting for proverbial gold in shit, I always tried to stay up to date on events in the now pacified Alemão. For $70 million, the state governor had built a giant cable car that was supposed to integrate the favela with the surrounding city. I enjoyed riding in the gondolas and looking down at the higgledy-piggledy pile of houses, especially on Sundays when people had barbecues and splashed about in rooftop paddling pools. All the funk, pagode and samba merged with chitter-chatter and noise into one unique soundtrack as I whizzed overhead, ever the voyeur. At the same time, I resented it. The cable car was a mind-boggling waste of money. Internal transport has never been a problem in the Alemão; independent local moto-taxi

3 / PEACE LOST: THE FAILURE OF PACIFICATION

and VW combi van services provide 24-hour access to all areas of the community. The favela needed sanitation, social services, conflict mediation and peace. Not an urban ski lift.

In my early days in Rio I looked forward to visiting the Alemão. To get there I used to take the metro, and then an old, rattling VW van service. Inside the van on my way to visit Claudia and her family, I used to get a warm feeling in my stomach as we chuntered and chuffed through the suburb of Inhaúma, with its wide roads, little gated communities, its calmness and on the hills overhead the vast orange–brown sugar-stack of the Alemão. Pile upon pile of houses, magnificent in its disorder. I didn't like the war, and I didn't want it to exist. I wanted things to be different. But away from the cosmetic privilege of the beachfront and the *Zona Sul* (South Zone), I often felt better there.[12] It made sense for me to be in the Alemão. At times I felt like a clumsy, invasive intruder. But I was always received with warmth. Before pacification there was always excitement in the air. As wrong as things were, with the gun display and the drugs and the terrible music, there was always a *baile funk* on Fridays, Saturdays and Sundays, and endless parties and there was happiness amid all the chaos. The favela made its own rules, and they were not good or right, but things worked, and people managed, in between police operations, to be happy. I learnt something from my visits to the Alemão, and I tried to give something back. I loved the Alemão, Claudia and her family. I still do. Her girls were now teenagers with Facebook accounts, growing pains and issues with boys. Claudia had adopted a baby,

---

[12] Rio's South Zone is the traditional middle and upper class part of the city that includes beachfront neighbourhoods such as Copacabana and Ipanema. Visitors to Rio tend to spend most of their time there.

Pedro, abandoned by a crack addict in the favela. She worked managing a team of cleaners in a condo in Barra. Her eldest daughter, Bia, who used to fit neatly under my armpit, was now 18 and as tall as me.

The light-heartedness and righteousness of my earlier visits had long disappeared. Now I dreaded the journey. There were no longer any bullet holes in the church and a priest even appeared to celebrate mass there now and then. A shiny UPP base sat where the traffickers used to hang around peddling their drugs, and just opposite lay a cable car station. Police in bulletproof jackets came in and out of the UPP. There was a constant to and fro and changing of shifts. At Claudia's the cable car moved silently over our heads, its individual gondolas usually empty. One of few open spaces in the favela, a mini square where children played football, used to lie in front of her house. Now even this had gone, and new houses and a church stood in its place. Despite everything, the favela continued to grow. Now there is only the path where the children used to play. But they didn't hang out in front of the house anymore. It was too dangerous. A gunfight could break out at any moment. It depended which police are on duty. Some patrolled peacefully, others sought out drug traffickers. You never knew what might happen. If not at school, the children stayed at home, inside. Their social lives were virtual.

At first in the Alemão, the UPP programme had reduced shooting. The number of officially recorded bullets fired there dropped from 23,335 in 2010 to 2,395 in 2012.[17] In some ways, life became more bearable. Even so, Claudia and her family were frightened. The drug traffickers continued to have eyes and ears everywhere and even minor contact with police could lead to accusations of being an informer, and consequent

3 / PEACE LOST: THE FAILURE OF PACIFICATION

expulsion from the community or worse. Relations with police were always tense. They turned up threateningly when residents held parties. They moved their base into Bia's school, which soon became bullet-ridden. And before long, gun battles were commonplace. Pacification brought war to the favela 24 hours a day. On hot summer nights Bia used to sleep on an open veranda but she stopped doing so when drug traffickers threw a homemade grenade containing nails and marbles that landed on top of her. Somehow she managed to wake up and get inside before the device exploded. The subsequent shooting went on for 40 minutes. The police put two bullets through Claudia's steel front door; the traffickers put one through a window. The next morning at first light the police returned to pick up bullet capsules and remove any evidence of the gunfight. They said they were sorry, but nothing more. The drug traffickers appeared later and offered to pay for a new window.

I watched the opening game of the 2014 World Cup on Claudia's sofa. Matches meant a temporary ceasefire, if not for the whole day, then at least for a few hours. For those hours the Alemão was at its best. The Brazil game days were public holidays and massive occasions in the favela. Residents covered alleys, houses and lampposts in yellow and green paint. Improvised big-screens stood outside bars and on corners. People wore the national strip, lit barbecues, stocked up on beers and invited friends over. They set off fireworks and made the most of the moment. No one had exceptional expectations but everyone wanted the team to do well. The longer Brazil stayed in the competition, the more parties there would be. Each match day gave a boost to the favela's micro-economy, another chance for the local entrepreneurs selling hooters, rattles and other World

World Cup match in the Alemão, 2014.

Cup paraphernalia to recoup their outlay. But you could not deny that Brazil's chances seemed cursed – from the moment their team kicked off the nation's campaign with an own goal.

I witnessed Brazil's catastrophic 7-1 defeat to Germany (like Flamengo football club, the German players wore red and black!) at Claudia's mother's, on a giant plasma TV. The image was so crisp and clear it felt like the match was going on in the room. When the goals started to go in, we reacted first with shock, dismay and eventually, laughter as endless German goals

3 / PEACE LOST: THE FAILURE OF PACIFICATION

pierced Brazilian hearts. It was unreal. At half time we walked across UPP police lines into "bandit country". Even though the Alemão was pacified, armed drug traffickers dominated and carried on as normal in large swathes of the favela. We followed a road in darkness for 300 metres. The gang allowed no lighting on this stretch that led to their part of the favela. In doorways, shadowy teenagers carried guns and shared sickly smelling joints. There were several massive speaker systems set up in the street.

It was the mix of party and gang enclave that I remembered from the days before pacification. Kids bounced on a trampoline. Small groups of people gathered in front of bars to watch the worst football humiliation in the history of the world. Now cheers and fireworks greeted German goals. At the end of the match, the street filled with hundreds of people for one last big party. We laughed, drank, danced and celebrated. I drank to forget the football calamity and to forget the police and traffickers preparing for battle. I drank to forget the ridiculous cable car.[13] I drank to forget everything bad that had happened in the last few years. I drank until I didn't feel anything any more.

Following the World Cup debacle, hopes for peace in the Alemão permanently unravelled. I continued to visit Claudia. Bia, hardly out of school, was pregnant with her first child. We did not go out much; it was too dangerous. The bars, beauty salons, pizzerias and bakeries of the Alemão that used to buzz with customers and activity were all but empty. In September 2014, Uanderson Silva, the 34-year-old Commander of one of the complex's three UPP bases, was shot and killed not five minutes walk from Claudia's house. The loss of this respected

---

13 The cable car ceased functioning in 2016, shortly after the Olympics.

commander, popular with residents and known for his ability to promote dialogue, was initially blamed on drug traffickers. Then, investigators discovered that he was killed with a single rifle shot in his back, fired by a junior UPP soldier. While they concluded that the shot was accidental "friendly fire", some locals believe the Commander was deliberately killed in order to wreck pacification in the Alemão for once and all. In April 2015, within a 24-hour period, police bullets killed Elizabeth Alves, a 41-year-old housewife, and Eduardo de Jesus, a 10-year-old boy playing in front of his house three minutes walk from Claudia's front door. The policeman who shot and killed Eduardo, from a distance of five metres, was not charged.

Even though Providência is much smaller than the Alemão, and was nearer to the forthcoming Olympic action, it did not take long for pacification to collapse there either. In September 2015, a group of UPP police apprehended and then summarily executed Eduardo Felipe, a 17-year-old faction member. From a crack in a window overhead, neighbours filmed the police as they faked a shootout, firing a revolver that they then put into the dead boy's hand. When the clip made national and international news, enraged residents protested in the streets near Central Station.

Ultimately, pacification constituted no more than a territorial re-arrangement. Pacification failed to reduce violence, and it failed to integrate the favela with the city. Without sustained governmental and financial support for the process, the perverse logic of political domination and the economics of corruption won. Rio de Janeiro all too quickly slid back into its natural state of fear, mistrust and chronic insecurity. Rio's big chance for peace was squandered.

PART TWO

THE GREATEST SHOW

"Every region of the globe needs one city where the rules don't apply, where sin is the norm, and where money can buy anything or anyone."

– THOMAS L. FRIEDMAN,
From Beirut to Jerusalem.

4

COCAINE: WHITE GOLD

Cocaine is integral to the contemporary drama of Rio de Janeiro. It's been that way for quite some time. Popular, early twentieth-century chroniclers of Rio's Belle Époque (well-educated, travelled men like Benjamim Costallat) documented the nocturnal decadence of the *carioca* establishment, particularly its men, who spent nights cavorting in environments where cocaine consumption was *de rigueur*. In 1924, the same year that he visited Providência, Costallat wrote about the city's cocaine neighbourhoods of Lapa and Glória, which at night "vibrated with light, the laughter of women, human spasms". In Glória, Costallat finds a street dealer who sells him German produced "Merck" cocaine, which he then takes to a brothel run by a Madame called Gaby. When he gives her two tiny glass flasks of Merck, she greets them with "shining eyes" and a "visible shiver of diabolical pleasure". Gaby, he observes, would probably deny bread to the poor, but if she needed drugs, she might even sell her last piece of jewellery.[18]

Cocaine remained a reasonably safe and popular drug for Rio's elite right through to the 1960s. Then Brazil began to follow the US-led war on drugs and UN-endorsed anti-narcotic conventions. These political shifts pushed cocaine further underground and further, as the stakes involved in buying and selling the substance rose, into the hands of criminals and corrupt officials. The tipping point came in the 1970s when, despite prohibition, worldwide demand for the drug blossomed. International traffickers began to move large quantities of cocaine through Rio de Janeiro.

THE REMARKABLY BEAUTIFUL CLAUDIA LESSIN came of age in the South Zone in 1977. Disco fever was at its height. Her elder sister, Marcia, was a well-known local actor who starred in a film adaptation of Tom Jobim's famous *The Girl from Ipanema*. The sisters came from a classic middle class Copacabana family, but their father, a civil aviation pilot, was not rich or powerful. They had lived in the same rented accommodation for 20 years. Claudia was sensitive and bright but, like many young people of any era, confused. Her father had recently travelled to the US to bring her home from Los Angeles where she had lived with Dusty, a gigolo boyfriend, and had been involved in all manner of scrapes. Back in Rio she plunged into a depression, stemmed only by psychoanalytic treatment and love for her cat Mouche.

She was just twenty-one when, one Monday morning, lifeguards found her naked corpse splayed on rocks at the Atlantic's edge. The discovery of an unknown female body – a white body – in this prominent spot, gripped the nation. Who was she? Who had killed her, and why? Claudia, face battered and disfigured beyond recognition, lay yards from the Avenida Niemeyer, a cliffside road leading from upper class Leblon to the neighbourhoods of São Conrado and Barra. In 1977, Barra was only beginning to grow and traditional South Zone *cariocas* regarded it as an undesirable neighbourhood, full of love motels and rum goings-on. Today, although Barra is a mecca for a certain type of moneyed Brazilian, for many *cariocas* its four-lane freeways, shopping centres and gated communities belong to an unwelcome dystopian nightmare.

If it had not been for a toothache, her murder might have gone unsolved. Indio, a migrant worker from the north-east, was unable to sleep the night before the discovery of her body. Cursing his bad tooth outside the precarious shack he shared with two other labourers, Indio spotted two men behaving strangely on the edge of the Niemeyer and noted down their license plate number. The car belonged to Michel Frank, son of a millionaire industrialist. But when a no-nonsense detective called Jamil Warwar publicly named Frank and his friend Georges Khour, a society hairdresser, as prime suspects, superiors removed him from the case. An Admiral and a Public Prosecutor offered and then withdrew an alibi for Frank. Rather than following up leads, police working on the case sought to slow it down. They did not carry out tests on the car, nor did they examine Frank, who had cuts on his hands and face. Eventually, Frank alleged that Claudia had died after an orgy of drug taking; that he and Khour dumped her body in panic. But the state autopsy said she had not taken drugs or even ingested alcohol. Claudia died from strangulation and head injuries. Following this revelation Michel Frank, who held dual nationality, fled to Switzerland.

Within a year of the murder, a prize-winning investigative journalist called Valério Meinel published a book called *Why Claudia Lessin Will Die*. Meinel meticulously picked apart the web of lies to discover that Khour and Frank were cocaine middlemen. Meinel believed they tried to force Claudia into sex, which she refused, threatening to expose what she had seen the night before in Frank's flat, when he had received a large quantity of cocaine that he promptly passed on in front of her to numerous Leblon society characters. Bombed on drugs and fearful of what she might do, Frank killed Claudia with his own hands. Khour helped to throw her body onto the cliffs in an attempt to fake the work of a sexual maniac. In 1980, the hairdresser, who had even cut little Claudia's hair as a child, was charged and imprisoned for accessory to murder. Frank remained in Switzerland where, in 1989, he was shot and killed by an unidentified assassin.

Naive young Claudia's horrific, public death – her naked corpse, her beauty and lost innocence – was a grisly portent of the havoc that the cocaine business was to wreak on Rio. Valério Meinel understood the symbolic significance of the murder as well as the implications of the subsequent cover-up. His book is both an investigative tour de force and a fascinating portrait of the South Zone at the end of the 1970s – that shines a bright, lucid light onto Rio's impending explosion of drug related violence. Meinel's genius is to get under the skin of his characters. He understood the petty prejudices, hidden hierarchies and social discomforts that drove *carioca* society and made life impossible for people like the detective Warwar:

> *I don't like Copacabana, nor anywhere in the South Zone. Everything is half-false, disguised by status. When I come*

up here, I always have the impression that some son-of-a-bitch is spying at me from a window the whole time. Things happen here that make me want to kick doors down and drag the culprit out. Like we do in the favela. There shouldn't be any difference, crime is crime. But here you can't. You have to be slippery, because everyone has a godfather. If we're not careful, when we get back to the station there are more than ten phone calls from bigwigs demanding our heads on a plate. Me, I'm from the suburbs, and proud of the fact.[19]

Meinel shrewdly identified the lethal opportunities for quick money and social ascension that cocaine opened up in Rio's torpid social matrix. He was empathetic with the principal victims of drugs – the young – and displayed extreme sensibility in understanding the needs, desires and fragilities that drive drug abuse. He describes a cocaine session that developed into an orgy in Frank's flat:

Paranoia floated in the air, revealing each of the participants as they were. Neurotic, needy, they seemed to reach the peak of their attention-seeking at that moment. They spoke, then, about themselves (...) Cocaine makes addicts frenetic and talented. Their eyes shine. Parties thrive on the powder, which raises the spirits and relieves memory, protects vigil, disguises emptiness, provokes euphoria, creates an illusion of self-sufficiency. And, above all, kills.[20]

But who supplied the suppliers? Where did people like Frank get their drugs? In Costallat's 1920s, cocaine was imported to Rio from Europe for medicinal use. Ninety per cent of it ended up on the black market, where an army of intermediaries and sellers distributed it across the city. According to Costallat, almost every profession – he cites chauffeurs, manicurists, barbers, dentists, doctors, fishmongers, waiters, gamblers and even journalists – had its share of cocaine suppliers. But although he had a clear grasp of the machine's inferior workings, he wondered who was at the top of the business:

> *But all this cocaine, spread across all these social classes, has a major wholesaler. He's the king of cocaine in Rio de Janeiro. He's the great pretender. A mysterious person who no one knows, but who dominates the clandestine market for the drug, setting prices and organising, unpunished and anonymous, its distribution and criminal sale.*
>
> *This king of cocaine, king of this century's great poison, with so many victims, must live surrounded by respectful peers. He must be rich and respected. He earns enough to be both things.*[21]

IN NOVEMBER 2013 A HELICOPTER carrying 450 kilograms of unprocessed cocaine landed on a farm in Espírito Santo state, just north of Rio de Janeiro. Police filmed the landing, arresting the two pilots and two other men as they unloaded the drugs into a car. But when it transpired that the helicopter belonged to a powerful politician from Minas Gerais, the investigation halted four days after the apprehension. In what appeared to be a cross between a cover-up and a damage-limitation exercise, federal police investigators called a press conference where they announced their conclusion that the cocaine had nothing to do with the member of the Minas Gerais state parliament, Gustavo Perrella, or his father Zezé Perrella, a federal government senator in Brasília.

The Perrella family are one of Minas Gerais' most powerful political clans, with strong ties to one-time presidential hopeful and former Minas state governor, Aécio Neves. Coincidentally, or not, Neves has struggled to stamp out consistent, long-standing allegations that he has been a lifelong cocaine user, if not addict. Neves' personal friend and ally, Senator Zezé Perrella served four terms as president of one of Brazil's most popular football teams, Cruzeiro, where one of the greatest living footballers, Ronaldo "Fenômeno", began his career. When the federal police and mass media dropped the matter like a hot potato, the "*Helicoca*" case was very quickly consigned to yesterday. However, dogged independent journalists discovered that the helicopter made a prior drop-off at a luxury hotel in São Paulo and that US DEA officers had visited the district judge in Espírito Santo to inform him that the drugs were probably Europe-bound. But by then the case was all but closed. The Perrella family denied all knowledge of the cocaine, laying the blame with the pilot, who they alleged had acted independently. But no one even arrested the pilot.

In *Zero, Zero, Zero*, an extensive analysis of the global power cocaine wields in the world today, organised-crime investigator Roberto Saviano argues that there is no financial investment in the world that gives better returns than cocaine; it is easier to sell than gold, its revenues can exceed those of oil, and in a few years cocaine speculators can accumulate the wealth that commercial organisations could only hope to achieve in decades. Saviano also asserts that:

For the most powerful families coke works as easily as an ATM machine. You need to buy a shopping centre? Import some coke, and after a month you'll have enough money to close the deal. You need to sway an election? Import some coke, and you'll be ready in a few weeks.[22]

In Brazil today, it's as if the "*Helicoca*" never existed. It simply vanished from the public domain, along with the half tonne of drugs. A minor detail – once processed, the shipment would have had a street value of $100 million. Another minor detail – at the end of 2013, Brazil's politicians, including the Perrella family, were gearing up for another costly presidential election. A final detail – who was incumbent President Dilma Rousseff's opposition rival? Aécio Neves.

THE MINAS GERAIS COCAINE CONNECTION reminds me of a turning point in my life. In 2001, whilst working on a report about torture in Brazil, I visited the civil police drugs unit in Belo Horizonte, the capital of Minas Gerais, with my co-worker at Amnesty International. The head of the station, a voluminous man armed with a sharp suit and wide grin, received us with a sweaty handshake in an uncharacteristically well-furnished office, which might have been more appropriate for the chief executive of a pharmaceutical company. He told us that 70 per cent of detainees in the unit, where there was 1000 per cent overcrowding, were not drug dealers but users and petty pushers. He was frank: "conditions here are subhuman".

The civil police he said, somewhat unfairly had to deal with detainees who should have been transferred to the prison system long ago, partly because of the slowness of the judiciary, and partly due to a desire to keep numbers in prison down. He thought a visit by Amnesty and consequent publicity for the overcrowding might better the situation. The chief also mentioned that he wanted to introduce us to some of his staff members, who had been demoralized by a recent state investigation into drug trafficking that made allegations of irregularities at the unit.

A white policeman with craterous pink skin and a shiny bald pate circled by hair that was tied back in a greasy ponytail, interrupted to whisper in his boss's ear. He looked like an informant straight off the set of *Miami Vice*. Ending our conversation, the chief walked us to the edge of his office, opened a door, and ushered us into a crowded room where more than a dozen station staff were waiting in seats. It was like walking out on to stage. The *Miami Vice* look-alike, keen and deferential, had been preparing our entrance. Whereupon the chief introduced us as visiting international human rights experts and invited us to speak.

There was a black female officer in the audience. Every time I caught her eye she looked away, as if her eyes might tell me something. At the end of our unplanned Q and A she invited us to see two tonnes of apprehended drugs in a small room that looked like an adapted broom cupboard, shelves stuffed with transparent bags containing marijuana, cocaine and rocks of crack. She showed us a handwritten notebook where seizures were registered. The lack of security for the drugs was surprising; as if they were intended *not* to be secure.

We entered the detention area after dark. The weather was cool and wet. A significant number of prisoners were held in an outdoor exercise area that effectively served as a huge cage. A bearded policeman with a pump-action shotgun walked across the reinforced wire mesh above our heads while we spoke to the men under the drizzle. They explained that overcrowding in the cells was so severe, that they had opted to face the elements outdoors. To stay warm our shivering interviewees, wearing woollen hats and sweaters, were constantly on the move.

Inside the lock-up, five cells opened onto a filthy, circular courtyard. Each one held an average of twenty-eight prisoners in spaces built to hold a total of four men. There was no electricity; overall conditions were squalid and disturbing. Light and ventilation for each cell came through a single barred door. A small room for meetings between lawyers and clients was used to cope with the overspill. In this room, that was so crowded prisoners took turns to sit, I was handed a note stating they had no toilet; they defecated in front of their cellmates in tin foil containers used for food. Several men mentioned a punishment room. When we asked about this police met our enquiry with theatrical puzzlement.

"There's no such place. They want to see a punishment cell? Oh, you mean *the deposit*?"

Guards escorted us outside the main lock-up area to a room with a heavy reinforced iron door, alongside a cell holding prisoners with special needs, including a paraplegic detainee in a wheelchair serving a four-year sentence for the possession of 50 grams of marijuana. The guards said they could not find the key to open the door, held shut by an industrial size padlock. We insisted on looking inside. Eventually someone appeared with a pair of bolt cutters to reveal a room filled with tables, desks, chairs, bicycles and other random bits of furniture.

"This," the guard said, with a dramatic sweep of the arm, "is where we keep stolen property."

As we left, the prisoner in the wheelchair called me over.

"They spent all this afternoon filling the room with that junk," he whispered.

The experience left me a different person. I wondered how human beings could survive what I had just seen. I would not have lasted 15 minutes. The visit repeated itself over and over again in a slideshow inside my head. I had a gut feeling that police from the drugs unit must run the city's narcotics business. Who would be better placed? By holding petty dealers and users in appalling conditions society had its bogeymen, providing cover for corrupt officials who could decide how, when and which drug dealers are caught.

While in Brazil this was the world of drugs that I witnessed, back in London I couldn't go out without someone telephoning a "bloke" who arrived in a car. Everyone would then be sneaking in and out of a toilet, hanging around, waiting for something to happen. The drug seemed to be everywhere. Weekend cocaine abuse went hand in hand with the bleak new millennium. Today, greater and greater quantities of cocaine pass through Brazil to satiate Europe and Asia's ever-increasing appetite for the super-stimulant. According to the *Guardian* newspaper, Calabria's 'Ndrangheta mafia move 80 per cent of European cocaine through the Brazilian port of Santos.[23] In reversal of the old slaving routes, much cocaine from Brazil now passes through West Africa on its way to these markets. Organised crime in the Middle East and Africa earns billions from the trade, which ferments corruption and instability. There were six coups in West Africa between 2008 and 2014, including an outbreak of civil war in Mali, formerly described by USAID as "one of the most enlightened democracies in Africa".[24] Meanwhile, back in Brazil, the illegal cocaine trade continues to wreak invisible, incalculable havoc in the realm of security, law and order, and politics.[14]

---

[14] In July 2019 a Brazilian Air Force Sergeant, on a special flight accompanying President Bolsonaro to a G20 meeting, tried to wheel a suitcase containing 39kg of undisguised high quality cocaine through Spanish customs. He told officials who opened his suitcase that he was bringing cheese to a cousin. The Sergeant, Manoel Silva Rodrigues, made 30 national and international trips for the Brazilian Air Force in five years.

5

THE ANIMAL GAME: MISRULE OF LAW

COCAINE WAS DEFINITELY A BIG PART of the problem; but after years living and working in the city I still did not understand how and why things in Rio de Janeiro had reached such despairing degrees of lawlessness. It didn't make sense for the favelas to be the source of all criminality. Aside from corrupt police and politicians, I wondered what other powers existed behind the favela-based gangs. The media and police officials describe these as organised crime, but they are often more like *disorganised* crime – retailers, not wholesalers. A teenager with a vest, Bermudas, flip-flops and a baseball hat is exactly that, until someone hands him an automatic pistol, or a rifle, at which point he becomes a criminal and a threat to life. But his power is limited to inside the territory where he lives – all the drugs and all the guns come from outside.

What else could lie behind this state of affairs? I continually struggled with the conundrum. One evening in 2011, I shared my anguished curiosity with Pedro, the pale-eyed, gentle *carioca* owner of the house where I had lived for many years. He motioned me to follow him to a bookcase, from which he pulled out an un-extraordinary looking book with a red and grey cover. Its name, *Eagle, Ostrich and Cocaine* (in Portuguese *Avestruz, Águia e Cocaína*), struck me as odd. Then I saw that Valério Meinel, the investigative journalist who had unravelled the Claudia Lessin murder, was the author. I read it in very few sittings.

The book tells the story of the gangsters who took over a very popular Brazilian illegal lottery, called the *jogo do bicho* (or "the animal game" in English)[15], in the 1970s and 80s; forming a mafia-style managing committee, a *cúpula*, that centralised all decisions related to their criminal operations. Meinel mentions them briefly in *Why Claudia Lessin Will Die*. Claudia's assassin, the South Zone coke dealer Michel Frank, repeatedly states that his supplier is a powerful man – a *jogo do bicho* banker – whom he refuses to name. Even though Meinel used fictitious names in the book, the publication of *Eagle, Ostrich and Cocaine* in 1987 lead to death threats, a kidnap attempt and six years of unemployment. When leading members of the *cúpula* were charged and imprisoned in 1993, the book was included as evidence and cited in her summing up by Denise Frossard, the judge who sentenced 14 *jogo do bicho* bankers to six years in prison under anti-gang laws. The year following the historic verdict, the book was reissued with a key explaining the real identity of each "fictitious" character. The book is a classic *Who's Who* of crime in Rio de Janeiro. It captures the spirit of the city's decadent 1970s and 80s, decades which saw the acceleration of Rio's slide into a quagmire of corruption and violence.

---

15 In Portuguese, the "ch" in *bicho* is pronounced like "sh" in English.

5 / THE ANIMAL GAME: MISRULE OF LAW

Meinel's central argument goes beyond discussion of the illegal lottery itself, to argue that, starting in the 1970s, the gangsters who formed the *jogo do bicho cúpula* (known in Rio as *jogo do bicho* "bankers") used their criminal networks to import and distribute cocaine in the city and elsewhere. Seeing that consumption, profit and corruption reigned in the city's affluent neighbourhoods, Meinel dared to question the much-vaunted state and media contention that it was criminals from favelas who were behind the cocaine trade. In colourful *carioca* detail, he describes the connections between the *jogo do bicho* bankers, the authorities and their mutually spun webs of criminal activity. The book's principal character is a chain-smoking crime reporter called Agostinho Seixas, last of an old guard of hard-nosed investigative journalists. Seixas is crippled by his obsessive, impulsive quest to find truth in what he refers to as Rio's "shitswamp" of immorality. Fired from his job for refusing to reveal his sources, he looks around the newspaper's editing suite and describes his ex-colleagues. Agostinho witnesses the death of investigative journalism in Rio de Janeiro and the beginning of the official propaganda-inspired crime reporting that dominated Brazilian media for so long.

> *Young men of twenty to twenty-five…who still believe in the profession…obedient, well behaved. They do what they are told, content to report on the collective interviews with ministers and secretaries, in the air-conditioned offices where the authorities' sensibility is frozen. They don't complain about their tasks, they don't have sources of information, they couldn't even cover a murder – they would vomit before a corpse – but soon they will be writing their reports on a text machine or a computer. The future belongs to them…*[25]

Meinel also described the birth of the powerful police death squads. These were illegal vigilante groups, a precursor of the sophisticated modern militia, who claimed to keep the streets crime free. They had names like "The Golden Boys" and the "Escuderie Detetive Le Cocq", and in 1970s Rio were associated with a police detective called Mariel Maryscott, who murdered suspects, innocents and enemies. He left messages with a card displaying a skull and crossbones and the letters "E.M" – *Esquadrão da Morte* (death squad) – next to corpses. Maryscott began his career as a lifeguard on Copacabana Beach before joining the police and becoming a minor celebrity. By the time of his murder – ordered by *jogo do bicho* bankers whom he betrayed – he was a major crime figure in Rio, a corrupt policeman who forced others to commit crime and pass the spoils to him. He killed those who refused, perversely displaying their corpses as an example of another dead criminal. Like the crooked Inspector Torres (the cigar-smoking self-styled Rambo whom we met in the "Waging War" chapter) in 2010, Maryscott was both villain and hero, embodying a toxic criminal pathology at the core of Brazilian law and order, whereby police are free to murder, torture, steal and extort – with the approval of society, as long as they target the poor and vulnerable.

In this underworld, the *jogo do bicho* bankers, known locally as *bicheiros*, sit silently at the centre of the action. Because their lottery is illegal – yet at the same time popular, and socially acceptable – they are, like Maryscott, both hero and villain. They have a symbiotic relationship with corrupt police – just as the *bicheiros* need the police to turn a blind eye, the police need the *bicheiros* to supplement their pay. Although the *bicheiros* always publicly denied any involvement with cocaine trafficking, I prefer to trust

Meinel, who died in 1997.[16] His evocation of a Rio that lay just out of my reach inspired me to study the *jogo do bicho* in depth. Although he won several prestigious awards, none of his books remain in print. I was lucky to have come across *Eagle, Ostrich and Cocaine*, because no one ever spoke to me about the *jogo do bicho*. *Cariocas* accept the game as a fact of life. But the more I researched and learned, the more I felt I was unravelling a golden thread that would help me better understand not only the dynamics of Rio de Janeiro, but also the history of modern Brazil. The *jogo do bicho* has deep roots reaching into all corners of Brazilian society. The more I learned, the closer I felt I was to the truth. I sensed the ghost of Valério Meinel at my shoulder, gently urging me on.

SEVEN DAYS A WEEK, RAIN OR SHINE, a man with ink-stained hands works outside a bar. He sits discretely on the pavement at a classic school desk that combines a wooden chair with a small writing surface. He is in his late fifties, with slicked-back hair and a thick moustache. He is unmistakably Brazilian but, all the same, looks as if he might be descended from Italians or Portuguese, with a smidgen of something else. He works long, hard days. When the sun hits his spot, he might move his chair across the road to the shade.

If you didn't realise he was there, you might not notice him among the men drinking beer, the hospital cleaners and doormen from the condos, with their brown overalls and *nordestino* faces. People, often older people, pause at his side and he listens carefully to what they say, noting their requests in

---

[16] In 2013 I interviewed a high-ranking federal policeman who recommended Valério Meinel's book about the *jogo do bicho*. When I replied that I had read it, he added, "Meinel describes what actually happened."

Handwritten jogo do bicho results in Rio's South Zone 2013.

swirling handwriting on a small pad. He tears these off, keeping a pink carbon copy, handing the top paper over. Customers sometimes confer lists of hand-printed numbers pasted on the wall behind him. There is always a discrete coming and going around this man, a palpable energy which emanates from him and him alone. The man is an *apontador* (a bookie) for the *jogo do bicho* and his betting point, something like an open-air office, is called a *ponto*. In Rio the "animal game" is everywhere. But if you don't know what it looks like, you might not realise it exists. I often stop and chat to the man taking bets for the *jogo do bicho*. He is one of the hardest working *cariocas* I know.

5 / THE ANIMAL GAME: MISRULE OF LAW

The *jogo do bicho* is based on a sequence of 25 numbers. A unique animal – perhaps a lion, ostrich, snake, deer or dog – is attached to each number. In turn, each number is attached to groups of four, in order that the 25 animals fit into a round hundred. So if I wager on the horse, which is group 11, I am betting on the numbers 41, 42, 43 and 44. A results slip contains seven different numbers, but if I choose one animal only, the alligator for instance, the only two digits that matter to me are the last two digits of the first result. If these include one of the numbers 57, 58, 59 or 60, I win. This is the simplest form of betting, one in which a child or anyone with a rudimentary grasp of numbers can partake. There are, however, endless permutations and possibilities. The animal game allows you to bet as much or as little as you wish on any combination of numbers you choose. Monday to Saturday there are four daily draws, with a single extraction on a Sunday. The animal game is illegal but because it's only a misdemeanour – like a traffic offence – it is a tolerated, common aspect of daily life in Rio de Janeiro. What is most surprising is its longevity: the *jogo do bicho* is more than one hundred and twenty five years old.

A flamboyant entrepreneur called Baron de Drummond invented the *jogo do bicho* in 1892. He was a property developer who founded Rio's first fully planned neighbourhood in the last years of the Empire. He built Vila Isabel, with its public squares and wide Paris-inspired boulevards, on the northern edges of the city; land that was formerly part of a plantation known as *Fazenda Macaco*, the Monkey Estate, from which Monkey Hill favela gets its name. Baron Drummond, as he is known today, was born and raised in Minas Gerais and therefore not a native *carioca*. Although an outsider, he achieved considerable status in Rio. He was a shrewd businessman who married into the city's elite. He belonged to a freethinking, abolitionist avant-garde and named his neighbourhood after renowned anti-slavery campaigner Princess Isabel, last heiress of the Empire. Drummond wanted to create zoological gardens, a European standard entertainment facility, to bring visitors and investment to Vila Isabel. Good relations with city councillors meant quick approval for his idea. All the same they made numerous stipulations, insisting that the zoo maintain the highest standards of hygiene, that it be free for students, and that it hold exhibitions and competitions for domestic animals. The zoo, which opened in 1888, should be world class.

The first years of the Brazilian Republic, established in 1890, were characterised by feverish business and financial speculation. Rapidly industrialising Rio de Janeiro lay at the epicentre of this boom; it was a vital pole for distribution of imported goods and home to a fast-growing local consumer market. However mass immigration and soaring living costs contributed to a crisis. In 1891, stock prices fell and the value of the currency plummeted. When his new zoo ran into financial difficulties, the ever-enterprising Baron proposed a simple raffle to raise funds. Each visitor received a ticket printed with one in a series of 25 animals. Every day the Baron would display a picture of one animal chosen at random. Winners earned a cash prize twenty times the value of the entrance fee. In July 1892, Baron Drummond drew the first winning animal, an ostrich, in the presence of a select group of local dignitaries, including the vice-president of the new Republic.

No one knows how the Baron chose his list of 25. It includes both the domestic – cat, dog, pig – and the wild – tiger, bear, snake. This unusual meeting of tame and savage beasts caught on. Visitors to the zoo multiplied. Police were deployed to maintain order on overcrowded trams transporting the public to Vila Isabel. Now people visited the zoo to bet on, rather than look at, animals. In order to save gamblers from the trip and ease congestion, the Baron also organised ticket sales in the centre of town. The innocent raffle had quickly outstripped its original purpose. It attracted the attention of the new authorities. Initial supporters of the enterprise, the same powers-that-be, now interpreted the animal fever as a moral threat to the new Republic. They rescinded their contract with Baron Drummond. However instead of ending the frenzy the game had unleashed on Rio, they drove it underground. Individual entrepreneurs continued to sell tickets, adapting numbers from the official state lottery to "generate" winning animals. The *jogo do bicho* was here to stay.[26]

Waves of violence and political repression troubled the Republic in its early years. The new political elite viewed Rio de Janeiro as the heart of a clash between civilisation and barbarism. After the 1888 abolition of slavery, the poor and working classes were subjected to increased surveillance. The moral scandal generated by the *jogo do bicho* was integral to this historical moment blighted by public order concerns, racial fear, political disunity and class conflict. Oppression of the raffle arose from efforts made to impose moral standards and define differences in the new Brazil. But criminalisation failed. Suppressed by the authorities and championed by the people, the *jogo do bicho* transformed itself into a clandestine numbers game, which made an ass of the law.

The subsequent decline of Baron Drummond's admirable zoo project, which lurched from financial crisis to crisis and from owner to owner, contributed to a general failure to create the progressive, Europeanised city the architects of the new Republic had envisaged. Suppression of his massively popular raffle consolidated a repressive, conservative regime, imposed on the city's populace by the authorities. Early attempts at prosecutions of gamblers and ticket vendors were however hampered by procedural vagueness. The *jogo do bicho* was classified alongside drunkenness and vagrancy as a *contravenção* (a misdemeanour) and acquittal levels were high. Despite efforts to extinguish it, the secret raffle's popularity and lucrative nature led to the creation of a sophisticated modus operandi, based on bribery, favours and alliances, to guarantee its survival. Newspapers published daily results, both explicitly and covertly, while individuals within the police force and the local authorities developed an interest in maintaining the lottery for their personal financial gain.

A concentrated attack on the *jogo do bicho* began in 1917, the same year that Brazil entered the First World War. The so-called *mata bicho* (kill the animal) campaign took place in the context of generalised fears of international communism and a wave of pre-emptive counter-revolutionary repression targeting the organised working classes. Despite the 25 years of attempted suppression, the animal game employed thousands, was as popular as ever, and had spread to other capital cities like São Paulo and Salvador. Although high-ranking police officers publicly attacked the game's immorality, lawmakers struggled to enforce prohibition.

Police officers on the streets made up the rules as they went along and their complicity became essential in ensuring the game's survival. By defining and offering a market for illicit privileges which could be bought or withheld according to the moment and the personal wishes of the actors involved, the *jogo do bicho* became a critical ingredient in the maintenance of the unpredictable relationship between the Brazilian state and its population. The pervasive, and at the same time malleable lottery provided lawmakers, enforcers and politicians with both a source of illegal revenue and a formidable tool for social control and oppression.

In 1941, a Federal Decree outlawed the *jogo do bicho* across the nation, removing any doubt as to whether regulation of the game could be decided locally. However, the decree determined that the game remain an ambiguous *contravenção*, not a crime. In 1946, gambling was prohibited in all its forms. When casinos across Brazil closed, tens of thousands of workers lost their jobs. Despite public ridicule, these legal developments forced changes. The commercial side of the *jogo do bicho* was the product of individual enterprise until the 1930s; some shopkeepers sold tickets on the side, while other vendors worked autonomously. These *jogo do bicho* vendors, the *apontadores*, were among the most mobile and independent of Rio's popular classes.

The loose, unstructured network of independent vendors and occasional entrepreneurs responsible for ticket sales could not however survive under the new restrictive conditions. Increased prohibition forced committed *jogo do bicho* vendors into closer alliances within law enforcement, while smaller, less powerful ticket sellers began to drop away. Modernising and protecting the *jogo do bicho* became essential in order to guarantee its survival, and to ensure increases in profit commensurate with new risks. This process contributed to the rise of a new generation of *jogo do bicho* operators, known in Rio as "bankers", who oversaw clusters of sales points in the city, and used violence to defend or expand their territory. These bankers established well-protected, secret business premises known as *fortalezas* (fortresses). The use of these fortresses combined with technological improvements, such as telephones, transformed the game's operations. The bankers also opened secret casinos and, as their illegal business interests expanded, more jobs became available for those working in the *jogo do bicho* infrastructure and more bribes became available to police.

The 1940s and 1950s were golden years for the animal game. It continued to rely for survival on a promiscuous relationship with the authorities. By the end of this period, another illegal creation that was to shape Rio de Janeiro's future began to emerge. General Amauri Kruel, head of public security in the city, founded an elite police special services unit, a precursor of the infamous *Esquadrão da Morte*, to which he gave carte blanche to track down and eliminate alleged criminals in favelas. According to historian R. S. Rose, Latin America's police sanctioned death squads began in Rio de Janeiro, where:

> *there were to be no questions, no paperwork, and no prisoners taken alive. When it was decided to go after a specific suspect, the individual's death had already been agreed upon.*[27]

While the special services police were judge, jury and executioner of faceless victims in the favelas, they also had other interests. Kruel was proficient in police corruption. He took money from illegal abortion clinics, prostitution rackets, drugs and the *jogo do bicho*. Forcibly removed from office because of such activity, he briefly served as Brazilian military attaché to the UN in New York, before returning to head the army in São Paulo. In 1964 he was the last general to join the coup that established the military dictatorship and went on to serve as a federal deputy in Brazilian Congress. The military regime nurtured Kruel and his

5 / THE ANIMAL GAME: MISRULE OF LAW

ilk, embedding manifold state criminality – murder, impunity and corruption – within the Brazilian criminal justice system.[28]

The 1960s were tumultuous in Rio de Janeiro. The national capital was transferred to Brasília, and for the next 15 years the city became known as Guanabara, before its rebirth as the capital of Rio de Janeiro state in 1975. During these years the *jogo do bicho* thrived in the shadows, according to social historian Mathew Vaz:

> *the illegal numbers game in Rio repeatedly surfaced in the political discourse as a problematic source of political and police corruption, a potentially useful stream of revenue for government projects, and an entrenched social practice tied into the larger landscape [...] at every turn it intersected with political and economic events, colouring Brazilian law, politics, economic exchange and social relations with ambiguity and inconsistency.*[29]

While the city attempted to come to terms with lost revenue and stature, the illegal lottery bosses moved from strength to strength. They financed public works and lined political pockets. They weathered crackdowns. By now, a few prominent bankers began to emerge as major players. Most famous was charismatic, debonaire Castor de Andrade. This private school educated law graduate, a "gentleman" from a traditional suburban family, expanded his practice to new dimensions, acquiring metal works, petrol stations and a fish factory. He even steered his local football team, the humble Bangu Athletic Club, to victory in the 1966 state championships.

The cold war military dictatorship that ran Brazil between 1964 and 1984 transformed the *jogo do bicho*. During its first years, *bicheiros* managed to keep a relatively low profile, but in 1967 a former police inspector called General Graça testified before a parliamentary commission investigating corruption. Graça explained how he had been forced from office because of his efforts to crack down on the *jogo do bicho*. He put forward his view that the authorities had a vested interest in prohibiting the game in order to draw illegal revenue from it. Although the *jogo do bicho* was seen as an acceptable way of supplementing policemen's salaries, his testimony sparked serious debate about police reform and legalizing the lottery. Proposals at state and federal level called for a legal version of the game, with taxation, for spending on social projects. The forward-thinking proposals, made before chronic police corruption took hold in Rio, were scuppered by an unlikely coalition formed by members of the Catholic Church, social conservatives and crooked politicians with a vested interest in maintaining the status quo.

The year 1968 was characterised by protests and demonstrations in the city, many ending in violence. The junta responded by implementing a sweeping piece of dictatorial legislation. Institutional Act AI-5 suspended constitutional rights for all Brazilians; it prohibited protests, trade union elections and extended censorship to the press and the arts. The act also did away with *habeas corpus*, paving the way for endemic torture of alleged subversives and political opponents in the regime's subsequent years. These became known as the *anos de chumbo* (the bullet years, or the years of lead). AI-5 also created an anti-corruption commission that led to round-ups of some prominent *bicheiros*, including Castor de Andrade. Investigators announced that the *bicheiros* were expected to provide information on corrupt police. Although most of those who got arrested were back on the streets after several months, repression of the lottery continued until the early 1970s. This was not mere crime fighting: the military sought to exploit the *jogo do bicho* and its street-corner network of thousands of *apontadores* to build up information on political enemies and undesirables. The process led to inevitable reciprocity between the game's principal organisers and the dictatorship, whereby the *jogo do bicho* provided information in return for protection and non-persecution. Smaller insignificant operators were targeted and turned into scapegoats. Castor de Andrade and his friends formed an alliance with the junta. The *bicheiros*, always adept at change, learnt from the military and centralised their operations.

Links between the *jogo do bicho* and the repression were further cemented throughout the 1970s when middle-ranking members of the military intelligence apparatus migrated from the dictatorship to the *jogo do bicho* infrastructure. One man who capitalised on this moment was Captain Ailton Guimarães Jorge. Captain Guimarães came to prominence in 1969 as part of a team that killed an 18-year-old dissident called Eremias Delizoicov. Before Delizoicov died – with 33 bullet perforations – he managed to wound two of his would be captors, including Guimarães, who he shot in the leg. For his efforts, Guimarães won the *Medalha do Pacificador*, a tribute meted out to regime darlings. Official reports described him as honest, spontaneous, dedicated and versatile. He was also a proficient torturer, so much so that he instructed others in the dark practice. However, during these years, criminality among agents was common. Guimarães drifted from anti-subversive activities towards contraband, specifically extortion of smugglers and robbery of their stock. He used his network of corrupt military officials and police to form a gang dedicated to seizing and re-selling contraband alcohol, clothes and perfume. Eventually he was denounced, investigated, captured and even tortured by his own colleagues. His reputation as an incorruptible agent of repression in tatters, Captain Guimarães turned to his network of crooked officials for introduction to major players in the *jogo do bicho*.[30]

He got his first break from an aging well-respected banker nicknamed Tio Patinhas (Scrooge McDuck) because of his resemblance to Donald Duck's uncle. Tio Patinhas put Guimarães to work with Guto, an unproductive Niterói banker, but Guto was murdered in mysterious and unresolved circumstances shortly after the captain's arrival. Another unresolved murder of a small-time local banker followed. Conveniently, Captain Guimarães now took control of their *jogo do bicho pontos*. When Castor de Andrade founded the *cúpula* (managing committee) of leading *bicheiros* who divided the city into indisputable regions, Captain Guimarães was at his side. The former torturer and medal-winning agent of the dirty war had become a prominent lottery boss in record time.[31]

DISCOVERING THE *JOGO DO BICHO* was my "eureka moment". I was beginning to decode the story behind misrule of law and disorder that constitute

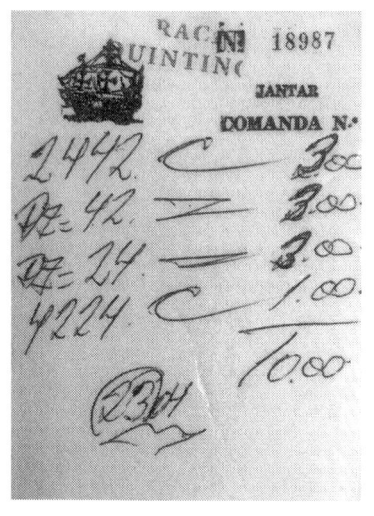

Jogo do bicho ticket purchased in Rio, 2015.

5 / THE ANIMAL GAME: MISRULE OF LAW

governance in Rio de Janeiro. Understanding the fact that the authorities not only tolerated but were complicit with the *jogo do bicho* at all stages in its history, helped me to navigate through the city's bewildering maze of concurrent criminal, legal and political interests. My understanding was enhanced greatly by Vinícius George, a civil police chief (himself under death threat for investigating militias) with decades of front-line experience. He once told me:

In every stage of the history of Republican Brazil the guys [bicheiros] are there. From Baron Drummond through to Captain Guimarães. From civilian dictatorship to the military dictatorship, in a democracy and under re-democratisation. Why? Because they play the game. What does political power want? 'You want an information network for a military dictatorship? Here you are. You want money to finance campaigns? Here. And I'll carry on with my business over there.' If you go deeply into this [the jogo do bicho], at the very minimum you'll be studying the history of the Republic, or better, the history of Brazilian politics since the proclamation of the Republic. The history of organised crime in Rio de Janeiro and Brazil begins with the bicheiros. The first criminal organisation in Rio de Janeiro and Brazil is [run by] the bicheiros. But there's no organised crime without the state – it penetrates the state. In our case it confuses itself with the state itself. You get to a point where you don't know what is the state, and what is a bicheiro.[32]

The coexistence and mutual dependability of the *jogo do bicho*, police corruption and politics as described by Vinícius, is also a constant in film director Fabio Barreto's 1985 thriller *Rei do Rio* (*King of Rio*), which tells the story of 20 years in the life of Rio de Janeiro from 1964 to 1984, a period spanning the beginning of the military dictatorship through to its end and the opening of the city's sambadrome (the purpose built avenue where samba schools compete during the annual Carnival). The film (which I watched for the first time at home after finding it hiding on a dusty shelf in one of Rio's last independent DVD rental outlets) is set during the early years of the regime, when two ambitious young petty criminals, Tucão and Sabonete, join forces to take over the area run by Cacareco, a traditional *bicheiro* who they betray and kill in a shootout. Business is good until the early 1980s, when they come under intense pressure from their corrupt allies – a police chief and a senator – to use their *jogo do bicho* network to distribute cocaine. Tucão, although ambitious, has inherited honourable, old-school principles from Cacareco and convinces his partner Sabonete to refuse. In retaliation, the crooked authorities launch a high-profile crackdown on the *bicheiros*, raiding their premises and using the media to accuse them publicly of being drug traffickers. When imprisoned, the former friends betray each other. Sabonete gives in, assuming administration of the city's cocaine business. In the final scene Tucão, shortly after declaring himself "King of Rio", is shot dead while his samba school parades in the newly built sambadrome. As he lies dying, the party goes on for the VIP guests in his box overlooking the parade.

Rei do Rio made me think about the relationship between *bicheiros* and Carnival. Just how far, I wondered, do the *jogo do bicho's* tentacles actually stretch?

6

BEIJA-FLOR: SAMBA IS POWER

IN ORDER TO DEEPEN MY KNOWLEDGE and understanding of the *jogo do bicho* and its power I joined a samba school; not because of sequins and dancing girls. Because of words; words muttered in private by journalists, by *sambistas*. Words whispered under their breath about money laundering and the crime kingpins who finance Carnival with illegal cash. So I joined Beija-Flor, a samba school famous for its extravagant, Carnival winning parades.[17]

Today, I like samba but for years I didn't. I couldn't contemplate the complex twisting footsteps I understood to be the samba dance. I felt out of place in expensive clubs where all Brazilians in the venue knew (or pretended to know) all the words to all the songs. I couldn't follow the rhythm. Carnival had me stymied, with its thousands of dancers and sumptuous, no-expense-spared floats; these tacky, often grotesque, creations

---

17 Beija-Flor (literally "flower-kisser") means hummingbird in English.

are watched by rich white Brazilians and gringo tourists paying exorbitant prices to gawp at semi-naked women gyrating on tiny platforms high in the air, helicopters overhead. Samba confused me. Carnival bemused me.

During my first years of living in Rio, I sometimes visited fascinating rehearsals of famous samba schools. I found them lovely to look at, but was baffled. So I watched from the sidelines while regulars – people of all colours, ages and backgrounds – immersed themselves in a collective ritual of music and words. In the months preceding Carnival, all schools hold rehearsals where the different groups forming the parade practice and sing that year's official song, called the *samba enredo*. When I was working in Providência, friends invited me to an open-air night rehearsal for Unidos da Tijuca, a samba school popular in the favela. Unidos comes from another part of town, but for many years conducted their rehearsals on a wide street between warehouses at the edge of the port. Samba enthusiasts in Providência only needed to walk out of their door and down the hill to join in.

Joining a Unidos da Tijuca rehearsal on a backstreet packed with supporters and members of the school, I felt I was finally beginning to grasp the importance of samba and Carnival for *cariocas*. I actually began to relax and enjoy myself! Much less the awkward gringo, I became more the happy foreigner. Under yellow neon streetlights, onlookers chit-chattered around stalls selling barbecued meats and drinks. An MC announced the start of the rehearsal and different components of the school began to walk down the grimy road. They chanted the *samba enredo* along with singers atop a huge mobile sound system. A beautifully turned out woman carried a flag. She was the *porta bandeira* (the flag carrier) and she danced in the company of an equally elegant man, the *mestre sala* (flag bearer). As the couple passed me the unappealing street turned into the setting of a plainclothes ball. A phalanx of drummers followed, rattling machine-gun polyrhythms on an array of percussion instruments; *repinique* (snares), tiny *pandeiros* (tamborines) and the outlandish *cuíca* (a friction drum with a high-pitched wail that sounds like forest animals screeching in the Amazonian night). The work of the drummers was founded on the *surdo*, the bass drums carried by strong, smiling men. Their beat – bom-BOOM-bom-BOOM – drifted back over the following *alas* (organised sections, literally called "wings") of the school as they followed time in disciplined groups. Kids I knew from Providência slipped between the singers. As the sound of the drummers faded away, the voices of the choir grew in volume. Now a group of elder women called *Baianas* passed by. Their song transported me to another world, far beyond the run-down docks and Providência and Rio.

SAMBA HAS MULTIPLE BEGINNINGS but only one root – the experience of millions of Africans who arrived in Rio after the horrors of the Middle Passage. Betrayed, captured, kidnapped, dislocated, relocated and whipped, survivors were left with a body, a voice and, sometimes the will to live. If given time to rest, the more resilient of these people might have taken the opportunity to sweep clear a space in front of their quarters to socialise. Proceedings then began with a ceremonial fertility dance called the *umbigada*. Dancers approached each other, moving closer until bellies touched. If drums were permitted, elders beat out simple rhythms and spoke about the week's work and events, or told stories of old and of home. They sang in

Yoruba and Kirongo, but also Portuguese, because this strange new language was often the only means of communication with fellow Africans, people stolen from different places and tribes at different instants. These precious moments of company and rest served to strengthen them for labour and enabled them to form bonds of friendship and mutual comprehension. Whenever the masters or their employees were present, the speakers disguised their messages with allusion, irony and subterfuge. Rhythm, word and dance converged to form a life-saving means of expression and communication. Little by little, the slaves began to rationalise their shared calamity.

Historically, samba encompasses prayer, dance and devotion – multiple expressions of joy. João do Rio, dandy, chronicler and acute observer of Rio street life in the early years of the twentieth century, used the word samba to describe Carnival songs in 1906. He observed that revellers singing a song about a shipwreck managed to combine the joy of celebration with a sad theme. "Only the people of this land of sun can look death in the face without fear in the macabre sambas of Carnival," he writes.

The revellers João do Rio saw belonged to a *cordão*, organised groups that took to the streets at Carnival in the mid-1800s. The *cordão* is the precursor of the modern samba school. Both slaves and nobles participated in *cordões* where, disguised as devils or clowns, they followed a group of men blowing whistles and beating drums. João do Rio describes a "pandemonium" of confetti, fireworks and lewd shrieks where alcohol, *lança perfume*[18] and cheap scent all contributed to an ambience of

---

18 An intoxicating mixture of ether, ethyl chloride and acetic acid inhaled for pleasure. *Lança perfume* remains popular, and illegal, in Brazil today.

promiscuity. He called them "irreducible nuclei of carioca folly […] which above all belong to the people, the earth and the enchanting barbarous spirit of Rio". João's guide explains that the roots of the tradition come from an African pagan rite, the *afoxé*, a celebration that makes fun of religion. He tells João that the *cordão* is rigorously hierarchical and orderly, despite its apparent chaos:

"Order in disorder?" João asks, incredulous.

"It's a national slogan," comes the reply.[33]

Such manifestations expressed the irreverent, riotous side of this new multi-racial nation, and they began to attract the attention of nervous authorities, particularly in post-abolition republican Brazil. The historical moment demanded the redefinition of social rules. Rio's cultural and social elite began to look for ways to reorganise the confusion of Carnival, and to redirect the energies of these expanding multitudes into more socially acceptable channels. But the authorities reacted with suspicion, as they always do with popular culture in Rio, especially black manifestations of popular culture. The first *sambistas* were persecuted, harassed and arrested by police. Such *sambistas* sang of the *malandro*, a popular social and cultural stereotype. The *malandro* is the *carioca* rogue par excellence; an easy living, sweet-talking hustler, who uses street savvy – dishonest if necessary – and cunning to come out on top of those situations where honesty and logic will not prevail. Such artistry is still a recognised, even acceptable form of social behaviour in the Rio of today. *Sambistas* were obliged to adopt the practice of *malandragem* to survive as artists. Because former slaves were granted a legal right to celebrate their religious beliefs without persecution, the *sambistas* transferred their guitars and song to the *terreiros*, holy places where the Afro–Brazilian religious rituals of Candomblé were celebrated. Here they used *malandragem* to convince suspicious eyes they were praying, and not singing for amusement. So original samba merged the sacred and profane with illusion; like the slaves, the first *sambistas* were obliged to camouflage their art, and to infuse their words with irony and double meaning.

Rio's samba schools, the unique social collectives that parade in official competition at Carnival, began to emerge in the early 1930s. Their original members were mostly, but not all, of African descent. In the years prior to the rise of the samba schools, repression of unruly and occasionally violent *cordões* had been turning Carnival into an exclusive party for the privileged. The authorities persecuted Afro–Brazilians celebrating informally in public places. So the nascent samba schools provided Rio's poor and excluded with a platform, a voice and a place where, once a year, they could be proper *gente* (people). Opinion formers and politicians, quick to realise the potential of samba as an expression of Brazilian "authenticity", were keen to incorporate the emerging culture into discussions about national identity, and despite its slave origins, samba eventually became, according to *carioca* musicologist Hermano Vianna, "an agent of internal 'colonization'. A national music born of indefinition came to define the rule, the only way of being authentically Brazilian".[34] This rule has stuck: even today a "real" Brazilian is supposed to know how to samba, be they rich, poor, white or black, and when people say that someone "has samba", this means they are quick-witted.

By the 1930s, samba's popularity obliged Rio's conservative establishment to take notice. The first collective granted legal

6 / BEIJA-FLOR: SAMBA IS POWER

Salgueiro samba school pays homage to the malandro, 2016.

status as a samba school was Estação Primeira de Mangueira. Known simply as Mangueira today, it remains one of the most popular in the city. Sponsored competition took place for the first time in 1932 and continued to grow throughout the 1930s and 1940s. Samba schools presented the authorities with an opportunity to regulate and incorporate the unruly *sambistas* into the Carnival infrastructure. These "democratic" spaces of participation and collective enterprise, proved from the outset to be formidable political and commercial weapons. Their birth coincided with a period of significant political modification. Rio was undergoing transformation; industrialisation and immigration had led to rapid development, growth and expansion of the city. Samba schools brought together the city's growing working classes. Alongside a widespread desire to promote new Brazilian culture in the context of a developing nationalism, official interest in the schools was also driven by the needs of politicians keen to capitalise on their popularity.

Sinhô, an original *sambista*, famously said samba is like a little bird: it belongs to whoever grabs it. The music began to emerge as a cornerstone of national culture over the course of the 1930s. The samba schools were powerful spaces for the opportunity of dialogue between the elite and the popular classes. Government subsidies were made available in 1935 (provided specific regulations were obeyed). Businesses were fast to catch onto the commercial potential of the new adventure, and as early as 1936, the Antarctica beer company used the image of a *sambista*, in traditional *malandro* uniform of hat, striped shirt and wide trousers, for advertising. Propagandists within the establishment targeted samba schools during President Getúlio Vargas' authoritarian regime (1937–1945), encouraging them to promote right-wing, nationalist policies, and imposing limits on parade content. International themes were banned. Political protest, criticism or allusion to current events could result in disqualification. The Portela samba school adhered closely to official requirements, winning the competition every year between 1941 and 1947, with *samba enredo* (official samba songs composed specifically for Carnival) such as *Glorious Brazil, Patriotic Motives* and *New World Dawn*.

Today the principal objective of a modern samba school is participation in the luxurious, fantastic parade at the heart of Carnival. This demands rigorous management and scrupulous attention to detail. The biggest schools, judged on minutiae by extremely high standards, garner supporters like football teams. The most successful belong to the *Grupo Especial* (Special Group) and parade through Rio's Oscar Niemeyer-built sambadrome. For two consecutive nights all eyes are on the thousands performing in this opulent display, which Brazilian media often refers to as "the greatest show on earth". The parade is a spectacular multimedia experience that combines dance, choreography, lavish decoration, song and music. Locals and tourists pay exorbitant prices for tickets in the stands. Millions watch live on TV. The omniscient Globo TV network holds exclusive broadcasting rights, transmitting live to all corners of Brazil and beyond. The event is Brazil's international public relations trademark and international media reproduce images of this unique party across the globe.

SUMMER 2014 WAS LONG, dry and boiling hot. Life on the Supervia suburban train service was a battle. Each Thursday I joined an exhausted mass of human bodies flowing towards the platforms at Central Station. Whenever I took the train, I always seemed to end up on an ancient click-clacking rusty model, with no air conditioning. On this particular day, I rushed up the platform looking for space, hoping for a spot near a door or window. It's important to stand where you can breathe and minimise the crush as people get on and off. Regular commuters know exactly where to be when the train pulls in. While it discharges passengers on one side, they crowd the closed doors on the other. Then as these open, ugly seconds of rough and tumble ensue as the strongest fight for a place to sit. Relaxation is a rare commodity for most Supervia users and every seat is occupied in a bad-tempered instant. Once a semblance of dignity is restored, grizzled snack and drink vendors begin to force a path through the passengers, shouting their wares.

An hour later I squeezed off the train at the apparently humble Nilópolis, which residents grandiosely refer to as Nilocity with typical carioca irony, and which is a small satellite suburb in Rio's outlying Baixada Fluminense district. It might be unremarkable, but it's home to one of Brazil's number one samba schools, Beija-Flor de Nilópolis – by 2020 already champion of Carnival 14 times. Beija-Flor's practice headquarters and home, the quadra, lies at the top of a gentle hill, 20 minutes by foot from the station. On Thursday summer nights the street in front of the quadra is one of the busiest places in the city.

Beija-Flor rehearsals are not for the soft-hearted. While richer fans of the school can simply purchase an expensive costume, and therefore must merely turn up on the day to guarantee their place in the official parade, I signed up as a componente (component) of one of the school's community alas (literally meaning wing). The Beija-Flor community is one of Rio's most devoted. Dedicated components must show up every week. Rehearsals, which rarely start before midnight, can go on past three in the morning. Community members earn free costumes and the right to compete for the school at Carnival.

Loyalty and passion sustain Beija-Flor. But money makes things happen and money wins Carnival. While the street outside the quadra teemed with locals who can't afford to pay the entry fee, the school's economic powers arrived at a back entrance in ostentatious air-conditioned SUVs with smoked windows. Doormen slid open a huge metal gate and waved these cars through to a large outdoor space at the edge of the quadra, where drivers park underneath an enormous sculpture of St. George spearing a dragon. The multicoloured, multidimensional sculpture towers over the throngs of components preparing for the rehearsal.

St. George is unofficial patron saint of Rio de Janeiro, and in the dual world of Afro–Brazilian religious syncretism he represents Ogum, the warrior orixá. Orixás, superhuman divinities inherited from Yoruba slaves, have special relevance for sambistas. The orixás are said to have lived on earth since its creation. They are invisible and omnipresent; neither natural nor supernatural. Devotees communicate with the orixá through prayer and offerings, and at Candomblé ceremonies where priests and priestesses choreograph the production of axé – the power to make things happen, a creative spiritual force akin to electricity.[35] Candomblé provides believers with social and spiritual roots that tap the sources of religious power hidden beneath life's surface. Many samba school quadras were built on holy spaces where Candomblé ceremonies took place. The gleaming silver and black SUVs conceal the sacred African history of samba.

A rotund, imposing man ruled the rehearsal. Laíla had been Beija-Flor's director of Carnival since the 1970s. Admired, at once disliked and imitated across the city, he dominated a packed central stage next to the formidable Beija-Flor *bateria* (drummers). Children, friends and assorted VIPs crowded around them. Most people were dressed in pale blue and white, the school's colours. The voluminous Laíla has a square face offset by a neatly trimmed beard, and was dressed in top-to-toe light cotton. His white smock shirt was embroidered with blue stitching. The cool, elegant outfit was adorned with a fine set of weighty necklaces made from beads, shells, feathers and seeds. Laíla is a devotee of Xangô, the fearsome *orixá* of justice, thunder and lightening. His famous necklaces are *guias*, physical reminders of Xangô's presence. When they disappeared once, Laíla appealed for their return on national TV. They were located within the hour.

Rehearsals took ages to start. We waited obediently while the school warmed up with rousing songs from victorious Carnivals past. All eyes were on the *porta bandeira*, the woman trusted to carry the school's blue and white flag, the *pavilhão*, which she holds for distinguished visitors and members of the public to kiss. The well-to-do and influential crowded a balcony that runs around all three sides of the *quadra*, overlooking the stage.

Eventually an MC opened proceedings, with the custom welcoming salute:

Bem vindos ao Grêmio Recreativo Escola de Samba Beija-Flor de Nilópolis! Lugar de gente bamba, gente forte no mundo do samba!

(Welcome to the Recreational Samba School Beija-Flor of Nilópolis! The place for true sambistas, heavyweights of the samba world!)

Naming them one by one, the MC greeted VIP guests and praised Beija-Flor's directors, at length. Eventually three or four distinctive chords announced the melody of the year's official song, the *samba enredo*. It was well after midnight when a thousand voices filled the *quadra*. We sang and danced under the watchful eye of Laíla and important gazes from the balcony above. As we moved slowly around the space, directors of *harmonia* walked up and down the *alas*, keeping the components in line, in time and singing properly. Singing properly meant really putting your heart into the occasion, filling your lungs and pumping out the words. Once the whole school was singing and moving in unison, I felt like one tiny element in an unstoppable gigantic throng. If I switched off, or got out of line, a director would soon be at my side, correcting me, urging me to do better. There was no space for slackers. Laíla is the sort of man you want to please, and when he ended the rehearsal with praise for the *comunidade,* I felt proud, hot, sweaty and tired. Beija-Flor works hard for Laíla.

At the edge of the *quadra*, behind the dancing *alas* and spectators, a sole granite bust stands on a marble plinth, before an impressive display of Carnival trophies. The minimalist sculpture is not a flattering portrayal of its subject, the beaky, aging Anísio. It owns a cruel face, lips curled downward in a snarl. Anísio is Beija-Flor's patron. He's also one of Rio's top *bicheiros*. And while we worked hard for Laíla, Laíla worked hard for Anísio. The community sang and danced, Laíla cracked the whip, and Anísio provided the money. His cash makes Beija-Flor what it is.

ANÍSIO WAS BORN ANÍSIO ABRÃAO DAVID in Nilópolis more than 70 years ago. His parents were immigrants. According to family history, his father was a travelling salesman who exchanged olive picking and poverty in Lebanon for long, gruelling days wandering the Baixada Fluminense on a diet of bread, bananas and water. The Abrãao David were one of several local families of Lebanese settlers. They developed strong links with another, the Sessim David, orthodox Christians from the same scorched region of Lebanon. The two families established themselves as local merchants, opening shops near the railway station and reinvesting their profits in property. The "cousins", known locally as *turcos* (turks), were united by hardship and their mutual immigrant status. They created strong inter-family kinship through shared meals, birthdays and weddings.

The dormitory town of Nilópolis grew fast, the population boosted by Brazilians fleeing rural poverty in the interior and favela removals in the city. Samba was a way of life. After starting as a humble street gathering, by the early 1960s Beija-Flor was a second division samba school. It fundraised through parties and donations from local traders. The collective provided newcomers with an important space for leisure and socialising with existing Nilopolitans. But even then, Carnival could be a violent business where thugs attended the parade with hidden knives in their costumes.

The 1946 national gambling ban had serious consequences for the samba schools then springing up in the city's suburbs. The 1940s saw rapid industrialisation in Rio de Janeiro, furthering urban expansion and immigration. Samba and the *jogo do bicho* were favourite activities of the city's popular classes and it was only natural, as they spread across the growing city, that the schools and the organisers of the illegal game should cross paths;

beginning most famously in the late 1950s with a one-armed *bicheiro* called Natal da Portela in the North Zone. Samba schools grew out of poverty, but needed discipline, a hierarchy, organisation and funding. Their survival depended on external intervention. Natal's successful patronage of Portela came at a time when samba was being consecrated as a national cultural manifestation, coinciding with the beginning of the territorial organisation for the *jogo do bicho*.

Samba had long been associated with gambling. *Pelo Telefone* (*On the telephone*), the first recognised samba song, is an ironic criticism of a 1917 crackdown. It was composed by a group of *sambistas* who suggest, playfully that the police chief is not being as thorough in his mission as he publicly declares. The song's original words implied police collusion with the game's operators: "*The chief of police/ Called to let me know/ That in Carioca/ There's a roulette/ That we can play*". The authorities subsequently censored the song, so the officially registered version of the samba – a synthesis of culture, illegal gambling and corruption – is altered.

Since the 1930s, different *bicheiros*, often using violence, acquired clusters of ticket sales points, establishing themselves as *dono* (owner) of a particular area. Disputes over these *pontos do bicho* had slowed down by 1960, with different territories recognised as belonging to particular *bicheiros*. Natal's support of Portela through generous donations towards floats, musical instruments and costumes enabled him to recast his role from *contraventor* to *sambista*, from criminal to cultural entrepreneur and investor in the neighbourhood. This secured a vital base of popular support in Madureira, the suburb where he ran the *jogo do bicho*.

Castor de Andrade, Captain Guimarães and all other major *jogo do bicho* bankers followed suit. Patronage of the schools provided these arch-*malandros* with a formidable multifaceted weapon in the negotiation of strategic partnerships, and with the opportunity of exploiting Carnival's universal popularity to camouflage their criminal interests. They used the schools to establish favourable relationships with the authorities, the media and businesses; and just as importantly, to cultivate public approval and an electoral base for their political allies. Carnival permitted *bicheiros* to portray themselves as benefactors of the poor, with a genuine interest in supporting the social life of the city. The schools were immensely valuable as a space for dialogue and interaction, providing bankers with a means of social integration at all levels, within both working-class and aspirant suburban society, as well as the traditional middle and upper classes of the South Zone. The marriage of samba to the *jogo do bicho* guaranteed its survival and, with national and international interest in Rio's Carnival increasing, it added further layers of complexity to Baron Drummond's invention.

When the military junta went on an offensive against the *jogo do bicho* at the end of the 1960s, the crackdown ended the careers of many low and mid-level *bicheiros*. But certain bankers, Anísio included, grew stronger under the centralising regime. A former petty drug dealer, he was a strategic opportunist who found himself allies in the dictatorship and who used police connections to drive rival *bicheiros* off the streets.[19] When he was not spending nights around tables at the pool hall, he visited Beija-Flor where Nelson,

---

19 Eliana Muller, his former wife, said she wrapped marijuana for Anísio as a teenager in a letter she wrote in 1991 denouncing his criminal activities. Two months after writing the letter she was executed on a Nilópolis street alongside her boyfriend. Anísio's brother, Nelson, killed himself one month later. Aloy Jupiara and Chico Otavio in *Os Porões da Contravenção* (Record 2015) pp. 180–186.

his younger brother, was popular with *sambistas*. When Nelson was elected Beija-Flor's president, Anísio became its patron. The brothers worked well together. Anísio now ran the *jogo do bicho* in Nilópolis. With money to spend, he set about resolving Beija-Flor's considerable material and financial problems and in 1973 the school won promotion to the elite *Grupo Especial*.

Year by year, Anísio progressively transformed Beija-Flor into his family fiefdom. His "cousins", the Sessim David family, went into politics, providing him with extra protection when necessary. He instigated growth and economic development, and used the samba school to eulogise the military regime. In 1973, 1974 and 1975, Beija-Flor celebrated Carnival in the form of direct tributes to the junta. The samba songs *Education for Development*, *Brazil 2000* and *The Great Decade* all eulogised the military government and the so-called "economic miracle". Generals enjoyed parties in the Nilópolis *quadra*. The sambas were pure propaganda, earning Beija-Flor the nickname "Official School of the Dictatorship". But mocking didn't worry canny Anísio. Using political clout, he made sure that the Arena, the junta's party, always won Nilopolitan elections. Military intelligence conducted a campaign against rival mayors and councillors in the region, accusing them of corruption and clearing the way for the Sessim and Abraão clans, leaving Anísio free to take over the *jogo do bicho* in the Baixada Fluminense. He reciprocated by finding work for former officials in his business structures, and even at Beija-Flor where they worked as security men. These employees included torturers who consequently infected life at the samba school with fear and their dirty war ethos. When Anísio was detained for several days immediately preceding the 1977 Carnival he described his arrest as a "subversive act of communists trying to cause revolt in the samba schools".[36]

For a considerable sum of money, Anísio hired Joãzinho Trinta, Rio's most successful *carnavalesco* (the creative producer who conceives and designs the parade). Joãzinho, a diminutive, genial northeasterner from the state of Maranhão, convinced Laíla, then director of Carnival at a rival school called Salgueiro, to join him. The choice proved a huge success when Beija-Flor won the championship in 1976, the first of three consecutive Carnival victories for the school, and the third in a series of five wins for Joãzinho and Laíla. A young local composer called Neguinho wrote and sang the winning 1976 samba, a homage to Baron Drummond and the *jogo do bicho*.

In addition to spending cash, Anísio and Nelson knew how to set up a winning team. Although Joãzinho Trinta is now dead, he stayed with the school until the 1990s. Laíla remained until 2018 and Neguinho still works there today. Success however came at a high cost for many longstanding members of Beija-Flor, now excluded from decision-making. "If you want to keep winning, then let us run the show," the brothers told them. Coercion replaced consultation and deliberation. Communal autonomy, a fundamental tradition at Beija-Flor, was no more. And as Anísio pumped money into Beija-Flor, other *bicheiros* followed suit with their own respective schools. As they competed for fame and status, the parade grew larger, taller, more sumptuous and more extravagant. Revered samba composers like Mangueira's beloved Cartola opted to stay away from Carnival, critical of the path taken by the *bicheiros*. Cartola called the new order a "cynical invasion" that had created a greedy industry. More tourists flooded the schools each

Carnival, increasing the already high numbers of components. The samba rhythm was accelerated to ensure that the thousands of dancers could get through on time. "I can't stand the rush," Cartola declared. "It looks like a military procession."[37]

Anísio's takeover of Beija-Flor preceded the creation of a centralised decision-making body for the *jogo do bicho*. Formation of the so-called *cúpula* in the late 1970s ended territorial disputes, dividing Rio into five regions governed by five *bicheiros*. Anísio ran the Baixada Fluminense.[20] The west of the city belonged to Castor de Andrade, patron of Mocidade Independente samba school. A gruff, coarse man called Miro Garcia controlled the South Zone; while Antônio Kalil, known as Turcão, ran the game in the city centre. Niterói, on the opposite side of the Guanabara Bay, now belonged to the ambitious, ruthless Captain Guimarães, who would in due course eventually become patron of Vila Isabel samba school.[38]

Their first grand show of strength was resistance to a concentrated *jogo do bicho* crackdown in 1982. Despite the arrest of 3,000 street level operators, the *cúpula* rode the storm unscathed. When they threatened to withdraw their samba schools from Carnival, the authorities buckled, calling off their campaign and sacking the head of the military police. After Carnival the *cúpula* held a banquet in honour of the president of Riotur, the government body responsible for the official side of the event. According to music journalist Sérgio Cabral (father of the state governor with the same name), Castor de Andrade personally handed Colonel Uzeda, the institution's military

---

20 In 2012, the cúpula was reduced to three members: Anísio, Captain Guimarães and Turcão.

president, a document praising his work. The colonel, moved to tears, responded:

I still believe in these men, good men, real men. Brazil needs men like these. I've received many decorations and homages in my life, including from the Air Force, but this is the most honouring document of my entire career.[39]

With the pressure off, the *cúpula* set about expanding their illegal gaming activities, which already included clandestine casinos and bingos, into electronic gambling machines. They imported these in bulk for nation-wide distribution. With the military on board, members of the *cúpula* were poised to become undisputed *capi* of Brazil's very particular tropical mafia. Now that the marriage of the dictatorship and organised crime was sealed, at Carnival time, Castor even set aside a VIP box for his military friends.[40] At this point, in order to protect their interests completely, the *bicheiros* needed to develop a communications strategy.

7

THE SHINING STAR OF BRAZILIAN COMMUNICATION

Beija-Flor was hot work. I sweated buckets. Beer was out of the question and water was hard to come by mid-rehearsal. But there was a point when the *alas* went beyond Laíla's range of vision. This moment meant that I could sneak away and bag a couple of mineral waters. Although people in my *ala* were friendly they kept a distance from the gringo. Even *cariocas* can be shy sometimes. All the same I shared sips and swapped names with some of my fellow components before we headed back into the glare of the *quadra*.

If you walked in time and sang the samba well, there was no great mystery to it. However, special attention was always paid to one specific corner of the *quadra*. Here, nervous directors appeared out of nowhere and shooed us into line, where we waited until called forward. This was a rehearsal for the beginning of the parade, when the whole school turns into the sambadrome, to ensure the *ala* can negotiate corners without breaking ranks. In the *quadra* the practice corner lies below a special balcony occupied by Anísio and his entourage – hence the need to get it right.

During one particularly humid rehearsal, someone out of my range of vision tossed some small packets over the edge of the balcony, spreading disorder among *ala* components, who elbowed each other to grab the items as they fell. I jumped and plucked one from the air. It was a polyester T-shirt in a plastic bag. Printed on the front was an awkward image of a man's face inside a TV set linked to an old dial telephone. There was no mistaking the face; it was stamped on all the year's official shirts. Beija-Flor's Carnival 2014 was dedicated to the man in question, Boni, whom the *samba enredo* called "the shining star of Brazilian communication". His image was splashed across an enormous multicoloured banner hung high above the stage, a hummingbird hovering near his grinning face.

I did my research and learnt that Boni had been Director of Content and Production at Globo TV for 30 years. A descendant of Spanish and Portuguese immigrants, raised in the interior of São Paulo, he joined Globo in 1967 at the age of 32. Boni (short for Bonifácio) was a natural publicist who grasped TV's money-making potential. He says that he applied mathematic models to pricing, created an automated system to demarcate publicity schedules, and implemented a commercialisation model based on extensive psychosocial market research. His stated aim: to give people "what they want", which was "popular material well done". Significantly, the "shining star of Brazilian communication" also says that he took orders from one person only – Roberto Marinho.[41]

7 / THE SHINING STAR OF BRAZILIAN COMMUNICATION

The eldest son of newspaper owner Irineu Marinho, Roberto Marinho had kick-started Globo TV at the beginning of the military dictatorship. His father had founded *A Noite*, an extremely popular evening newspaper, which he subsequently lost to rivals. Not to be beaten, in 1925 he established *O Globo*, although he died suddenly shortly afterwards. His son, Roberto, was already an apprentice at the newspaper. He spent the next six years preparing for the role of editor-in-chief, which he took on at the age of 26. A competitive sportsman and bon vivant, he amused himself with horses and boxing by day, women and samba by night.[21] At work he channelled his considerable energies into the newspaper, purchasable for the price of a coffee. The cheap cover price kept profits low but canny Marinho generated extra income by re-selling American comic books in translation and investing in property. *O Globo* defended and promoted traditional values. Marinho had spent his adolescence in a big house in the middle-class Tijuca neighbourhood. Hidden from the beaches and city centre by lush forest and mountains and home to industrious immigrant families, Tijuca is fertile ground for an inward-looking, ungenerous Brazilian conservatism. Residents call themselves *Tijucans*. Marinho's Tijucan outlook gave him the ability to read and tap into the fears and desires of Brazil's silent majority.[42]

Before long Marinho expanded the business into radio, founding Radio Globo in 1944. He won his first state TV concession in 1957. TV Globo was launched in 1965, the year after the military coup. Extensive (and illegal) foreign financing

---

[21] In 1923, Sinhô wrote a composition called "*A Cocaína*" which he dedicated to "my friend Roberto Marinho".

from US publishing company Time Life gave Marinho the edge he needed. The dictatorship prioritised telecommunications and his TV service spread rapidly, winning state concessions across the country. In 1969, Globo launched *Jornal Nacional*, its nightly news programme, shortly after the arrival of censorship via the draconian AI-5 legislation. Globo obeyed, never questioning the status quo. Marinho intervened only when necessary to protect his staff. They might be communists, he said, but they are my communists!

With the advent of colour TV in the 1970s, Globo developed a sophisticated roster of *novelas* (soap operas) and magazine programmes. The ever-resourceful Boni raised production standards. In 1975 he invited Hans Donner, an Austrian designer, to create a unique Globo logo and typeface. Boni even invented a sound effect, called the *plin-plin*, to separate programming from commercials. He conceived magazine programmes with names like *Fantástico* and *Globo Reporter*. These remain immensely popular today. His inventions and innovations constitute the visual and intellectual essence of the network's identity. In Brazil it's referred to as *padrão Globo* – Globo standard – and Boni devised it.

By 1984, at the beginning of the transition back to democracy, Roberto Marinho ruled sovereign over a unilateral national communications empire. The ambitious Tijucan was now Brazil's most influential civilian. Names of potential ministers were submitted to him for endorsement. Globo's *novelas* and *Jornal Nacional* commanded 95 per cent of audience figures. Boni pioneered product placement and sponsorship schemes, transforming programmes into sophisticated money-making devices. While Marinho and Boni grew rich, critics accused Globo, with its hypnotic logo, repetition and continual self-reference, of distorting Brazilian reality. Globo, they said, was the provider of false dreams and the guardian of privileges. Marinho himself watched every transmission of *Jornal Nacional* with a telephone at his side, censoring and motivating news editors with criticism or praise. He told the *New York Times* "we give all necessary information, but our opinions are in one way or another dependent on my character, my convictions and my patriotism. Yes, I use this power [...] but I always do so patriotically."[43]

During Brazil's dictatorship, when the number of TVs in the country went from half a million to 27 million, the network exploded from state TV franchise into national media monopoly and the world's fourth largest network. Like the *jogo do bicho*, under the junta Globo grew powerful and organised. Today, where there is a Brazilian TV, there Globo will be. Before the arrival of the internet, Globo held absolute power. Even now, Globo often decides what is and is not news. Brazilians of all ages and classes still look to Globo for the latest in fashion. Globo continues to supply the nation with myriad fantasies and its unique "*global*" reality. It explains the world to Brazilians and offers them a blueprint to define their place within it.

Roberto Marinho wasn't Boni's only powerful associate; the TV producer was also intimate with Castor de Andrade. The friendship began in 1974 when a Globo set designer took him to visit the *bicheiro*'s samba school, Mocidade Independente. That same year, Boni paraded with the samba school, wearing a green and white *diretoria* (director) shirt. Globo transmitted Carnival until 1984, when there was a stand-off with Leonel Brizola, Rio's leftist governor. Brizola was a charismatic, straight-talking southerner who had favoured deposed President João Goulart's timid reform proposals, that so alarmed the establishment in the run up to 1964. After the coup, Brizola fled the country alongside the deposed President, only returning to Brazil after the 1979 amnesty declaration.

In 1982, Brizola ran for election as governor of Rio. Proconsult, a new company with links to the SNI (the National Intelligence Service), was contracted to carry out an electronic vote count.[22] The counting programme was rigged to credit null and invalid votes to Brizola's chief opponent. In advance of the vote, Globo had been publicising false opinion polls predicting his defeat. However, before votes were taken to Proconsult for counting, they were totalled at local polling stations. When the figures did not tally, the final Proconsult figures were contested. Radio Jornal Brasil denounced the rigging, and after days of delay, Brizola's victory was announced. Although Globo denied participation, the SNI had been tapping Brizola's telephone and passing information back to Roberto Marinho.

Unsurprisingly, Brizola and Marinho were enemies. Brizola believed what was good for Globo was bad for Brazil. He called Marinho "the Stalin of Brazilian communication". Brizola favoured education, agrarian reform and external debt cancellation. He appointed brilliant anthropologist Darcy Ribeiro as his state Secretary of Science and Culture. The pair established a new education system aimed at providing children in Rio with a full day of activities, a radical idea in Brazil, where public education was – and sadly still is – carried out in shifts, leaving children at other times to their own devices. Oscar Niemeyer, Brasília's architect, designed pre-moulded concrete

---

22 The SNI was extinguished in the 1990s to make way for today's ABIN, Brazilian Intelligence Agency.

installations called CIEPs, *Centros Integrados de Educação Pública* (Integrated Public Education Centres). These contained libraries and offered free extra-curricular sports, cultural activities, school materials, textbooks, full meals, showers, onsite healthcare and dental treatment. Brizola and Ribeiro dreamed of changing the destiny of the nation by raising healthy, well-educated generations of poor Brazilians. Brizola also curbed violent state incursions into favelas, obliging police to secure judicial authorisation for operations.

Brizola and Ribeiro aimed to provide opportunity, hope and safety for Rio's poor. They also planned to bring Carnival and the samba schools closer to the ambit of government. In 1983, Brizola asked Oscar Niemeyer to design a permanent structure for the parade, to replace the existing venal, highly expensive practice of mounting and dismounting temporary metal structures each year. Ribeiro and Niemeyer envisaged a place where the people of Rio could take ownership of Carnival. They called it the *sambódromo*, the sambadrome. Outside Carnival time, the installation would be a CIEP, a public facility,

Niemeyer added a large open space to the end of the parading avenue, which he called the *Praça do Apoteose* (apotheosis square). This feature caused concern among samba school directors. Used to parading in a straight line from start to finish, they did not know what to make of it. Roberto Marinho attacked the construction through *O Globo*. According to the newspaper, the structure would collapse. It was too high and would not be ready in time. However the project was completed in a lightening 110 days, ready for Carnival 1984. Brizola did not forgive Marinho's posturing and granted Manchete, a rival channel, exclusive TV rights. When Mangueira won the sambadrome's first hugely successful Carnival, Globo was absent.

But thanks to Boni and his friendships, Globo would never miss another Carnival. He had already represented Globo in meetings about the new sambadrome where he clashed with Darcy Ribeiro, and following the channel's exclusion he contacted the *cúpula* for help. The *bicheiros*, tired of Brizola's interference, were in the process of founding their own independent association of samba schools called LIESA, the Independent League of Samba Schools. LIESA provided them with a perfect weapon for the stand-off. Castor was emphatic: Globo transmits the parade or we will do it in Niterói, he said. Brizola would not speak to the *contraventores* in person, so it was Boni who knocked on his door to announce LIESA's creation and intentions. The governor, outraged, picked up the telephone and called Rio's mayor, Marcelo Alencar, to set up a meeting with the *cúpula*. Boni, Castor, Anísio, Luiz Drummond – patron of Imperatriz Leopoldinense samba school – and Captain Guimarães all took part. Full organisation of the parade and all concession rights now belonged exclusively to LIESA. [23]

The antipathy between Boni and Darcy Ribeiro encapsulates the two irreconcilable versions of Brazil that have pursued me since I first came to the country. Boni's vision for Globo TV promoted ignorance and alienation. A Brazil of opportunity and exploitation, camouflaged with superficial propaganda for the masses – obey the law, stay where you are and consume. For years, Globo, hypnotic, omnipresent, omnipotent, followed my every step.

---

23 Boni describes these meetings and his intimate friendships with the *bicheiros* in his autobiography where he makes the *faux pas* of describing the Beija-Flor community as based in Nova Iguaçu, not Nilopolis! *O livro do Boni* pp.402–403.

The only place I could avoid Globo was in my own house, which is where, after carrying the dense 400-page volume back and forth across the Atlantic, I finally sat down to Ribeiro's *The Brazilian People*, a full 13 years after purchasing it. For many years I had just looked at the blue cover, with its shaded green fonts, and the book's subtitle, written in small white letters – *the formation and meaning of Brazil*. For years I didn't dare to open it, daunted by the language and the 400 plus pages of ideas. But when I finally did, I read it with speed.

Ribeiro was one of Brazil's great public intellectuals and activists, at once anthropologist, indianist, ethnographer, writer, politician and educator. Published in 1995, *The Brazilian People* traces the tangled roots of Brazilian racial, sexual, social and ethnic relations. It is as accomplished in its account of how Brazil came to be, as Boni was with his marketing devices. Ribeiro believed that the first Brazilians, born of Indian mothers by European, and then African fathers, were born into *ninguendade:* "nobodyness". Brazilian civilisation, this "tropical Rome", according to Ribeiro, is founded on *ninguendade* and washed in African and Indian blood. He believed that Brazil's tropical *mestiços* were suffering today to build tomorrow's world. *The Brazilian People* is a complex and generous book. Ribeiro taught me everything about his country that Globo TV never would. Unfortunately for Brazil, the information and ideas so beautifully expressed in *The Brazilian People* were not those beamed daily into the nation's homes. On the contrary, those were Boni's. For decades, Boni's Brazil was the version consumed daily by Brazilians, and was the one they regurgitated to the world outside. Boni won the cultural war.

Before he died in 1997, Darcy Ribeiro wrote:

Recently, things have got more complicated because traditional institutions are losing all their powers of control and doctrine. Schools don't teach, the Church doesn't catechise, parties don't politicise. What we have is a monstrous mass communication system that bullies people. It imposes unattainable standards of consumption, unfulfillable desires, deepening the marginality of these populations and their tendency towards violence. Violence unleashed on the streets has something to do with the abandoning of this population to socially and morally irresponsible radio and television, which only seeks to sell more fizzy drinks or bars of soap, with no concern about the moral and mental confusion provoked.[44]

BONI KNEW WHAT EFFECTIVE COMMUNICATION could achieve. All communication is strategy, he wrote in his autobiography. Perfect communication only occurs if the message is clear, if the means are used correctly, and if the recipient responds. All means interfere and modify the message. Efficiency of communication, he said, can only be evaluated by constant measuring of the answer.[45] In 1989 he used his knowledge and position at Globo to influence Brazil's first democratic election, post military dictatorship. A few days before the second round of voting, the popular trade unionist Lula was in the process of beating the establishment candidate Fernando Collor in opinion polls. Globo, naturally, was to host the final televised debate. Lula was rising, Collor falling. As Brazil's streets emptied in the minutes leading up to the debate, Globo's director of programming indulged in a little carnivalesque magic. Small touches to make Collor appear less elite, less distant from Lula's *povo* (the "people"). Using glicerine gel to fake earnest sweat on his brow, Boni loosened his tie to make him appear less bourgeois, softening Collor's starched image. Then he placed a pile of yellow and green folders on the plinth in front of Collor.

'These,' Collor said, waving his hand over them theatrically, "contain serious allegations of corruption against Lula."

The folders contained blank pages.[46]

Following the debate, highlights were produced to showcase Lula's worst moments against Collor's best. Collor occupied one minute and ten seconds more than Lula in the edit, which was broadcast non-stop in the days that followed, and which proved decisive in reversing polled voting trends. Collor was elected and swiftly plunged Brazil into economic chaos. Octavio Tostes, one of the editors asked to manipulate the edit, later described it as an exemplary piece of bad journalism; in fact it wasn't journalism, he said, "it's the most sordid piece of work I ever produced in my life."[47]

Today, the partnership Boni and the *bicheiros* cemented remains in place, unchallenged. LIESA controls all organisational and commercial aspects of the Carnival parade. Exclusive transmission rights belong to Globo. Which is why in 2014 – for the 30th anniversary of the foundation of LIESA, the inauguration of the sambadrome, the sealing of LIESA's partnership with Globo, and the historic, definitive victory over Brizola – who was it better for Beija-Flor to eulogise, than Boni?

Back in the heat of the Beija-Flor *quadra*, under Laíla's watchful eye, it was important to sing with all your heart. The shining star of Brazilian communication appeared at a few of the rehearsals, alongside an aging Anísio. He stood near Laíla on the stage, waving his index finger as we sang and danced in obedient, orderly rows. I passed by under Boni's hand. He pointed at me. I pointed back. We sang together, laughing, looking each other in the eye. I put on my happiest face, smiled, threw my arms in the air and filled my lungs:

Boni!
Tu és o astro da televisão
Fiz da sua vida minha inspiração

(Boni!
You are the star of television
Your life is my inspiration)

8

XANGÔ'S CURSE

SUMMER 2014 WAS VIOLENT. WHITE-HOT days. Blood-red sunsets. Unease, insecurity and a lynch-mob mentality contaminated life in Rio de Janeiro. Trouble broke out one Sunday afternoon at Ipanema and for the first time in decades, the media resurrected the phantom of the *arrastão*, mob beach robberies. I met a white Brazilian who had been chased by a group of teenagers. He was bemused; they did not try to steal anything, they just ran after him into the water saying "let's kill the gringo, kill the gringo!" The incident was captured and broadcast repeatedly on TV. Riot police lined up behind sunbathers at Arpoador Beach on Sunday afternoons. Bohemian Lapa, safer than it had been for years, suddenly and inexplicably became dangerous again overnight. Outside the famous Circo Voador music venue, a barefoot chain snatcher tore a cheap necklace from my friends' neck and sprinted into the night. The theft was over as it happened. If it had not been for the physical loss of her chain it might have been a hallucination.

On Tuesdays I used to attend another of Rio's most loved samba schools, Salgueiro, in Roberto Marinho's favoured Tijucan heartland. Numerous hillside favelas, including Morro do Salgueiro where the school was born in the 1950s, service the staunch middle-class neighbourhood of Tijuca. Rehearsals were joyous, ebullient occasions. Neither *quadra* nor the street outside could contain the crowds. So in the weeks before Carnival, Salgueiro moved to a nearby street, Rua Maxwell. Thousands turned up. Above the road fans crowded the windows and balconies of high-rise condos. Down below spectators trampled clipped lawns in front of the buildings, fighting for standing room alongside drink vendors carrying heavy iceboxes, just to catch a glimpse of the red and white riot of Salgueiro passing by.

Salgueiro was once part of a coffee plantation. Like all Rio's hillside communities built on the edge of precipices, its residents are resourceful, tough people. The tight-knit favela, founded by former slaves and immigrants from the state of Minas Gerais and the north-east, was popular with visitors coming to all night parties on the hill. Then torrential rains destroyed the young samba school's *quadra* and in 1966, it moved down onto the Tijucan asphalt. Now the doormen, porters, house cleaners and clothes washers who lived on the hill had a place to mix with the aspirational middle-class families they worked for, many of whom, like Roberto Marinho, were descendants of immigrants from Portugal and Italy.

Salgueiro also has a Beija-Flor connection. Before moving to Nilópolis, the creative genius Joãzinho Trinta was Salgueiro's *carnavalesco*. Formidable Laíla was born and raised in the favela. For me, the organised anarchy of Salgueiro street rehearsals was a welcome antidote to Laíla's midnight military-style exercises at

Beija-Flor. Salgueiro's Carnival was dedicated to Gaia, primordial goddess of nature, with a samba that sang of African *orixás* and the Earth's origin. Salgueiro's spiritual celebration of earth and heaven was an ontological universe away from Beija-Flor's toadying of Boni. Religiosity has long been associated with the favela of Salgueiro, known for its *benzedeiras, rezadeiras* (holy women) and dotted with *terreiros* (temples) where Candomblé priests and priestesses celebrated weekend rituals for the *orixás*. The school's red and white colours demonstrate Salgueiro's long association with Xangô, the tempestuous thunder deity. According to Yoruba legend, Xangô recklessly experimented with a leaf that had the power to bring lightening down from the skies. In doing so he set his own palace on fire, killing his wife and children in the blaze. Wild with guilt, Xangô hanged himself.[48]

Although *orixás* have no hierarchy, none would dispute Xangô's power. A *bicheiro* called Miro Garcia financed Salgueiro for many years. Miro was a gruff, coarse man who had spent his childhood in state institutions and began work in the *jogo do bicho* at 14. Starting as a humble street-corner bookie, he rose to dominate the *jogo do bicho* in Rio's South Zone, becoming a respected member of the *cúpula*, so rich that the other *bicheiros* called him the "Bradesco bank of contravention". He owed much of his fortune to Tio Patinhas. The legendary *jogo do bicho* banker, who got Captain Guimarães started on his career, was also godfather to Maninho, Miro's son, heir and business partner. Maninho, a sports lover and a womaniser, lived the life of a typical beach-loving *carioca playboy* (Brazilians use "playboy" as slang for middle and upper-class kids). But while Miro was respected and admired, Maninho made many enemies. Barely into his twenties, he accused a group of young men of making eyes at his girlfriend at a restaurant in Leme. The accusation led to an argument, then a car chase and gunshots, which left one of the group paralysed from the waist down.

Xangô is born for power and dies for power. In 2004, assassins shot and killed 42-year-old Maninho one morning in front of Body Planet gym academy in the West Zone Jacarepaguá neighbourhood. Maninho's 15-year-old son, Mirinho, with him at the time, was hit by a bullet but survived. When the 77-year-old patriarch Miro died in hospital a month later, Salgueiro was left with no patron. The concurrent deaths of Maninho and Miro triggered a bitter, bloody dispute within the Garcia family. Maninho's wealth was to be split four ways between his wife, son and twin daughters, Shanna and Tamara. But Tamara accused Shanna of selling off some of their father's wealth without consulting other family members.

Xangô judges and destroys. The dispute over Maninho and Miro's spoils now turned into a bloody feud, with frightening implications for Salgueiro. The Garcia family split. Tamara and her brother took sides with their uncle, Maninho's brother Bid. Shanna, already in her early twenties, joined Zé Personal, Maninho's former sidekick, who she was engaged to. Bloodshed ensued. First, Miro's adopted son, Guaracy, vice-president of the samba school, was murdered with his wife in 2007. Then in 2008, an early evening drive-by attack on the road outside Salgueiro's *quadra* led to four more deaths, all of men linked to the *jogo do bicho*, including the brother of the school's then-president.

Xangô is more powerful than death. Also in 2008, Shanna allegedly organised a failed attempt to kill Rogério Mesquita, Bid's right hand man and manager of the $25 million, 300,000-hectare family ranch. He was ambushed on a lonely road at the vast country estate. His would-be assassins, believed to be members of Shanna's own security detail, were all former policemen, and included ex-members of the elite BOPE military police commando unit. Even so, Mesquita survived the rural ambush. But his killers caught up with him in January 2009, just one day after he had visited homicide detectives to ask for protection. Walking in sports gear mid-morning along a high-end shopping street not a hundred metres from Ipanema Beach, talking to his personal trainer on the phone, Mesquita was executed with three shots fired into the back of his head at point-blank range. His assassin fled on the back of a black Honda motorbike, leaving the dead 54-year-old face down on the pavement.[49]

Two years later, in 2011, three masked gunmen burst into a spiritist temple in Jacarepaguá during a religious consultation and killed Zé Personal. At this point the Garcia family lost its grip on Salgueiro. Regina Celi, a popular, maternal figure who referred to school members as "my children", was elected president of the samba school. Even so, her rivals still competed to regain control. In 2012, Regina Celi, who had once been close to Maninho, denounced death threats, which she attributed to "people who want to get their hands on Salgueiro".

In 2014, Salgueiro's reverence for Gaia did not protect the school from the violent summer. Marcello Tijolo, Regina Celi's vice-president, was leaving a meeting in Vila Isabel when unidentified assailants on a motorbike gunned him down him in the street. He was rushed to hospital. The next day the authorities announced that Tijolo was lucid, orientated and out of danger. His recovery was widely reported.[50] Then his family moved him to a private hospital. Out of nowhere Tijolo was pronounced dead. His family declined to comment on the medical cause and the press dropped the matter. To the mournful thud of a bass drum held by a samba drummer, Tijolo was buried with Salgueiro flags and a red and black Flamengo shirt. His teenage daughter collapsed. His tattooed son, also wearing a Flamengo shirt, wept alongside. I asked acquaintances at the school if the murder might be linked to the *jogo do bicho*. They looked blank. They changed the topic.

The Garcia family is not the only *jogo do bicho* clan that turned on itself following the death of a patriarch. Like Miro, Castor de Andrade had a son involved in the family business. Like Maninho, Paulinho had a playboy reputation and was nowhere near as popular as his father at Mocidade. So when the debonair Castor died of a heart attack during a card game in 1997, his *jogo do bicho pontos* (betting points) were supposed to pass onto his business-minded nephew, Rogério. When Paulinho refused to hand them over, Rogério, allegedly, had him killed. The murder triggered a war over the family empire. Fernando Iggnácio, Castor's son-in-law, stepped into the fray. Rogério travelled with a large security detail and seemed untouchable. But in 2010 enemies nearly got him with a daylight car bomb that brought panic to the affluent West Zone Barra neighbourhood.

The explosive had detonated shortly after Rogério left an exclusive gym after his daily morning workout with his youngest son, Diogo. That morning Rogério let 17-year-old Diogo take the wheel of his bulletproof Toyota Corolla. When the bomb beneath the vehicle went off, the teenager took the full force of the explosion. He died instantly. Rogério suffered facial injuries only. Diogo was buried in pieces. The off-duty police who provided security for Rogério all escaped unharmed. Apparently organised by Fernando Iggnácio, the assassination attempt involved men close to Rogério. These included his own head of security, a sergeant in the fire brigade who, a few months later and reportedly on Rogério's orders, was shot and killed while riding his Harley Davidson near Barra Beach.

At the time of the car bomb, federal police estimated monthly turnover for the West Zone electronic gambling-machine business at $5 million a month. Organisers forced bar and bakery owners to install virtual poker units on their premises. The machines meant more profit, less paperwork and less daily stress. The venomous de Andrade family dispute even divided Rio's civil police force, with different groups of police aligning themselves to either side.[51] These years saw the fortification and further emergence of militia organisations linked to police and fire services across the West Zone. These groups carved up and took control over whole neighbourhoods, charging residents for security and provision of basic services such as gas, water and electricity. Without the firm hand of Castor, the "gentleman" godfather who had reigned absolute for decades, quarrelling *bicheiros*, police factions and militia turned western Rio de Janeiro into a war zone. Mocidade samba school also suffered. Castor, resplendent in green silk shirt and white suit, used to entertain politicians and celebrities with French champagne. But Mocidade failed to win another Carnival until two decades after his death.

After Tijolo's burial I carried on going to Salgueiro rehearsals and detected some unease. But violent death is not uncommon for *cariocas* who grieve, then proceed to get on with things. Life in Rio de Janeiro is too unpredictable to dwell on what might have been, especially with Carnival around the corner. The state governor Sérgio Cabral blamed insecurity in the city on enemies seeking to destabilise his authority. In an emergency, police were nowhere. Citizens took matters into their own hands. Vigilante *playboys* caught and beat an alleged thief, then padlocked him, naked and bleeding, to a lamppost. Shoppers at a supermarket in Copacabana attempted to lynch a crackhead shoplifter who threw a rock at a staff member. Mob members told passers-by who intervened that if they cared for such a criminal then they *should take him home*. In the Baixada Fluminense suburbs, there was no intervention and no arguing when a driver filmed a mid-afternoon summary execution on a busy street. The driver recorded a youth sitting on the ground, covered in blood from a beating. His killer stepped off a motorbike and fired a pistol into his head. The anonymous witness uploaded the images and they were viral within hours. In the Complexo do Alemão, someone shot a young female police officer in the back. Her murder, attributed to drug traffickers, triggered more war in the favela's tangle of narrow alleys.

THE FAMILY CLANS behind the *jogo do bicho* manage complex criminal and commercial interests that extend far beyond samba schools. They kill each other at the beach, outside gyms and on busy shopping streets. They employ BOPE hitmen. While they run organized crime in Rio, their criminal empires spread far beyond the city into other states of Brazil and abroad. Their money laundering, drug trafficking and gambling interests connect them to Sicilian and Corsican mafias. Yoram El-Al, member of the Israeli Abergil crime syndicate and international ecstasy kingpin, was imprisoned for 13 years in Rio in 2013. Linked to a North Zone *bicheiro* called Piruinha, he is believed to have provided the explosive for the car bomb that killed Diogo Andrade.[24]

The golden age of the *cúpula* ended with the heart attack that killed Diogo's great-uncle Castor. During his lifetime, Castor de Andrade courted celebrities and the media. Judges kissed his hand. He was an intimate friend of the world's most powerful *carioca* of that era – João Havelange, former International Olympic Committee member and president of FIFA between 1978 and 1998. Havelange, who sat at Castor's table for the *bicheiro*'s daughter's wedding banquet in 1986, once wrote a character reference describing him as an amiable, pleasant, loyal friend and family man.[52] Whilst alive, Castor cultivated the public image of an honourable *malandro* who limited his criminal interests to gambling and *jogo do bicho*. However in Valério Meinel's *Eagle, Ostrich and Cocaine* he does not cut such a fine figure. According to the scrupulous Meinel, it was Castor who introduced the *bicheiros* to cocaine dealing.

Early one morning in December 2011, a black helicopter hovered over an exclusive seafront apartment block metres from Copacabana Beach. A second helicopter containing journalists captured images of masked gunmen carrying assault rifles as they dropped from the helicopter onto the garden rooftop of the luxury penthouse on Atlantic Avenue, one of Brazil's most prestigious addresses. As the elite police commandos ran across

---

24 Judicial documents pertaining to "Black Ops", a 2011 federal investigation, identify Yoram El-Al as the subject of an Interpol arrest warrant related to the seizure of 1.4 million ecstasy tablets in Los Angeles. In 2017, hooded gunmen executed Piruinha's son and heir, Haylton Escafura, and his girlfriend, a serving military policewoman, in a Barra hotel bathroom. "The Crime Office" death squad, linked to Marielle Franco's assassination, is believed to have carried out the attack.

the roof and into the building, the TV cameras zoomed in on a *beija-flor* (a humming bird) painted onto the bottom of the rooftop swimming pool. The police were armed with an arrest warrant for Anísio, owner of the penthouse. This he had acquired shortly after the death of its previous owner, Roberto Marinho, founder of the Globo empire and Boni's former boss. Anísio was not at home, but was picked up in the street a few weeks later.

The cinematic raid was the climax of Operation Hurricane, a four-year federal police investigation into the *jogo do bicho*. In 2012, Anísio, Captain Guimarães and a third member of the *cúpula*, Turcão, received 47 years each. Although they were briefly detained, the jail sentences soon evaporated in a vacuous puff of legal appeals, house arrests and petitions of ill health. The judicial verdict, which runs to 1,500 pages, depicts in minute detail the sophistication of the modern-day operation:

the current penal action portrays the workings of a gigantic criminal organisation, rooted in the Brazilian state apparatus, principally Rio de Janeiro, with special focus on the state, federal and military police […] which even extends its tentacles to the financing of electoral campaigns for state and federal parliaments and executives[…] [It is] a Mafioso style organisation, which illegally exploits gambling games in the state of Rio de Janeiro and various other states in the federation, and which spans from the jogo do bicho through to slot machines and electronic bingos. Functional support for this organisation has been identified as coming from an enormous web of corrupt officials, not only in the police but also in the judiciary, which has served, and probably still serves, as a protection network. [53]

Moreover, the verdict declares, "it is precisely the criminal organisation here in question, that dominates and exploits, in fact, the *carioca* Carnival, one of the largest tourist attractions in Brazil and the world". The central LIESA office in downtown Rio, it says, is headquarters to "one of the most dangerous and articulated armed gangs in the country". [54]

The razzamatazz of the "greatest show on earth" hides the dark heart of Brazilian organised crime. And in 2014 I took part in the parade to discover how it felt to belong to the party…

9

THE PARADE

Beija-Flor was the last school to parade on the first night of the 2014 Special Group competition. One of thousands of components, I waited outside the sambadrome under heavily pregnant rain clouds. Drinking alcohol in the "concentration", as the immense queue is called, was forbidden. All the same, some of us sneaked beers bought from vendors through the steel fence that separated us from the late-night/early-morning city on the other side. Half-cut revellers on their way home squinted through the fence, alongside wily street urchins looking to raise funds. In my little group the surreptitious drink flowed. We had worked hard during the past months and we intended to enjoy the show.

At the entrance to the Avenida Marquês de Sapucaí (the name given to the road the sambadrome runs along), "son of Xangô", the indomitable Laíla, puffed hard on a thick cigar and waved the smoke in the air. Beija-Flor directors in official shirts scurried around him pouring the contents of cans of beer

9 / THE PARADE

The author, 2014.

and bottles of *cachaça*[25] onto the road at his feet. Salgueiro, the preceding school, had put on an excellent display. But Laíla believed that these ceremonial offerings for his *orixá*, Xangô – which included bouquets of red roses, would clear the way for Beija-Flor.

A bellicose fireworks display kicked off our performance. Now the much-loved Neguinho da Beija-Flor, who has represented Anísio since the 1970s, sang the first lines of Boni's samba in his fabulous honey-smooth baritone. The moment had arrived. My *ala* were dressed as cockerels. Our emerald green lycra outfits made us look more like pheasants, but officially we were the crowing cockerel; arch communicator and eternal harbinger of the proverbial new day. I found a director to tighten my headdress, and huge breastplate of sharp artificial feathers called an *esplendor* that jutted out from my chest. With the headdress and *esplendor* as tight as possible, there was less chance of something going wrong. Woozy and beer-fuzzled, I needed to pee but there was no more time to make a dash for the chemical toilet. We shuffled forward ten metres or so every few minutes with a clanking of rattling costumes and rustling feathers. You could be forgiven for thinking we were some sort of kitsch army.

Communication was our "message". In the beginning was "the word". The first Beija-Flor *carro alegórico* (float) to drive into the *avenida* was manned by a sumptuous mélange of dancing Mesopotamians and Sumerians astride a moving tower of Babel. A fierce blue-bearded head dominated the centre of the float. His serpent-like tongue, decorated with hieroglyphs, circled

---

25 A powerful alcoholic spirit made with sugar cane.

downwards from his mouth, wrapping itself around the feet of dancers. At the very top of the float, high above the road and at eye-level with the crowds in the stands, a golden blonde woman gyrated, gesticulated and celebrated with the joy of a veteran revivified. This was Anísio's wife, Fabíola, who first appeared for Beija-Flor in 1989. Today she was here to honour their friend Boni. Underneath her danced Anísio's young daughter Micaela, plumed in gold and blue.

A Godzilla-like fire-breathing dragon, accompanied by orange, red and green geishas, white and blue carrier pigeons and Red Indian chiefs, followed the Tower of Babel and its dazzling dancers. The American Indians were remembered for the smoke signal, the Chinese for early forms of paper. Next came a float dedicated to Hermes, with *alas* representing telephones, telegraphs, Greek rhetoric, Julius Caesar and Roman newspapers. Winged messengers dangled underneath hissing serpents. Now dancing bunches of grapes, chefs and more than two hundred drummers announced the arrival of bon vivant Boni. Bowler-hatted, moustachioed Boni and the Beija-Flor *bateria* were all dressed as Charlie Chaplin. For his big night at the sambadrome, Boni pays homage to his hero; the grand master of wordless communication.

At five in the morning I was halfway along the *avenida*, under the floodlights following scores of dancing microphones. Ahead of me, on a float honouring "the book", The Little Prince, Harry Potter and Don Quixote waved to the crowds. By now I was in severe pain. The metal mesh frame holding together my rooster headdress dug at the sides of my skull. The pain was strongest just above and behind my ears where the straps were drawn fast. The elaborate *esplendor*, my breastplate of artificial feathers, was crushing my chest. It hurt me to breathe and my bladder was set to burst. The secret beer I had drunk in the queue was punishing me, trying to escape. My internal organs screamed. Crushed from the outside, exploding inside, I sang to distract my attention from the suffering. I sang and kept in step. Eventually we must reach the end. The crowd of dancing microphones parted ahead, revealing Laílá. He was standing in the middle of the *avenida* with eyes that focus at once on all and none of us. Despite the extreme pain, I was relieved by his presence. As I passed Laíla I sang even harder. I wanted him to know I had done my best for Beija-Flor. Sweat mingled with blood oozing from a cut behind one of my ears and dripped onto my costume.

Towards the end of the parade, Beija-Flor was close to the official time limit. We needed to exit the sambadrome quickly to make space for the remainder of the school, or risk losing precious points. I got trapped in an unruly crush and for a frightening moment lost my balance in a group of walking TV sets. Eventually we emerged into the street behind the sambadrome. Dawn was visible; streaks of grey began to appear among the black, heavy clouds. The rain that had been threatening Beija-Flor since the beginning of the parade had somehow held off. Maybe Laíla's offerings had worked.

Back in the sambadrome the final Beija-Flor floats made their way past the judges. The penultimate car paid homage to Globo TV through a construction filled with *globais*, the name given to actors and presenters who, thanks to Boni, are some of the most famous people in Brazil. Giant LED screens broadcasted unforgettable moments – kisses and fights in equal measure – from countless Boni-commissioned *novelas*. The last float was supposed to represent the future of communication, but in reality it was yet another homage to Boni's perceived brilliance. Inside a giant conch, an LED orb broadcasted highlights from his career. The globe displayed photographs of Boni with celebrities, including the deceased Formula One hero Ayrton Senna. Next came Boni with Jorge Castanheira, the current LIESA director, and then Boni with Anísio. Images of *bicheiros* and heroes gave way to a digital inscription in Globo font, reading "*padrão Boni da qualidade*" (Boni quality standard), a reference to the Globo standard catchphrase invented during the Boni decades to refer to the much-imitated, but never superseded, Globo way of doing things. These words closed the parade.

Still dressed as a green chicken, I walked home through streets knee-high in discarded beer cans, food wrappers and other twenty-first-century bacchanalian detritus. Rio's street cleaners, the popular orange-suited *garis*, were on strike. By Monday, revellers, tourists and police would be fighting through a sea of trash. I joined a stream of people in various stages of costume dress. The pain in my bladder was worse than ever but I could not find a chemical toilet anywhere. Urinating in the street is an arrestable offence in Rio, especially at Carnival time, when the media conduct a sanitation campaign against the *mijões* (pissers), publishing photos of revellers mid-pee and delighting in arrest statistics for such behaviour. But there were no toilets in sight. I found a parked lorry and – with some difficulty – rolled my tight green lycra outfit down below my waist. Luckily no authorities witnessed my moment of shame.

AFTER RESTING UP, that night I went back to the sambadrome to watch the remaining schools competing for the *Grupo Especial* title. Away from the VIP boxes and tourists, in the cheaper stands, *carioca* passion for the parade is most vocal. Visceral emotions ride high as each school enters the avenue. Supporters sing the year's sambas by heart. Some appear to know the words of every samba for every school. Imperatriz Leopoldinense paid special birthday tribute to football legend Zico. He rode on a truck carrying dancers who kicked footballs high into the stands. União da Ilha, from the Ilha do Governador neighbourhood, featured trapeze artists swinging back and forth on long bending poles in a graceful airborne dance, high over the road. A swirling sea of blue and white female dancers, called *Baianas*, following a majestic, screeching eagle, opened Portela's electrifying parade, which incorporated explicit references to the street protests that swept the country in 2013. A float passed with a huge rock split wide open, giving birth to a giant, in direct reference to the awakening giant that swamped Brazil's cities. The rock opened and closed several times along the avenue. But when it left the sambadrome, the giant was back inside his rock, once again asleep and hidden from view.

During pauses in the entertainment I flicked through an official Beija-Flor magazine, one of 60,000 copies of the 100-page glossy colour publication handed out each year to spectators at the sambadrome. The shining star of Brazilian communication grinned Cheshire Cat-like on the cover. Anísio dominated the opening pages with a full-page photo and his editorial. He praised entrepreneurialism and the "unnamed citizen" who has put aside "dreamy discourses of equality and state super-protection to act, work and achieve his dreams". Anísio's brother Farid, president of the school and three-times mayor of Nilópolis, wrote a second opinion piece, and yet another celebration of Boni:

Until today Boni lived secretly in the life of each Brazilian, without their knowledge. The mage of communication is a genius at what he does, and with his competence, dedication and simplicity he created a standard of quality that gave Brazilians dignity through programmes of the highest quality.[55]

Boni and Beija-Flor share the will to succeed, according to Farid. There were photos of Boni with his children, Boni with his fine wine collection, Boni with Anísio. Handwritten letters from the parents of children who attend a crèche founded by the Abrãao David family described the importance of Anísio's social work in Nilópolis. A mother thanks "Mr Anísio" for making sure her children were well fed at times when there was no food at home. "I adore the Beija-Flor family," she said. Another article praises the *malandro*, that traditional Rio scallywag and entrepreneur who lives on his wits. Many *malandros*, the text reminds, got rich from gambling. "These individuals practiced charity and invested part of their earnings in charity and cultural investment, like samba." Tucked away among the propaganda, singing Anísio's praises as grand benefactor and provider to the needy, were telling advertisements for luxury casino hotels in Las Vegas and a Beija-Flor stud farm called Haras Beija-Flor. After all, what is Anísio but the *malandro* supreme? He was not there in the flesh. Anísio had not appeared at the sambadrome for some time and 2014 was not to be any different. Since they received their lengthy Operation Hurricane sentences in

2012, most of the *cúpula* of the *jogo do bicho* were keeping a low profile.

For the 30th anniversary of LIESA and the sambadrome, despite his absence, the 60,000 Beija-Flor magazines made sure however, that no one overlooked Anísio's contribution to Carnival. Captain Guimarães, on the other hand, turned up in person to mark the occasion. According to Boni, the captain is "the great mentor and articulator of LIESA, always calm and low-profile and another personality to whom Carnival owes a lot".[56] According to many, the captain still rules from behind the scenes, where he is known as *nosso comandante* (our commander). Sambistas say no significant decision about the parade is taken without his permission.

While the older generation of *bicheiros* were more discreet, Castor de Andrade's nephew set out to make a big splash at Carnival 2014. Only a few weeks before the competition, Rogério Andrade had announced his takeover of Mocidade Independente. The move took Rio by surprise. Rogério had not been seen near the sambadrome for years. The late 80s and early 90s were the samba school's glory years. Castor, resplendent in green silk shirt and white suit, would host a box where he entertained VIPS, like João Havelange, with cases of imported champagne. Mocidade had still not won since the death of Castor. Now Rogério planned to revitalise the school. But for Carnival 2014 he had only stepped in at the last minute. There was no chance of turning Mocidade into a champion in the space of a few weeks. All the same, he made sure that no one failed to notice his return. He hired four VIP boxes and loaded them with an entourage of pneumatic blondes and beefy security guards. The Moët & Chandon flowed. Wearing Uncle

Castor's characteristic outfit of white suit and green silk shirt, Rogério informed the press that next year he was going to "fill Mocidade with money".

On Ash Wednesday, when the confident Beija-Flor team sat down with the other samba schools at the results ceremony, their Nilopolitan ebullience rapidly soured. The extra millions of reais, LED orbs and float full of Globo stars led to Beija-Flor's worst result in 21 years. Laíla blamed politics. Boni cried foul – the judges fixed the result, they have too much power, the judging system is old and must be changed! Never mind the fact that the same judges gave Beija-Flor victory two years ago. Laíla threatened to resign.

No one else was surprised. Rio de Janeiro was underwhelmed by a samba centred on Boni. Beija-Flor's parade was technically competent, but unremarkable. The Nilopolitan school only missed the annual champions parade by one place but the combination of Anísio's money and Boni's story failed to bestow honour on Beija-Flor. The more than generous sprinkling of Globo celebrity stardust did not work. Unidos da Tijuca took the title with a parade dedicated to Ayrton Senna. Almost immediately Paulo Barros, victorious *carnavalesco* at the Tjucan school (and best paid man in Carnival) announced his move to Mocidade. Rogério Andrade asked him to get to work on Carnival 2015 immediately. Mocidade's next theme? *What would I do if today was my last day on Earth?*

That night I had a Carnival dream. I was in the *avenida* dressed as a clucking chicken that transformed into a green Pinocchio with an expanding nose. I danced on strings held by a cackling airborne blue-bearded Boni, hovering in the night sky. He pulled me into the heights where, with a white flash

View from the stands at the sambadrome, 2015.

and almighty crack, I exploded. Tiny multicoloured fragments of shit, piss, bones and blood fell shimmering onto the parade; a fiery artery ablaze with sound and colour far below. My soul floated free. Underneath, the sambadrome cut like a knife through the heart of the metropolis.

A YEAR LATER I bought spectator tickets for both nights of the Special Group parade. I wanted to discover what Paulo Barros, perhaps the greatest living *carnavalesco*, would achieve with Mocidade. Would Rogério Andrade win Carnival for the first time since Uncle Castor's death? I also wondered how Beija-Flor would fare after the previous humiliating result.

On the first night the heavens opened. It poured non-stop. Along with everyone else in the stands I sat wrapped in a transparent plastic sheet that made us look like human embryos from *The Matrix*. But it was worth every minute to see Mocidade. Rogério Andrade spared no expense to bring to life a song that asked "if the world was about to end, tell me: what you would do if you only had one day?". Giant heads filled with living humans spun 360 degrees. Sexy couples (even triples!) caroused under white sheets in beds hung like pouches from the side of a giant float playfully called "Motel Mocidade". The lovers came in all flavours – women with men, women with women, men with men. Another float transformed a typical Barra multi-storey shopping centre into a classic Rio gym crammed with pumped lycra-clad *cariocas*. Mocidade's Carnival even included a float that carried a car with an exploding engine. To all purposes, it looked very much like a homage to the young Diogo, killed when he left the Barra gym with his father in 2010.

I wondered what Valério Meinel would have made of it all. *Eagle, Ostrich and Cocaine* ends in the sambadrome; while Adamastor, Meinel's pseudonymous Castor de Andrade, sprays champagne over Mocidade components, a police chief and senator discuss a transformational expansion of Castor's organised crime empire – the introduction of electronic gambling machines. In 1987, Meinel was as prescient as ever. In the 1990s, the Sicilian mafia helped Castor flood Brazil with electronic gambling equipment (for a few years such machines were legally authorised in the country). The Corleone family allegedly appointed two men, Fausto Pelegrinetti and Lino Lauricella, to oversee the operation and subsequent laundering of cocaine money through the *bicheiros*' gambling empire. Of course, the Italians paid them handsomely to do so. When Lauricella turned informer back in his home country, he told Italian investigators: "In Rio de Janeiro a *cúpula* exists, called the *cúpula* of Rio de Janeiro, a *cúpula* in the way we understand it, with a boss and district sub-bosses." [57]

Once again, we find Castor de Andrade at the centre of the action. Castor had long-established Mafia connections. In the 1960s, he befriended Antonino Salamone, a member of the first Sicilian mafia commission. Salamone had fled to Brazil during the so-called First Mafia War, after a car bomb killed seven police officers and soldiers in Palermo. Castor helped his Italian friend, who was convicted in Italy and subject to an international arrest warrant, to acquire Brazilian citizenship, which was ceded without question by the military authorities in 1970.[58] After decades of toing and froing between the US, Italy and Brazil, Salamone died in São Paulo in 1998, one year after Castor's fatal heart attack.[26] The criminal network Castor founded with the *cúpula* had crossed borders for decades. From street corner bets, through Carnival and beyond, in partnership with Boni and abetted by the Brazilian military dictatorship, Castor and his associates were prime players in the international underworld of global organised crime.

---

26 According to the website of the Instituto Brasileiro Giovanni Falcone, Salamone was once married to *capo dei capi* Totó Riina's sister, and was described by *pentito* Tommaso Buscetta as a "sphinx".

9 / THE PARADE

FOR THE 450TH ANNIVERSARY OF RIO DE JANEIRO in 2015, Anísio was looking further afield than Italy. That year, his samba school's Carnival parade paid extended homage to Equatorial Guinea. Beija-Flor had visited the tiny, oil- and gas-rich West African country in 2013. Wearing a pale blue smock, then 45-year-old Teodorin Obiang, Vice President and Minister of Forests and Agriculture and also son of the country's president, watched the homage to his country from the Beija-Flor VIP box. Teodorin was an international playboy who often travelled to Rio. He owned a penthouse in São Paulo where he kept a fleet of sports cars, including a Maserati, a Lamborghini and a Porsche Cayenne. Until recently, he had also owned mansions in Paris and Malibu but French and US authorities investigating money laundering confiscated these properties, along with more sports cars and Teodorin's collection of Michael Jackson memorabilia. In 2018, Brazilian customs officials apprehended more than US$16 million dollars worth of cash and diamond watches from Teodorin's entourage, when he landed by private jet at a small airport in São Paulo state. In 2020 France fined him $33 million for money laundering.

I found Beija-Flor's parade uninspiring, unlike the judges. Most of them were new – 21 out of 40 had been replaced after Boni's complaints in 2014. They crowned Beija-Flor grand winner of Carnival 2015. While Boni and Anísio danced a celebratory tango back in the Nilópolis quadra, Brazilian newspapers asked why Beija-Flor was eulogising a corrupt and poverty-stricken country. The ever-bombastic Laíla rounded on the school's critics, accusing them of double standards, pointing out that the Brazilian government had established diplomatic links with the African nation.

How might Valério Meinel have interpreted Beija-Flor's homage to Equatorial Guinea? Political connections aside, I couldn't help remembering that West Africa is a hub for global cocaine trafficking. Historically speaking, Brazilian and West African supply chains have long had deep roots in the slave trade. Today, international cocaine smugglers favour the same trajectory, but in reverse: black souls have become white powder.

PART THREE
TRUTH AND LIES

"The flat-earth hard-line colonels have arrested the spiritual development of what is potentially a brilliant country of liberal creative instincts and the most lively intellectual capacity."

– Sir John Russell,
UK Ambassador to Brazil, 1969[119]

10

TRUTH

I N 2014, THE YEAR I SANG AND DANCED FOR Beija-Flor and for Boni, the 50th anniversary of Brazil's 1964 military coup cast a sombre shadow over Carnival. There was also hope, however. Dilma Rousseff, a survivor of regime torture, was President. State and national truth commissions worked hard to eke out truth from the shady corners of Brazil's two decades of military rule. Eager teams of lawyers and prosecutors sought to establish exactly what had happened in the dungeons of the dictatorship. While the commissions exposed the sordid practices used to terrorise opponents of the junta, Amnesty International offered me consultancy work at their recently opened Rio office, run by Brazilians. The dream of establishing a permanent local base had been high on the organisation's agenda for a long time. Finally, it had invested resources in a converted house in Laranjeiras, a leafy South Zone neighbourhood.

I was pleased. I always felt uncomfortable in the role of foreign finger-wagging do-gooder. Brazil needed a strong civil society if it was to move towards being a safer, more humane

Inês Romeu, survivor of the "House of death" interrogation centre, speaking to reporters at the Rio de Janeiro Truth Commission, 2014.

country. A strong national Amnesty office was a step in the right direction. The organisation's biggest challenge was to restore the public concept of human rights, from attackers who had successfully disqualified it over the years. Powerful populist voices, which consistently call for more punishment, say that human rights protection works for the defence of criminals. Amnesty International, they snarl, makes Brazilian society less, not more safe. They shout for more prisons, more walls, more guns! *Bandido bom é bandido morto!* (A good criminal is a dead criminal!) Such rhetoric, with roots in death squad activity and the military dictatorship, ruins coherent public discourse and paves the way for violent policing, torture and extrajudicial executions. Worst of all it is extremely popular.

I knew little about the military dictatorship. Just that it was a heavy, black cloud that hung over recent Brazilian history. I did understand that the military were very close to the establishment; that in many cases they *were* the establishment. I only ever had limited contact with people from this class. For many years I associated the army with an advertisement I saw on Brazilian TV in 2003, shortly after Lula was elected for the first time. It showed a jungle, apparently only trees and shrubs. The foliage rustled, came to life, and soldiers in jungle dress appeared. "You might not see us: but we're always here," announced a voiceover as they faded back into the forest. I read the advert as a not very thinly veiled threat.

So when the opportunity arose to improve my knowledge of what happened during the dictatorship, I jumped at the chance. I worked on a project to record and publicise the stories of people defended by Amnesty. We interviewed former "prisoners of conscience" (people imprisoned for non-violent expression of their beliefs), whom Amnesty had campaigned for in the 1970s and 80s. These women and men, survivors of such sombre times, were inspiring for their vivacity and the fact that they had since achieved so much. Their testimonies of resilience filled me with admiration.

I attended long hearings packed with students, reporters, cameras and flashing lights, where unremarkable elderly men and women sat and listened quietly. I wondered whether they were victim, dissident, relative, perpetrator or collaborator? When called to testify, most former military men claimed ill health, manufacturing dubious medical notes like dishonest schoolboys. Those that did appear, denied all knowledge or memory of what went on behind the scenes during the period of Brazilian history that supporters of the junta call the "revolution". Even so, lies sustained for decades quickly unravelled to reveal elaborate pantomimes. Worn collages of deceit peeled away to expose tragedy, torture and murder. Investigators began to piece together the facts behind hitherto unsolved mysteries, like the "disappearance" of Rubens Paiva.

Paiva was a left-leaning civil engineer and politician who made the mistake of travelling to Chile where he contacted exiled dissidents. In 1971 the military began to pay attention to him, believing he might lead them to their then nemesis, a former army captain turned insurgent called Carlos Lamarca. When men claiming to belong to the Air Force knocked on Rubens Paiva's door, he said goodbye to his family and accompanied them without fuss. He even drove himself to his own interrogation wearing a suit and tie. Paiva was never seen again. Producing a machine-gunned, burnt-out VW Beetle, the authorities later alleged that, in a daring operation, subversives had rescued him on a lonely road that cut through hills high in the Tijuca forest.

This official version of events remained intact for four decades. Then a retired general, Raimundo Campos, admitted to receiving orders to spray bullets into, and then set fire to, an abandoned VW Beetle. But no one could say what happened to Rubens Paiva until a septuagenarian former colonel with a red, cratered face spoke to investigators. Formerly known by the

Punishment for military regime torturers, graffiti in central Rio 2014.

codename Pablo, Paulo Malhães, former intelligence officer and expert in disposing of bodies, was not driven by remorse – he said he would do it all again if necessary, to prevent Brazil from becoming Cuba – but he did feel that the dead man's family deserved to know what happened.

Malhães said he did not murder the politician but that superiors called on him to dispose of what was left of Paiva's body. The remains had been poorly buried in sand on Recreio Beach and the military wished to avoid their possible discovery.

So Malhães organised and disguised a search party as tourists. They secretly dug for Paiva in between swims. Eventually they found what they were looking for and sent it out to sea, via the Rio yacht club. Or dumped it in a river. Malhães changed his story, his memory was blurred. He confessed to losing count of the number of dissidents he had killed. His job required cutting the fingers off corpses and removing their teeth, to prevent identification.

Critically, Paulo Malhães broke the "no-squealing" rule upheld by his former colleagues. He gave several interviews to the Truth Commission, his 20 hours of testimony opening an unexpected breach in the wall of silence. He confessed that when he wasn't faking the tourist at the beach, he directed operations at the *Casa da Morte* (House of Death), an interrogation centre hidden in a residential house in Petropolis, mountain seat of the Imperial Court. Lawyers believed that at least 22 dissidents were tortured and murdered there. When Paulo Malhães retired from the military he moved to a secluded house on the outskirts of Nova Iguaçu in the Baixada Fluminense. The torturer and body disposal expert was soon working for Anísio, and was a regular visitor to Beija-Flor.

GENTE BOA, THE GOSSIP COLUMN in *O Globo*, mostly hosts photos of plastic soap stars and equally plastic socialites. Occasionally, however, it yields unexpected fruit. One Saturday in the run up to Carnival a few lines in the column caught my eye. Captain Guimarães, *bicheiro* and LIESA *comandante* had been called to testify at a Truth Commission hearing the following week. I made sure to attend. Maybe I would catch a glimpse of the famous captain?

The public hearing took place in an air-conditioned auditorium inside the elegant building that houses Rio's National Archives. Somewhat predictably, Captain Guimarães didn't appear, alleging ill health. But the hearing didn't disappoint. Chief speaker was Roberto Espinosa, former member of an underground resistance group which specialised in stealing arms caches from military depots. Espinosa's testimony was frank and clear. In 1969 he was detained with his girlfriend, Maria Auxiliadora, and a young Jewish student from São Paulo called Charles Chael. Intelligence services traced the trio to a house in Lins de Vasconcelos in Rio's northern suburbs. When Espinosa answered the door he was bundled away. His co-conspirators tried to resist, but not for long. All three were detained together.

"We weren't innocent," he said. "We felt a moral obligation to re-establish Brazil's constitution and democratic government. So we joined the armed opposition, exercising what we saw as legitimate rebellion against tyranny."

Chael died under torture. Maria Auxiliadora survived and fled first to Chile, then to Europe. In 1976, she threw herself under a train in West Berlin. Espinosa is the only member of the remaining alive. His interrogators had suspended him from a pole by his arms and legs and applied electric shocks to his naked body. The torture had been bearable, Espinosa said, when he could see who was doing it. That way he could hate them. Hate gave him strength. Even today he mixes up the words *sala* (room) and *cela* (cell). He survived by sleeping between torture sessions, convincing himself he had a moral obligation to do so. In his dreams he felt free and recovered strength. He never suffered from insomnia again. But the mere sound of keys turning in a lock terrifies him.

Ten men had tortured Espinosa, Chael and Auxiliadora. Officials had flown in from across Brazil to participate in their suffering. Those still alive now claimed they were too elderly and infirm to testify. But Espinosa insisted on naming all those who had been present, including a torturer whose codename was Dr. Robert. Dr. Robert, Espinosa told the Truth Commission, "is Captain Guimarães – the connection between the tyranny of the dictatorship and organised crime."[27]

Espinosa's words rang in my head as I stepped into the thermal blast that is Rio at midday in high summer. Because it was nearby, I walked to the sambadrome. Construction workers scurried around preparing the avenue for the upcoming parade. I tried to imagine what it must be like to be tortured, to be at the mercy of human beings who intend to destroy you. I could not. However, I did remember a passage from *The Brazilian People* where Darcy Ribeiro talked about torture. Back at home I found the page. His lucid words trace the prevalence of torture in Brazilian society to the historic treatment of Indian and African slaves, punished constantly with executions, routine whippings, beatings and mutilations. Brazilians, Ribeiro says, have the propensity for violence scarred on their souls:

> *No people that experienced this as a matter of routine over centuries, will escape without indelible marks. All we Brazilians are flesh of the flesh of those slaughtered Indians*

---

[27] 1987 SNI intelligence service reports in Rio de Janeiro's National Archive discuss the suspected involvement of the Captain with supplying Uzis to drug dealers in Vila Isabel's Macacos (Monkey Hill) favela, where many members of Vila Isabel samba school live. As noted by Jupiara and Otavio in *Os Porões da Contravenção (Record 2015)* pp. 171–172.

and Blacks. All we Brazilians are, equally, the same hand that slaughtered them. The most tender sweetness and most atrocious cruelty come together to make us into the feeling and suffering people that we are and the insensitive and brutal people that we also are.

Descendants of slaves and slave owners, we will always be servile to the malignity distilled and installed in us, as much for the feeling of pain produced with the intention of being more painful, as for the exercise of brutality against men, women and children, converted into objects of our fury.

Our most terrible heritage is to always carry with us the torturer's scar branded on our soul, ready to explode in racist and classist brutality.[59]

BY THE MID-NINETEEN SEVENTIES, the authorities had crushed any coherent armed opposition to the military government. Despite this, a pathological hard-core of military officials and police remained committed to defending the dictatorship, even if this meant acting illegally and outside official chains of command. They called themselves the Brotherhood, or Secret Group. Financed by powerful *bicheiros* and businessmen who stood to lose benefits from a transfer to democracy, they aimed to preserve the status quo at any cost.

The port and state capital of Espírito Santo in Vitória is a blander, smaller version of Rio de Janeiro. It is picturesque, but lacks Rio's painterly drama of mountains and tropical rainforest. Plain buildings and docks circle its scruffy bay. Cláudio Guerra was a civil police chief from Vitória who proved useful to hardliners during the crackdown on dissidents in the early 1970s. Like Paulo Malhães, he was an expert at disappearing corpses. Guerra was close to some fascist landowners who ran a sugar cane plantation, where he could dispose of bodies sent from São Paulo or Rio. The factory owners turned a blind eye while Guerra dumped them in the incinerator. His affiliation with both the SNI (the military intelligence service) and the Secret Group was inevitable. He belonged to an inner circle of military officials and regime sympathisers who frequently met in Angu do Gomes, a restaurant in downtown Rio. While discussions at the dinner table always celebrated the junta, conversation remained discreet and cordial. But after the long meals, smaller gatherings took place in a sauna next door, where, amid the steam and prostitutes, Secret Group members and military men planned and organised violent attempts to destabilise a possible return to democracy. Cláudio Guerra was a business partner in the sauna, which served as a fundraising front for the Brotherhood's terrorist activity. According to Guerra, Boni was a regular visitor; the shining star of Brazilian communication, he says, enjoyed both restaurant and sauna.[60]

In 1981, the Brotherhood mobilised a final push to prevent re-democratisation. This included bombing a Mayday benefit concert in Rio. The Secret Group, and its anonymous high-ranking supporters, wanted a public tragedy; they would blame the bomb on leftist dissidents and society would reject the political opening-up. On the night of the attack, the head of Rio's military police – a co-conspirator – prohibited police vehicles and other emergency services from circulating around the Riocentro, the concert venue. Within it, some of Brazil's most famous contemporary musicians performed to a crowd of 20,000.

The doors of the venue were locked from the outside. The Secret Group divided into four units; one to plant bombs inside the venue, another to graffiti the initials of the VPR – an extinct guerrilla group – in the vicinity of the show, thus attributing the attack to enemies of the regime. A third team would deactivate the Riocentro's electricity generator, to cut off power. Cláudio Guerra was to arrive at the venue with a prepared list of innocent dissidents to arrest and accuse of responsibility for the atrocity. But despite considerable support from the intelligence services and police, and allies within the military, the ambitious plan went awry. A bomb accidentally exploded inside the first terrorist car to arrive at the venue, instantly killing one of its two occupants and thereby ending the operation before it had begun. Gonzaguinha, a hugely popular singer, announced to a terrified young audience that a bomb had been detonated in an attempt to halt the spread of democracy. The bungled attempt cut short the desperate hard-liners' attack on re-democratisation. The botched bombing also led to one of the biggest cover-ups in Brazilian history, which presented the dead sergeant as a martyr – an innocent victim of a leftist terrorist attack. This is the official version of events.

Despite their efforts, the Secret Group and its supporters failed to prevent Brazil's democratic enlightenment. With Cláudio Guerra out of a job, his mentors introduced him to Castor de Andrade, who in turn appointed him head of security for the *jogo do bicho* in Rio de Janeiro. This role brought Guerra close to Captain Guimarães. Forming a partnership, the pair subsequently planned and successfully executed a takeover of the *jogo do bicho* and organised crime in Espírito Santo.[61] Eventually Guerra served a seven-year sentence for another failed bomb attack, this time on an Espírito Santo *bicheiro* who Guimarães wanted out of the way. Guerra, during his time in prison, found Christ – he repented and began a new life as an evangelical preacher.

THEN SOMEONE KILLED the Truth Commission's chief witness. Within weeks of testifying, Paulo Malhães, the retired colonel who exposed Rubens Paiva's disappearance and the macabre machinations of the Casa da Morte, was murdered. Despite widespread suspicion that Malhães was killed for talking, the regional civil police homicide department declared, almost immediately, that amateur robbers had murdered him. The alleged reason for this violence – theft of the colonel's very modest gun collection from his secluded house in the Baixada Fluminense, where he had lived, undisturbed, for decades. Despite protests from the federal government, and even a request from the UN, the investigation was quickly closed.

The converted Cláudio Guerra, however, drew his own conclusion. In his subsequent testimony for the Truth Commission, the former dirty war operative recalled the 2012 killing of another retired army colonel, Júlio Molina. Police investigators also attributed the murder of Molina – also connected to Ruben Paiva's disappearance – to weapons thieves. Guerra reminded the Commission that disguising political executions as common criminal activity was the very modus operandi of the intelligence services during the dictatorship. Unequivocally, Guerra stated his belief that Malhães was killed for talking. [62]

Guerra's ghost-written memoir, *Memories of a Dirty War*, captures the schizoid horror of the fusion of organised crime with fascist repression, at the rotten core of the military regime. Arms trafficking, eliminating his own colleagues, falsifying murder scenes, strategically feeding fabricated versions of events to the press and bombing civilian targets, were his regular business:

> *In the name of Brazilian state security, members of the intelligence community could do anything: persecute, wiretap, investigate, judge, condemn, interrogate, torture, kill, disappear with bodies and lie to families on the whereabouts of their loved ones. No ethical code, formal or informal, directed our conduct. Everything was allowed.*[63]

Under the junta there were no limits. And if Cláudio Guerra is to be believed (and why shouldn't he be?) the truth is that there are still no limits today. Paulo Malhães told his version of the truth and was promptly eliminated. Perhaps, because the country has maintained a national narrative for so long constructed on deception and subterfuge, Brazil no longer knows where the truth lies.

WHILE THE TRUTH COMMISSIONS turned up plenty of new information, they were shunned by the military hierarchy, who remain shielded from prosecution by a 1979 Amnesty Law – despite rulings in international courts defining torture and "disappearance" as crimes against humanity. Among a handful of high-ranking officials to publicly acknowledge the work of the Commissions, then army chief-of-staff General Sérgio Westphalen Etchegoyen dismissed the findings as "pathetic" and "wishy-washy".[64] Both his father and uncle had been named in connection with torture. According to Paulo Malhães, it was

General Etchegoyen's uncle, Colonel Cyro Etchegoyen, who had given the orders at the Casa da Morte.[65]

After Dilma Rousseff's shabby impeachment, when the cadaverous 74-year-old Michel Temer assumed the Brazilian presidency in May 2016, he immediately appointed 64-year-old General Sérgio Etchegoyen as head of his Office of Institutional Security. Etchegoyen, reporting directly to Temer, was now responsible for advising the interim President on matters of national security and federal intelligence. According to military sources quoted in the *Folha de São Paulo* newspaper, Etchegoyen's immediate mission was to monitor social organisations and leftist movements, in order to identify and pre-emptively snuff out, any resurgence of the mass street protests that paralysed Brazil in 2013.[66] The appointment of this committed military hardliner, to such a sensitive and powerful position, sent a shudder down my spine.

On the evening that Brazilian Congress voted to impeach Rouseff in April 2016, I had watched live on TV as Jair Bolsonaro, then pre-candidate for the 2018 Presidential election with more than three million social media followers, cast his vote in favour of impeachment with a eulogy to Colonel Carlos Brilhante Ustra, "the terror of Dilma Rousseff". Ustra had been regional head of military intelligence when President Dilma was tortured for three years.[28] "You lost in 1964 and you've lost again in 2016," said Bolsonaro, who represented a formidable group of populist, conservative evangelical fundamentalists. This group favoured relaxation of gun ownership laws, a reduction

---

28 In 2019 President Bolsonaro described Ustra, who is credited with institutionalising torture in Brazil, as a "national hero". The first public report on Paulo Malhães' killing was published on a website linked to Colonel Ustra, who died in 2015.

in the age of criminal responsibility and a tightening of Brazil's already severe abortion legislation.

Brazil's inability to prosecute junta atrocities, unlike neighbouring Chile and Argentina, has effectively embedded state impunity for human rights violations in the legal system, and denied the country a much-needed reckoning with the past in order to move forward. This failure permitted Bolsonaro and his fascist ideology to flourish.

11

MOLOTOV

PRIOR TO THE MASSIVE 2013 STREET protests, quality of life in Rio de Janeiro had apparently been slowly and painfully, improving. But cracks eventually showed on the official façade of success and cordiality. Ancient inefficiencies in the gas and electricity infrastructure led to random but frequent episodes of exploding manhole covers, which made walks downtown into a form of pedestrian Russian roulette. A city centre restaurant exploded. A 23-storey building collapsed. Leaked mobile phone images captured chubby Rio state governor Sérgio Cabral and business partners in Paris, cavorting frat-house style, napkins tied round their heads (his group was henceforth nicknamed 'the napkin gang'). *Cariocas* were incensed. The moment was the apex of Cabral's folly – two years later he was imprisoned for corruption and massive embezzlement of public funds.

Next, an American tourist was raped in front of her boyfriend in a pirate taxi. Thousands of these semi-licensed vans provided *cariocas* with a cheap, fast travel alternative. But the rape of a foreigner became a public relations fiasco. Mayor Paes used the moment to close down many such operations, favouring his relationship with the city's bus syndicates.[29] An unlikely coalition of indigenous people, leftist students and middle-class families stymied government plans to bulldoze both a school and the National Indian Museum, in order to build a multi-storey car park next to the Maracanã football stadium. Then the southern city of Porto Alegre's *"Passe Livre"* movement, that mobilised street protests against spiralling transport costs, spread north, turning 2013 into an unexpected *annus horribilis* for Rio's authorities.

Times were tough in São Paulo too. When thousands marched in support of the *Passe Livre*, police greeted them with riot gear, stun grenades, tear gas and baton charges. In Paris, São Paulo governor Geraldo Alckmin, whilst promoting the city as potential host for the 2020 World Expo, dismissed demonstrators as "thugs and vandals". In Rio several thousands marched but there was, initially at least, very little violence. President Dilma and Sepp Blatter were booed at the Confederations Cup opening ceremony in Brasília. Blatter appealed for "more love" but protestors dug in and demanded high quality "FIFA standard" schools and hospitals. When hundreds of thousands occupied central São Paulo and Rio de Janeiro on 20 June 2013, the rallies were now clearly about much more than bus fares.

I was on a plane to England at the time. I couldn't believe it. Something big was finally happening and I was missing it. Randomly, the day I arrived in London, the *Guardian* asked me to write a comment piece about what was happening. I centred

---

29 Eduardo Paes was mayor of Rio between 2008–2016.

my argument on words used by the taxi driver who had dropped me at the airport in Rio. We're tired of being treated like suckers, he said, using the *carioca* slang "*otários*" to describe a generalised national disaffection.

The protests continued and I followed the news from afar. While street rallies objecting about a wide array of ills, from public transport through to corruption, spread across Brazil, the focus in Rio turned on Globo TV. Demonstrators accused Globo of telling systematic lies, and of manipulating news stories to provide a distorted and perverse retelling of the events. Even with a revocation of the fare increases that sparked the protests, activists continued to demand transparency regarding the relationship between the bus cartels and the mayor's office. They gathered outside the Copacabana Palace Hotel, during a high society wedding reception for the granddaughter of Jacob Barata, a local transport tycoon known as "king of the buses". From the balcony, wedding guests responded by throwing banknotes at the protestors and even a heavy glass ashtray, slicing open one protestor's head.

In the enormous Rocinha favela, pacification police detained a local man called Amarildo, leading to his disappearance. "Where's Amarildo?" chanted protestors, who also set their sights on state governor Sérgio Cabral. They occupied Cabral's exclusive street in the Leblon neighbourhood, where one night masked rioters attacked shops and banks and battled police. Nevertheless the *Ocupa Cabral* movement, as the spontaneous anti-governor protest became known, was mostly peaceful. Sympathetic local residents even sent pizza down to the young campers.

The protests had meanwhile generated an intriguing boom in internet street journalism. Perhaps "citizen reporting" could finally challenge Globo's hegemony? Two stories in particular had grabbed my attention; the bungled arrest of a young man called Bruno Teles during Pope Francis' July 2013 visit to Rio, which appeared to be a case of mistaken identity, and the rise of a guerrilla media collective called Media NINJA. Learning more about these matters might, I felt, help me to discover what were the dynamics behind these protests and what were the opportunities that might lie behind them.

ON RETURNING TO RIO DE JANEIRO in September, I caught the tail end of the rebellion. Although hard-core protestors were still on the streets, overall numbers had plummeted. One evening in early October, I went to meet friends marching in support of striking teachers. I was late and when I arrived, most demonstrators had gone. Avenida Rio Branco, downtown Rio's business centre, looked as though a hurricane had passed through. I stopped outside a battered bank building where a man in his sixties was looking at an apparently intact cash dispenser, which appeared to still work. The gentleman – a *senhor* by all accounts – was well dressed in that casual Brazilian way, wearing dark jeans, a white shirt slightly rolled-up above the wrist, with a neat haircut and greying moustache. I watched him take his money and then walk towards me. His feet made the noise of wading through slush. He stopped, shaking and stamping his shoes to remove the fragments of glass stuck to them.

"This is the very minimum," he announced, to no one in particular.

Two photographers in crash helmets captured the sight of this stylish man in the freshly wrecked bank forecourt. Despite the alarms going off, the smoke and the fact that everything except the cash machine itself was in pieces, he had decided this was the place to withdraw money.

"This is the very minimum," he repeated. I wondered what he could mean by this?

"So do you agree with all this, sir?" I asked.

He nodded and looked at me.

"Yes," he answered, "this is the very minimum they should be doing. They should bust the banks, and now they should go to Brasília and blow up the whole damn place."

He slid his wallet into the back of his jeans and walked back across Rio Branco towards the metro station. I heard shots and explosions. Groups of people, mainly passers-by and office workers, came running down Rio Branco towards me. As they reached me, and were covering their faces, I felt the sting of tear gas. I ran for cover in a side street leading up to Rua México. But only for a moment; another group of police arrived on the corner and prepared to fire again.

On Rua México I came upon a scene reminiscent of *Escape from New York*, John Carpenter's dystopian film where Manhattan becomes one big prison and Broadway is taken over at night by "crazies". A man with a T-shirt wrapped around his head was pulling a street sign out of the road with his bare hands. Encouraged by whoops from comrades, he succeeded and made a clumsy attempt to toss it through an office window. Youths set fire to a pile of rubbish in the middle of the road. A well-dressed hipster couple documented the scene on their phones. More tear gas canisters landed next to me. An office doorman in traditional blue short-sleeved shirt and black trousers looked on, aghast. I ran towards the nearby US consulate for safety, pausing to catch my breath beside a homeless man pushing a cart. A group of crazies then ran in our direction and as they reached the corner, one of them pointed to the consulate.

"Estados Unidos!" he explained in an adrenaline-choked voice. His confederates paused and then stood back to hurl cobblestones at the bombproof glass.

I TRACKED DOWN BRUNO TELES, eager to find out what had happened the day Pope Francis arrived in Rio. While the Pope was shaking hands with President Dilma in the Governor's Palace, police and protestors were at the same time clashing just outside. When someone had thrown a Molotov cocktail, 27-year-old Bruno found himself at the epicentre of a most unholy row.

Bruno agreed to meet me at the house he shares with his parents in Vila São Luiz, on the outskirts of Duque de Caxias, a satellite city in the Baixada Fluminense. Caxias is oil-rich and vital to economic and political life in the state of Rio. It has shopping centres and luxury condos, as well as favelas and forgotten rural corners. Zeca Pagodinho, Brazil's favourite *pagode* (pop samba) singer lives there. Vila São Luiz is a quiet, hilly neighbourhood where elderly residents relax in front of their painted two- or three-storey houses. Young middle-class people in Caxias tend to work hard. Most have jobs in Rio, many study law, engineering or accountancy at night. They arrive home late, see their families, eat, watch TV and go to bed.

When his mother saw a gringo in the house she looked ill at ease. She was clearly upset by what had happened to her son. Bruno told her not to worry. His gentle manners made a good impression on me, being soft-spoken with an engaging smile. We sat on his roof terrace, where a breeze took the edge off the late afternoon heat. Bruno chatted easily. He explained

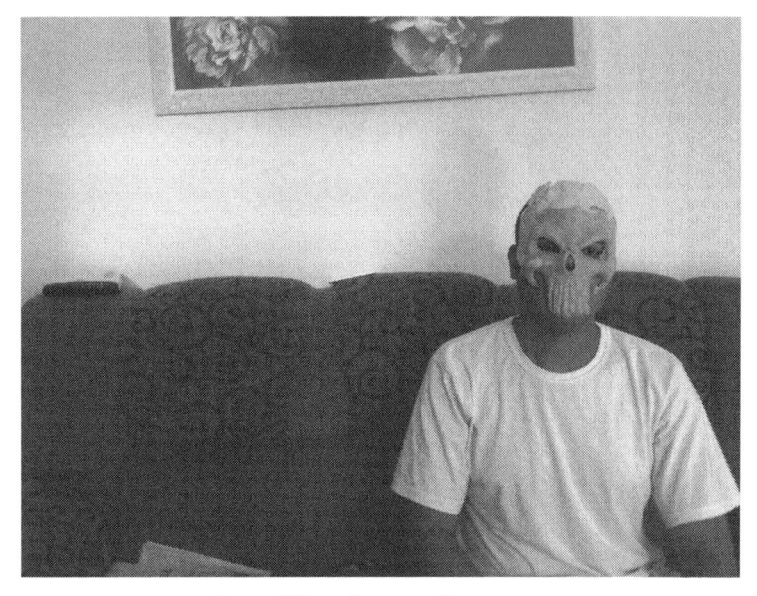

Bruno Teles at home in Caxias 2013.

that he was good with figures and had worked in an engineering firm for a couple of years, where he did well and rose quickly to become team leader. But the monochrome world of numbers and equations left him cold. He took a course in sculpture during lunchtimes, learned to mould plastic, and quit. Now he designed masks and costumes for computer graphics nerds who held US superhero costume parties. A Captain America mask might earn $60 and he could make $100 for Nemesis from *Resident Evil*. He liked making masks as they let people be whoever they wanted to be, and who doesn't put on a mask to disguise their real feelings?

"There isn't much to complain about in Caxias," he told me. "It's the sort of place where hard work gets you ahead. At the same time, like Brazil itself, it's very unequal. There are corners of the municipality, Gramacho for instance, where people live alongside animals."

According to Bruno, his friends describe him as *chato* (a drag). When the time comes to discuss things, anything – the universe, or why a certain girl will fall for a certain guy – Bruno is hard work. He likes arguing. He likes to try to understand why things are the way they are – especially regarding "the system" and politicians. When it comes to talking about politics, they say, Bruno is a real pain in the ass. He's always been *chato*.

Bruno first became aware of something going on when he went to buy a digital image mixer at the electronics bazaar in central Rio. He had seen news pieces about bus fare protests but not much else. He heard some distant noise and walked to the Candelária Cathedral where a crowd was gathering. There were placards, and people chanting, and homeless people hanging around. Bruno was fascinated. The marchers spoke about change and he saw something in their eyes. The crowd grew and grew, and he then walked with them down Rio Branco, turning left towards the state assembly, where they met another march coming from Presidente Vargas. A few hundred individuals had become a sea of people. He took a call from his mother outside the legislative assembly.

"Do you know there's a million people on the streets?" she asked.

She urged him to stay safe. After dark Bruno saw people preparing for violence. Feeling insecure, he decided to call it quits, and caught the late bus back to Caxias. Once back home, he calmed his mother down and switched on the television. The protests were all over every channel and, as Bruno had predicted, there had been some trouble. Reporters were criminalising the events, comparing protestors to drug traffickers and organised crime. But apart from a tiny number of agitators, Bruno had only seen middle-class kids, professionals and students. It did not make sense. He realised the TV was telling Brazil a different story.

That first day Bruno just watched and analysed what he saw. Then he began to look into what was behind the protests. He began to attend other demonstrations. Always watching, analysing, supporting. Not waving a banner or shouting for a cause, but listening, looking and learning. He felt the need to be present; not just to support, but also to understand. He liked to go unaccompanied, although sometimes he ran into friends, mainly middle-class types from the South Zone. When they walked together, it was, however, only a matter of time before a stun grenade might explode nearby and separate them. The protests were always unsafe. Revolutionary zeal had become fear. Even so, Bruno kept going. But numbers at the marches had begun to drop – a few hundred thousand became tens of thousands, then thousands.

In Caxias, Bruno worked on a university design course at a small local campus where he often sat in to observe other classes. There was plenty of talk about the marches. One day a law professor invited students to debate the matter. She asked those who were attending the protests to raise their hand. Bruno was the only one. Bruno told the class that they shouldn't just swallow what the media showed them – if there were 900,000 people at the protest, and 30 of them were violent, the media will always focus on the violent minority. Even after he had spoken, others in the class said it was still wrong; that people shouldn't attack property. He knew they did not know the other side of the story, about all the demonstrators getting injured by the police.

Bruno decided that the protests were for those Brazilians who wanted to see things as they really were. The security forces did not know what to do – nor did the protestors. There were no leaders. Some of them shouted about education, some about security, some people simply seemed annoyed with the world at large. Some police were trying to keep things calm, and some even sympathised. Other cops just weren't prepared psychologically to deal with the situation. In fact, everyone was unprepared. There was a lot of truculence and repression. The demonstrators were very nervous; people were scared and didn't know what might happen. Bruno kept going anyway, even though he too was fearful.

After a month he was tired; he wasn't working, he had marks on his legs from plastic bullets, had spent all his money on transportation and food, and was tired of headaches and the explosions that rang in his ears. Numbers of protestors were continuing to drop sharply. Since the beginning he had been watching and observing, and he realised if he didn't make an effort to record some of his thoughts soon, that he would have nothing to show others. The protests were about his future and his generation. There was a political awakening going on, and he was part of it.

MEANWHILE, IN SÃO PAULO, another Bruno's life was also undergoing rapid change. Until recently, Bruno Torturra had held an editorial job at *Trip*, a glossy lifestyle magazine for the fashion conscious. In his own time he participated in cultural collectives, including an internet TV channel that examined alternatives to the traditional media. The group created a name for their activities: NINJA, which stands for

Narrativas Independentes, Jornalismo e Ação (Independent Narratives, Journalism and Action), and set up a Facebook page to publicise them. Members of the collective attended the World Social Forum in Tunisia for their first online broadcast. Although no more than 30 internauts viewed the live transmission of a pro-Palestine march, it paved the way for the coverage of Brazilian human rights questions that NINJA engaged in, slowly building up a national following at home. The time was a fertile one for activism. The appointment of a homophobic evangelical preacher as National Human Rights Secretary had enraged liberals; and with life getting more expensive, Brazil's economy was slowing down, and the national currency, the *real*, depreciating. To cap all this, the constant exposure to glossy FIFA World Cup public relations and marketing exercises, grated on public nerves.

In São Paulo journalism was in crisis. Magazines and newspapers were laying off staff left, right and centre. Bruno Torturra was already known for his interest in alternative media so it was no surprise when *Trip* magazine invited him to join the growing ranks of unemployed former hacks. Torturra believed radical change was imminent. In the first week of June he published a call to arms on his blog entitled *Ficaralho*. *Ficaralho* is a hybrid word invented by Torturra that refers to the unexpected sense of relief he detected in himself and those other journalists who had lost their jobs. The general gist of it is "if you stay behind, well stay and get fucked". *Ficaralho* refers to the sacking of dozens of media professionals, and the inherent paradox of his happiness and sudden sense of freedom. Torturra compared it to the depression he perceived among those who remained at their desks:

The consolidation of social networks, information hyperflux, streaming and the emergence of a connected mass, ready to absorb and share news and stories, has made traditional vehicles all the more dispensable. By confusing themselves with their name in copy and conditioning themselves to the false comfort of a salary, journalists have turned their backs on autonomy, their greatest asset. And they end up playing the comfortable and cynical role of victims of the death of journalism.

He finished his manifesto by calling an open meeting for media professionals "unemployed or wishing they were unemployed", in order to establish:

a broad, decentralised communications group, which exploits the possibilities of coverage, discussion, repercussion, remuneration and radical freedom of expression that the internet offers.[67]

The proposed date, 13 June, clashed however with another *Passe Livre* protest, and Torturra was obliged to cancel. He reiterated his belief in the future of independent street journalism, and urged all sympathetic journalists, photographers, filmmakers and communicators to participate in live "real time" coverage of the event. At the demonstration, Torturra found himself near the front of the march of thousands. Despite it being a peaceful protest, riot police fired concussion grenades, rubber bullets and tear gas into the crowd. Torturra witnessed it all. The march disintegrated but again and again police fired more rubber bullets, stun grenades and tear gas. They chased protestors into side streets where they attacked them with truncheons. Seven journalists from the *Folha de São Paulo* newspaper were injured.

One of them almost lost an eye. The next day the establishment broadsheet switched from attacking to supporting the protests. A slapstick NINJA clip filmed that night shows a protestor, clad top to toe in black, dancing disco steps in front of a line of police to a superimposed soundtrack of "Staying Alive". The 16-second montage halts suddenly when a rubber bullet fired at the disco-protestor misses, striking the camera. The Youtube post was NINJA's first big hit.

Wasting no time, the *Passe Livre* movement booked its next march for 17 June. NINJA, this time better prepared, deployed its first mobile headquarters. It looked like the device E.T. mounted to phone home; a shopping trolley carrying an old generator plugged into two laptops, a mixer for sound and video editing and speakers, all protected by a plastic sheet and umbrella. The streets swarmed with a multitude of demonstrators, united by frustration and mutual incomprehension. While eager participants railed against everything from communism to corruption, NINJA sought to register the movement's polymorphous impulse. Two photographers and cameramen sent images to a team who then posted these online. But with so many marchers and mobile web users present, the internet crashed.[68]

The following day was NINJA's grand Brazilian première. A much smaller gathering turned violent when a suspect group of several dozen masked, Black Bloc style anarchists began to attack property on the Avenida Paulista.[30] Coming across an advertising sculpture made out of Coca-Cola cans, they attacked it with gusto. Two NINJA correspondents relayed the episode live to

---

30 "Black Blocs" are protesters who wear black clothes, cover their faces, and are sometimes violent.

Brazil and the world via their mobiles. When the anarchists set fire to the Coca-Cola stand, erected for the Confederations Cup, 50,000 virtual spectators watched the Black Bloc victory celebration live online.

RIO OFTEN SEES BIG CROWDS but when Pope Francis descended on the city for World Youth Day in July 2013, it was like Carnival and New Year combined. The faithful crowded the buses and the metro. They stood in endless lines at tourist spots. They built a city of tents under Sugarloaf Mountain. The faithful were everywhere. The Pope arrived to the acclamation of crowds, and he enchanted them with his simplicity. He asked Catholics to shun ephemeral idols of material success, power and pleasure. The Pope urged *cariocas* not to grow accustomed to evil, but to defeat it.

When Bruno Teles heard the Pope was coming, he expected a hullabaloo. Constitutionally Brazil is a secular state, yet huge sums of money were involved; the Brazilian authorities had put $52 million towards this, the first papal visit since 1990, in a country where one in four of the population now declare themselves evangelical Christians. Bruno researched gay and gender-based protest movements. He decided he was going to make a video the day the Pope arrived, and then he was going to take a break. The mood of the city was too dangerous.

For this, his last mission, he left little to chance. He kitted himself out with protective goggles, earplugs, a mouth protector and a light iron chest plate – which came from an Iron Man costume he was working on. He planned to film from the front and reckoned that the chest plate might protect him from plastic bullets. He used a pair of iron armbands that were also part of the Iron Man costume and covered it all with a light denim jacket, zipped up. With the goggles on his head, he looked ever the futuristic fashion eccentric as he caught the Supervia from Caxias to Central, crushed inside the train alongside eager fans of the Pope.

At Largo do Machado, Bruno stopped to film the crowds packing the square. Gay rights campaigners were staging a kiss-in next to a group of the faithful praying before the church. On the steps, worshippers, surrounded by leftists waving red flags, engaged in heated debate with demonstrators in Anonymous masks. Bruno mingled as the unconventional congregation of LGBT activists, sympathisers, onlookers, worshippers, communists and anarchists drifted in no apparent order towards the governor's palace, where inside Pope Francis was finishing his meeting with President Dilma. "Let me knock gently at the door to the heart of the Brazilian people. I ask permission to come in and spend this week with you," the Pope said. "I don't have gold or silver, but I bring Jesus Christ."

Night had fallen. Phalanx upon phalanx of riot police separated protestors from the faithful. When the Pope left the palace, Bruno put his camera in his pocket and moved to the waist-high iron barricades dividing him from the police. He called out to them, above the sounds of drums and horns and the helicopter overhead

"Your children study in schools where there is no investment in education!" The line of police remained unresponsive. "I'd prefer to die here than in a public hospital! My high taxes pay for your clothes and your helmets. They should be going to schools!"

Suddenly the streetlights went out. The road flooded with shapes and shadows, flashes from cameras, lights from houses. A group of protestors wearing hoods and gas masks huddled near Bruno.

"When the Pope leaves, you're going to attack us, because those are your orders!"

The police watched Bruno, who now was leaning over the iron barricade, hand outstretched, pointing. In anger, he appeared to double in size. Demonstrators projected the words "More dialogue less bombs!" onto the side of an apartment building.

"You sell your services cheap. Human life is priceless!"

Suddenly the barricades clattered to the ground. The crowd scattered backwards from the police. There were moments of panic among them, and calls for calm. When the line of protestors began to regroup, Bruno ensured that he remained at the front. Today was to be his last protest and he wanted to make sure it counted. Then someone from behind launched a Molotov cocktail, over the heads of protestors and into the crowd of riot police. The bottle smashed, covering one policeman in flames. Chaos erupted. Rubber bullets, tear gas and concussion grenades rained down in turn on the protestors as they ran for cover.

Bruno came forward in the midst of the pandemonium. He stood facing the police. When one leant forward to grab his arm, he turned and fled. Footage of the incident later showed a lone grey-clad figure, goggles atop his head, streaking away from a multitude of baton-wielding riot police. His steps are long and graceful and easy. When a well-built man wearing a black backpack and a black T-shirt attempts to intercept him, Bruno delivers a high-speed flying kick. He takes the man clean out. He sprints for more interminable seconds but eventually slows and halts, hands raised. There's an almighty flash, a stun grenade and Bruno falls to the ground.

The first people to reach Bruno's outstretched body are a police officer in uniform, a second man in black T-shirt and jeans – almost identical to the one Bruno felled with his Bruce Lee kick – and a press photographer. Bruno is motionless, but even so the cop leans over and thrusts a taser gun into his chest. Now an unruly scrabble develops. A riot police officer delivers a truncheon blow to a passer-by who attempts to intervene. The man in black kicks at a photographer. Other police officers appear and drag Bruno away, limbs limp, head lolling to one side. As they do so, the man in black removes his T-shirt and mysteriously wraps it around his head. Masked and now indistinguishable from so many other protestors, he fades away into the gathering throng.

What might have happened without his homemade Iron Man armour, is anyone's guess. The last thing he remembered before his arrest was putting his hands in the air. He did not remember the stun grenade or his fall to the ground. He did not remember the uniformed policeman who knelt over and shot him point blank with a taser gun. He did however remember standing on his feet in the middle of a crowd of very irate police. There were reporters, lights and cameras, and a barrage of questions.

"Who are you? What's your name? Where are you from?" They ripped off Bruno's Iron Man plate and held it above his head like a scalp. "And this! What is this?"

Then, as if on cue, a policeman in regular uniform stepped forward, his finger in Bruno's face.

"It was him!" The cop turned as he shouted so that everyone could hear.

"It was him who threw the first Molotov cocktail!"

A furious bald officer pushed himself to the front, and all but garrotted Bruno with a headlock.

"You're under arrest!"

The bald officer bent Bruno forwards and over until he was bent double, his head at his feet. He choked, coughed and gagged.

"*Calma!*" cried voices in the crowd. "*Calma!*" The long, ugly incident only ended when other police intervened. For a moment the scrum around him calmed and Bruno tried to breathe again.

"Whose prisoner is he? Who caught him?"

"It was the P2!" someone shouted. "The P2 caught him!"

P2 is slang for the plainclothes police. The protest had been swarming with them that night. Most were not hard to identify – neat military haircuts, crisply shaven, well-built, all in black. The man wearing a backpack whom Bruno had kicked to the ground, was a P2. So was the second man who melted away after his arrest, wearing his black T-shirt like a mask. All the P2 looked neat and observant, and out of place, among the starry-eyed religious devotees and the angry protestors.

A short walk away, another P2 was making life difficult for a NINJA reporter called Felipe Peçanha. The P2 held a mobile to his ear and spoke to an unseen central command. He put his spare hand in Felipe's pocket.

"Are you a reporter?" Felipe asked, filming all the time. "What channel do you represent?"

The P2 announced he was taking Felipe into custody. "My battery's running out," Felipe shouted. "I need another smartphone!"

Before his battery faded, 14,000 internauts watched as the P2 muscled Felipe into the back of a police car.

Bruno Torturra had made the journey from São Paulo to follow the Pope's visit for NINJA beside Felipe. He was happy to follow the peaceful crowds to the palace, happy to record the gay kissathon, and happy for once that a protest appeared to be passing peacefully. But when the Pope left the palace he heard the first explosions. He took cover and then ran, following the crowds to Largo do Machado, where he watched the moment that they arrested his fellow reporter for NINJA. When they took Felipe away for questioning, hundreds of eyewitnesses and fellow protestors were present, and many recorded, photographed and shared the incident. They began to chant:

"*Ei polícia! Cadê a Mídia NINJA!?*"

"Hey police! Where's Media NINJA!?" they cried. The crowd decamped to the ninth district police station, where Felipe had been taken in for questioning. The chanting continued:

"*Ei polícia! Libera Mídia NINJA!*" (Hey police! Free Media NINJA!)

Felipe's detention was illegal, and after a short time he was released to a hero's reception. However, other protestors remained inside, including the injured Iron Man Bruno Teles. When a lawyer asked the NINJA team if they could help these detainees, Bruno Torturra agreed to try, and slipped into the police station.

After the violence of his arrest, the inside of the police station seemed to Bruno Teles to be a small bubble of tranquillity. That is, until he was charged with affray, incitement to violence, carrying an explosive device, causing bodily harm and attempted murder. He called his parents. His mother was hysterical. She had already been asking Bruno to stay away from the protests. His father – a manager in a department store supplying uniforms to the army and navy – stayed cool. "He'll be home in the morning." After all, Bruno was just one more among dozens of kids getting picked up at the protests. Bruno wished his parents good night. He did not tell them the police had accused him of throwing petrol bombs, or that he had been accused of trying to kill people.

When he put the phone down Bruno felt the full weight of the night's events for the first time. He had been shot with rubber bullets, knocked out by a concussion grenade and zapped with a taser gun. He had been arrested and filmed by the media, and now he had been made to sign a charge sheet with the words "attempted homicide" on the page. He was reflecting on all this when a woman appeared and asked him if he would like to do an interview for NINJA. A man called Bruno Torturra held up a smartphone.

The next morning Bruno Teles' father switched on the news and saw his son. Without finishing his breakfast, he called his work and made his way straight to the police station, where police told him that Bruno had already been transferred to prison. Strangely the officers seemed relaxed. They did not appear angry, and they did not recriminate him for being the father of a kid who'd tried to kill some cops with petrol bombs. They told him not to worry.

What Bruno's father didn't know was that thousands of people had seen his son's interview with Media NINJA. Bruno had appealed to everyone present to upload images of the events to prove he had not thrown a single object, and that he was not carrying a black backpack as the police had publicly alleged. In the hours following the live broadcast, the NINJA email inbox was flooded with eyewitness clips and statements. A team of volunteers worked through the night crosschecking material to create a video narrative that disproved the charges. The images spoke for themselves. Bruno had not been carrying a backpack, Bruno was unarmed, unmasked and standing in front of the police lines when someone threw the Molotov cocktail from behind him.

Rio's military police press department posted an official clip of footage filmed by their own cameraman that showed the moment the Molotov was thrown. Two heavily built men with T-shirts wrapped around their heads are working together, lighting a petrol bomb, that one of them then skilfully lobs into the assembled riot police. This official footage was removed after a few hours, but not before the NINJA team had downloaded it for use in their independent reconstruction.

By now the internet was alive with images proving Bruno's innocence; and by the time his father reached the prison, his son was already free and heading home. Back in Caxias, Bruno took a shower before turning on the computer, to encounter a virtual whirlwind of information about him. He had even been on CNN in the US. In Brazil, on the other hand, there were people claiming he was a right-wing agitator behind a sinister North American plot, and that this was clearly proven by his metal chest plate!

Bruno Torturra was at a meeting at Rio's Federal University when he learnt that NINJA footage had been used on *Jornal Nacional*, Globo's primetime nightly news programme. Globo showed Bruno's interview and appeal, and then, like the dozens of witnesses who had sent NINJA images and reports, Globo broadcast its own camera footage which also showed Bruno unarmed, unmasked and without a backpack. Torturra was elated.

NINJA had averted a possible miscarriage of justice and even the all-powerful Globo corporation had been forced to follow their own street-produced story. Citizen journalism had saved the day.

There still remained unanswered questions. If Bruno Teles did not throw the bomb, then who did? The montage of footage painted a very strange picture; it looked as though a plainclothes P2 operative had thrown the Molotov cocktail. Even the military police's own footage incriminated undercover officers; two men with military haircuts, black T-shirts and jeans whose behaviour had been suspicious throughout the protest. These were the two men present at the moment of Bruno's arrest; one of them felled by Bruno's flying kick, wearing a backpack, and the other wearing a T-shirt that he removed and wrapped around his head, as Bruno was being carried away.

The two men star in a plethora of independent footage. In the seconds following Bruno's apprehension, they run together into the police lines, where a riot policeman barks at them to sit down. They refuse. There is then a frantic standoff and one of the P2, bare-chested with his T-shirt now wrapped around his neck, pulls some form of ID out of his jeans, waving it furiously. His colleague with a black backpack raises his hands to his head, in sheer desperation. The apparent stand-off only ends when another uniformed police officer intervenes. Before dozens of spectators and eyewitnesses, he gesticulates to the two desperate men to move on. As the P2 with the backpack turns, the pack swings, and a nearby camera records the unmistakable sound of glass bottles clinking against each other. The two men are then allowed to jog away, under the eyes of a throng of bemused riot police. When they reach the end of the cordon, the P2 with the backpack rips off his T-shirt, removes the bag and runs into the night.

Minutes later, Globo TV reporters register the discovery of an abandoned backpack containing unused petrol bombs made out of small beer bottles. "This," a police officer says to the camera, holding up one of the Molotov cocktails, "is what kills police officers."

Despite this strong evidence suggesting that undercover cops were responsible for throwing petrol bombs at their own colleagues, before attempting to frame Bruno Teles, there was no investigation into the incident. The military police press office eventually produced a scrappy montage of images, asserting that alleged differences in T-shirt designs worn by the petrol bombers and the P2 proved their innocence. With the Pope's visit occupying the news once again, the matter was buried.

In the months following the papal visit, the marches across the nation continued to decrease in size. However, the hard-line activists were down but not out. A mob attacked the Globo HQ in São Paulo, spraying the building with manure. In Brasília a police captain was recorded on camera telling peaceful protestors that he used pepper spray on them, "because I felt like it". In Rio, demonstrators forced governor Cabral to abandon his Leblon residence. The protests almost always ended in violent clashes that were attributed to leaderless, masked Black Bloc anarchists. Activists across the country occupied council offices and state parliaments, where legislators debated initiatives to prohibit the wearing of masks. Violence overtook Rio's city centre on a weekly basis. Black Blocs smashed banks to bits. In the face of extreme police truculence, the established media sought culprits. It denounced the so-called "professional protestors" and accused them of belonging to international networks. TV bombarded the general public with tales of property destruction and the protests were slowly but surely transformed into synonyms for disorder and danger. With the word "vandalism" now attached to them, most *cariocas* avoided the demonstrations altogether.

In December, the dogged authorities triumphantly produced an official scapegoat for all the violence. Rafael Braga Vieira was a 25-year-old homeless recycler, whom police picked up during the 20 June mega-protest, the night Bruno's mother told him there were a million people on the streets. They arrested Rafael outside the derelict building where he was sleeping in Lapa, well away from the main march. There were no witnesses. Rafael was carrying two plastic bottles filled with disinfectant and cleaning fluid. The police called these articles "Molotov cocktails". Rafael's defenders pointed out that Molotov cocktails are made with glass bottles and petrol, not plastic bottles and cleaning fluid. Rafael's profile could not have been more unlike that of the middle-class students who constituted the vast majority of protestors. Rafael was uneducated, black, homeless, jobless and barely literate. In an interview with the state human rights commission shortly after his subsequent conviction, he could not even name the mayor. Human rights lawyers called his five-year conviction a gross miscarriage of justice and called for his release. *O Globo*'s account differed:

> *The first condemnation for a suspected vandal, the can collector Rafael Braga Vieira, must serve as a paradigm [...] it is an example of how public power must act in response to aggression against the rule of law.*[69]

No one filmed Rafael's arrest.

Turnstile protest, Central Station 2014. The placard reads:
We want Fifa standard trains.

11 / MOLOTOV

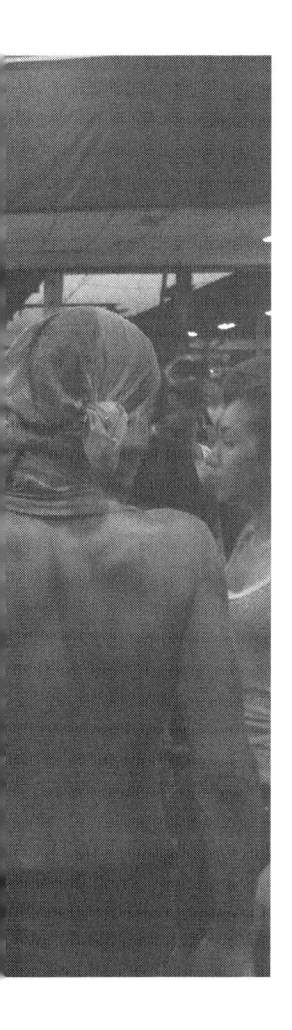

IN FEBRUARY 2014 RENEWED protests about transport fares once more got out of control in Rio. This time, the focus was the overcrowded and inefficient Supervia suburban train service. Hundreds of protestors invaded Central Station and occupied the area leading to the platforms, where they encouraged commuters to jump the turnstile. When police responded with tear gas and stun grenades, thousands of rush-hour commuters became embroiled in disorder, as it spilled out of the station and onto one of Rio's busiest commuter arteries, Avenida Presidente Vargas. Here mask-wearing protestors, many of them with T-shirts wrapped around their heads, clashed with police amid the rush-hour traffic.

Santiago Andrade was a well-known, respected cameraman who worked for BAND, one of Brazil's prime TV stations. He was filming the disturbances that afternoon when a firework – a skyrocket of the type fired at Copacabana Beach on New Year's Eve – exploded next to his head. Santiago fell to the ground with a massive head wound. As he lay in hospital with a severe brain haemorrhage, the media went into overdrive. The attack on Santiago had become an attack on the news itself.

While Santiago lay in a coma, the incident dominated all broadcasts. Footage of two young men lighting the rocket leaked out. One of them appears to light it, the other drops it to the ground and runs, back turned, as it skews, launches and explodes beside Santiago's head. Within 24 hours, a 22-year-old called Fábio Raposo handed himself in. He said he had handled the rocket but had not lit it. Jonas Tadeu, a lawyer with a history of defending West Zone militia leaders, took up his defence for "the love of the cause".[70] Bizarrely, Tadeu wasted no time in leaking details of an alleged conversation he had had with a well-known protestor connecting violence at the protests to Rio's most popular leftist politician and human rights advocate, Marcelo Freixo. Coincidentally, or maybe not, Freixo had risen to fame for helping to send militia leaders, associated with Tadeu, to prison. At the time, it seemed strange that a lawyer who defended militias, suddenly wanted to protect violent protestors.

Santiago's tragic death a few days later triggered a generalised media lynching of politicians known to sympathise with the protests. Tadeu, theatrically, led Globo TV to Bahia to arrest Caio de Souza, the second of the young suspects, alleged to have lit the rocket, and announced that Caio was paid by politicians to cause trouble. Subsequently, newspapers and TV stations publicised a list of politicians and leftist figures that made donations to a Christmas lunch for homeless people. The expenses include costs for plastic cups, plates and *rabanada*, a traditional sweet pudding served at Christmas. Somehow, segments of the media managed to link the Christmas meal to the rocket that killed Santiago. Jonas Tadeu – his social media page peppered with the sayings of Gandhi, Mother Teresa and Bob Marley – alleged that agitators linked to councillors, state deputies and senators, had paid the two suspects. But he named no names. While no questions were asked about the strangely opportunist appearance of Jonas Tadeu with his militia links, the city's press cranked up its smear campaign against social welfare movements and human rights defenders.

For Bruno Torturra, Santiago's death was a tragedy foretold. He had stopped reporting on street protests in August 2013, after almost being hit by a firework himself. The next demonstration he attended (wearing a helmet) was his last. Violence was emptying the protests of demonstrators. Radicals accused Media NINJA of being involved in a government plot. Conflict between Black Blocs and police was inevitable. Broken banks and rubber bullets had replaced argument and reasoning. The protests were reduced to a battle between police, who had turned into a leaderless militia, and protestors who were now guerillas without a plan. Torturra observed that Santiago was neither protestor nor policeman, but a cameraman whose job was to be "our eyes on the street". "Santiago's death," Torturra wrote, "only makes us more blind."[71]

FOR A WHILE IN 2013, if you searched "Molotov" on Google, images of Bruno Teles would come up. People still approach him in the street: "It's you – the guy who was there the night the P2 threw the Molotov cocktail!" Bruno however refrains from judgement. He is careful not to jump to possibly false conclusions. There remain many omissions to the story, and incoherencies. Sometimes he thinks it might have been a weird accident. At other moments, he admits that the facts all suggest a plainclothes police officer threw the petrol bomb, part of the organised deployment of *agents provocateurs,* using violence to sabotage and destabilise the protest movement. But he tries not to think too hard. He finds such mental speculation difficult to process. He sticks to what he knows to be true. Nor does he blame the police. Even after what happened, he will not condemn them as individuals, believing that they were only doing what they were trained to do. He says they have been taught to repress, to beat and injure people. Bruno thinks Brazilians are very all-or-nothing. "We're either peaceful and well behaved, or we're cutting someone's head off. Brazil still doesn't belong to anyone. You won't find a Brazilian who wants to die for his country – although I almost got killed that day."

We will probably never know for certain who threw the Molotov cocktail that night. What the arrests of Bruno Teles and Rafael Braga, and events surrounding the death of Santiago Andrade did all show, was that the establishment and the authorities seized every possible opportunity – to promote narratives that disqualified the demonstrations and criminalised the protestors, regardless of the facts, or in an attempt to hide them.

PART FOUR

THE HORNET'S NEST

A passerby looks at posters asking "Who ordered the killing of Marielle?" pasted in central Rio for the first anniversary of the assassination of Marielle Franco, 2019.

12

MARIELLE

During my life in Rio, two instances marked my transformation into an adoptive *carioca*. The first, when I stopped caring if people addressed me as *gringo* and allowed this to become a term of endearment, not a slight. Once I embraced the fact that I was always going to be a gringo, I was comfortable in my *anglo-carioca* skin.

The other moment also concerned how I felt in my skin – but only in the strictly physical sense. Rio can get very, very hot. *Cariocas* say there are only two seasons in the city: "summer" and "the apocalypse". In summer I was usually OK. But I agonised during the apocalypse! Warm air and sweat got trapped under my T-shirt sleeves. While I sweated and suffered, friends in favelas offered a simple solution. Why didn't I dress like the locals and wear a vest with no sleeves. A wife-beater? Me? Never. For years I refused. I stoically ploughed on, ever the sweaty gringo. Until one day I capitulated. The simple garment change added years to my residency in the city. Wearing a vest in apocalyptic Rio equates to free personal air

Marielle Franco, 2011.

conditioning. I instantly became less hot, less sweaty. More *carioca*.

I clearly remember when I got to know Marielle because it predated my wearing vests. In 2007 she worked for a citywide campaign to end the use of police armoured vehicles in favelas. She wanted to extend this to the Complexo do Alemão and through a mutual friend asked for introduction to my contacts. We spent a long, boiling day hiking up and down alleys looking for MC Playboy. We could not locate him. The longer we searched the hotter I became. The hotter I became the more I sweated. Eventually, I couldn't bear it any more and took off my T-shirt. Was this proper? Should a skinny gringo lead a human rights defending colleague around a favela with his top off? Appropriate or not, at the time it was a matter of survival. And she didn't seem to mind. From that day on I regularly encountered resolute, charismatic Marielle at events across the city and we became friends.

ON 14 MARCH 2018, more than ten years after our visit to the Alemão, Marielle was a rising force in Rio politics. Presidential and state level elections were due that October. She had a formidable public profile and planned to stand as vice-governor for the state of Rio. Charming, popular and tenacious, Marielle had embarked on a potentially transformational political journey.

Shortly after 9pm that day she finished a public meeting entitled *Black Women Changing Power Structures*. Outside, she got into a car driven by Anderson. He came from the Alemão and was working part-time for Marielle (her regular driver was off sick). Marielle usually liked to sit in the front but this time she sat behind to talk with her assistant Fernanda. Before they were halfway home, Marielle and Anderson were dead. Fernanda survived without physical injury.

When I learnt about the murders I was a long way from Rio, working in a school in northern England. I cried in the toilet. It was late winter and underneath my shirt I wore my *carioca* vest to keep warm.

WHOEVER ORDERED THE ATTACK underestimated the reaction to it. Thousands turned out to see her coffin. National and international media outlets ran the story for days. The killing was denounced at the UN Human Rights Commission. Interim President Temer called for a quick resolution. He had recently sent the army to Rio, allegedly to reduce violence. The attack made him look weak. Pope Francis telephoned her family. Katy Perry, then Twitter's most popular artist, brought Marielle's sister and daughter onstage at her Rio concert.

Initial inquiries pointed to a professional assassination. A few kilometres from the meeting, a silver Cobalt car that followed Marielle's vehicle had drawn up alongside it. An occupant fired 13 gunshots into her car. There were, apparently, no witnesses. Reliable security cameras on the stretch of road where the murder took place were switched off. The bullets belonged to a federal police shipment "lost" in 2009. Alarmingly, ammunition from the same stolen batch had been used in a drive-by death squad attack that left some 20 people dead on the streets of a São Paulo satellite city in 2015.[72]

The homicide investigation was shoddy from the offset. On the night of the murder, police sent bystanders away without taking statements. When a veteran Rio journalist visited the crime scene one week after the event, she located eyewitnesses the homicide investigators had failed to identify. They reported seeing a man leaning out of the window of the attacker's vehicle, firing shots from a gun with an extended barrel that looked like a silencer.[73]

The month of May saw an apparent breakthrough. Rio's *O Globo* newspaper published an exclusive piece based on leaked documents. An anonymous source had denounced Marcello Siciliano, a fellow councillor of Marielle's at city hall. The informant made statements to police saying that he attended numerous meetings between Siciliano and Orlando Curicica, an ex-policeman, where they had discussed killing her. The pair allegedly ran militia activities in West Zone neighbourhoods where her human rights work had been unwelcome. Precise details given included times, places, names and information on related killings and crimes. The grass even quoted Siciliano verbatim, alleging that he had said, "*We have to do something about Marielle. The woman is getting in my way.*"[74]

However, days after the accusations, Orlando Curicica (held in prison on other charges) issued a handwritten rebuttal via his lawyer claiming not to know Siciliano. He also vehemently denied any involvement in the "barbarous crime" and said "with all due respect" to the dead councillor, he had not heard of her prior to her murder.[75] Curicica's lawyer expressed fears for his safety, alleging that someone had already tried to poison his client. Curicica was subsequently transferred to a high security prison in the North of Brazil. Siciliano also flatly rejected all accusations against him. He said he had enjoyed a warm professional friendship with Marielle. A picture of the two smiling and hugging appears to corroborate his claim. Despite these refutations, Rio's homicide department still insisted on following the Siciliano-Curicica line of enquiry.

But in August *O Globo* published information about a completely different line of investigation. Detectives had discovered the existence of a group of killers for hire called "The Crime Office". Formed by police and ex-police, The Crime Office was an elite death squad that performed high-profile hits. Technically sophisticated, highly skilled, The Crime Office would kill anyone for the right price and usually worked for the *jogo do bicho*. The group was linked to Marielle and Anderson

Jair Bolsonaro and supporters at a protest calling for military intervention, Rio 2013.

by mobile phone records placing one of their members at the scene of the murders.[76] Concurrently, newly assigned federal prosecutors took testimony from Orlando Curicica in his high security prison in the North of Brazil. Under pressure at home and abroad to deliver results, Brazilian national authorities had grown impatient with the slow investigation in Rio.

MEANWHILE, A DIVIDED BRAZIL SUFFERED under a deeply unpleasant presidential campaign. Popular former president Lula was out of the race, imprisoned in April 2018 on corruption charges understood by many to have been politically motivated. In his absence, Jair Bolsonaro, former army captain and longstanding ultra-right parliamentarian known for glorifying the military dictatorship, was gathering momentum under a national unity banner. Dressed in green and yellow, he promised to end corruption, fight crime and save Brazil from communism. Then in September, while out campaigning, a lone-wolf assailant stabbed him. For his supporters, Bolsonaro's survival – evidence of divine grace – remodelled the populist politician into indestructible messianic hero.

Jair Bolsonaro is not the only member of his family involved in politics. Two of his four sons were also contesting government seats. Flávio Bolsonaro, his eldest, sought to make the jump from Rio state government to Brazil's federal senate.[31] His brother Eduardo, aimed for re-election to federal congress. A third son, Carlos Bolsonaro, already a councillor in Rio's city hall for nearly twenty years, opted to stay where he was. In 2018, the family stood both to consolidate old territory and to make radical gains. The Bolsonaro clan was on an unstoppable roll.

Marielle's assassination inevitably possessed political capital. Supporters fought for her legacy of human rights and social justice. Detractors celebrated the murder. At a Rio campaign meeting, Bolsonaro affiliates brandished a broken memorial to her memory. The blue and white plaque had previously been

---

31 Each of Brazil's 27 states elects three senators who sit for eight-year terms. During his senatorial campaign, Flávio canvassed for votes in Nilópolis alongside *bicheiro* Anísio David's brother Farid, mayor of Nilópolis, and Simão Sessim, Anísio's cousin. Sessim held a congressional seat in Brasília for 40 years. After failing to win re-election in 2018, Sessim was appointed official representative for Rio's state government in Brasília.

fixed to a street sign outside the Rio city assembly. Now local candidates wearing black and white Bolsonaro T-shirts waved its two halves in the air like a trophy, promising to clean leftists from the face of earth.[32] Eventually, the electoral dust settled on a comprehensive victory for Bolsonaro and his sons. In Rio, consolation came for Marielle's supporters with the election of three former members of her team, all black women from favelas, to the state parliament.

Following the election, public attention refocused on the murder inquiry. In November 2018, *O Globo* published an interview with Orlando Curicica, based on statements he made to federal prosecutors. The former militiaman claimed that in May, Rio's chief police investigator had attempted to coerce a confession out of him. By way of explanation he referred to the existence of The Crime Office:

What I have to say, no one would like to hear: there is a battalion of hired killers working for money in Rio today, most of them connected to the contravention [jogo do bicho]. The homicide department and civil police chief know who they are, but receive money to not investigate, so creating a protection network for the contravention to kill whoever they want.[77]

---

[32] Rodrigo Amorim, one of the candidates, is a close friend and political ally of Flávio Bolsonaro. He was successfully elected to the Rio state assembly with the highest number of votes for any candidate. Subsequently, he framed one half of the broken memorial plaque and hung it behind his desk at his public office in the parliament building. In April 2020, prosecutors from the Baixada Fluminense municipality of Mesquita charged him with embezzling more than $20,000 in public funds between 2014–2016.

When federal government eventually conducted an "investigation into the investigation", the Siciliano-Curicica theory was discredited and discarded for good. The original witness who claimed to have seen the pair planning the killing admitted to lying. Apparently a group of police with West Zone political pretensions had concocted the story in order to eliminate Siciliano as a rival. But would they really go to such extreme lengths just to score political points? Or were they protecting others?

WITH SICILIANO AND CURICICA RULED OUT, attention turned to The Crime Office. A January 2019 police operation revealed that leaders of the death squad conducted their activities out of Rio das Pedras, a West Zone favela and militia enclave of more than 60,000 residents. The raid led to several arrests and the revelation that the same rogue police who led The Crime Office also ran the Rio das Pedras militia. Members of the gang laundered money through illegal real estate development, while practicing extortion, protection racketeering and a wide range of mob activities. While the swoop led to several arrests, The Crime Office's alleged leader, a former BOPE policeman called Adriano da Nóbrega disappeared.

Also known as Captain Adriano, Nóbrega's past was well known. Once regarded as the finest police sniper in the city, in 2003 he was arrested and later convicted of murder. A group of police had tortured and extorted money from Leandro da Silva, a 24-year-old favela resident. The day after officially denouncing the torture session to a police internal investigations unit, Leandro was shot dead on his doorstep. The state governor at the time ordered the arrest of all the policemen involved in the incident.

Convicted by jury and sentenced to 19 years for murder, Adriano was later acquitted. Following his discharge, he ostensibly returned to work as a policeman. However, his famed ruthlessness as a killer now earned him extra employment as head of security for Shanna Garcia, daughter of the legendary *bicheiro* Maninho, granddaughter of Miro, *jogo do bicho cúpula* member and patron of Salgueiro samba school. Adriano subsequently became a key player in the Garcia family conflict. In 2011, he was expelled from the police force as a result of this activity.

Acknowledgement of the existence of The Crime Office was no surprise. That Rio's police did not investigate, or falsified investigations into, certain killings would seem obvious to the informed observer. Payments to police are as old as the *jogo do bicho*. Rio's civil police have the prerogative to investigate crimes in the city – or not. With rare exceptions, the institution has almost always answered to organised crime.

But the connection of The Crime Office to both *jogo do bicho* and militia was novel. The Crime Office was acting as gatekeeper for organised criminal activity in Rio de Janeiro. But however

Mangueira samba school's homage to Marielle, 2019.

shocking that development was, it still did not offer a motive for Marielle's killing. Since the beginning of the investigation, rumours abounded that she had ruffled the feathers of West Zone militiamen. But no one took these seriously. Marielle had fought human rights violators across the city for years. No single militia group stood to benefit from her death. And there was no reason for the *jogo do bicho* to kill her.

WHEN BRAZILIAN EYES turned towards Rio's annual Carnival parade in March 2019, Mangueira samba school cruised to victory with a crowd-pleasing history lesson that included a significant homage to Marielle. The triumph focussed public attention on the upcoming first anniversary of her death. With national and international media now wise to the many obstructions affecting the investigation, Rio's authorities were under pressure to deliver.

Results came soon after Carnival. Dawn raids led to the arrest of two former military policemen, both alleged members of The Crime Office. Ronnie Lessa, was charged with firing the shots that killed Marielle and Anderson; Élcio de Queiroz, with driving the car. Simultaneously, police and prosecutors searched numerous addresses across the city. They discovered 117 M-16 assault rifles at a property belonging to a childhood friend of Lessa: the largest weapons seizure on record in Rio at the time.

Both Lessa and Queiroz had extensive historic connections to organised crime. Queiroz was fired from the police in 2011, having been accused of arms dealing. Lessa retired from the military police after losing a leg in a car bomb attack in 2009. Like Captain Adriano, Lessa moonlighted for the *jogo do bicho*. At the time of the car bomb incident he worked as hired gun for Rogério Andrade, patron of Mocidade samba school and nephew of charismatic *capo* Castor de Andrade. Detectives believed that whoever bombed Lessa also planted the explosive that killed Rogério's son, Diogo, in a Barra car park in 2010.[78]

Wilson Witzel, Rio's newly elected state governor, called a press conference to promote the arrests (and himself). While commemorating technical matters relating to the investigation, he sidestepped questions about who might have ordered the killings. His chief homicide detective, the same man who allegedly attempted to coerce Orlando Curicica into taking responsibility for the murders, even suggested that Lessa and Queiroz, known contract killers, might have acted independently, targeting Marielle out of hatred for her political activity; a ludicrous hypothesis. However, one significant matter proved less easy to fudge. Barra resident Ronnie Lessa was Jair Bolsonaro's neighbour.

13

BARRA VILLAS

RIO IS BIPOLAR AND CONTRADICTORY – chaotic, hedonistic, endlessly fascinating, chronically corrupt, and very cruel. You might witness a ferocious gun battle in the morning, spend the afternoon on a beach and then dance the night away. The very physical environment is anarchic. Gravity defying favelas cling to impossible escarpments. Sea, mountain and forest clash with glass, concrete and metal. The sensation that the unexpected lies around the corner is difficult to escape.

Then there is Barra. Aseptic, orderly and predictable, Barra is unlike any other part of the city. Rio's wannabe Miami is the contradiction within the contradiction. Shopping centres, multiplexes, luxury condominiums, wide highways and a visual of gleaming towers and straight lines define the beachfront neighbourhood. Barra is a dissenter – an anti-Rio. With its own 27-metre high Statue of Liberty replica and one of the nation's highest human development indices, Barra suits a certain type of Brazilian – former policeman Ronnie Lessa, for example; or Jair Bolsonaro, Brazilian President.

In 2018, the former policeman and the congressman lived on the same street in Vivendas da Barra – Barra Villas in English – one of the area's many gated communities. Its inhabitants live behind high walls and electric fences. Paid staff monitor comings and goings, and guarantee privacy for residents. After his election success, thousands of Bolsonaro supporters gathered outside. Behind the walls, the candidate made his victory broadcast to the nation. "You will know the truth and the truth will set you free," he began.

Seven months prior to the celebrations, not long after 5 pm on 14 March 2018, Ronnie Lessa and Élcio de Queiroz met at Barra Villas. They left the residence shortly afterwards, prosecutors believe, to kill Marielle Franco. Neighbours knew little about Lessa, except that he ordered his own water and installed security cameras facing the street. He spent many free afternoons down at a seaside restaurant called Varandas, where he could be contacted for jobs.[79]

The revelation that Lessa lived almost next door to the soon-to-be president generated inevitable comment and speculation. During an organised breakfast meeting with journalists, Bolsonaro responded dismissively, claiming not to have heard of Lessa.[80] Asserting that he did not socialise with neighbours he emphasised that other Barra Villas residents had been arrested for criminal activity in the past. Reports that his youngest son dated Lessa's daughter did not bother him. Never to miss an opportunity to trumpet Bolsonaro hetero-virility, he boasted that 20-year-old Jair Renan had been with all the girls in the villas. Then, he returned to his standard tactic when deflecting questions about Marielle's murder; comparing it to the knife attack he suffered during the election campaign.

13 / BARRA VILLAS

AT THE END OF OCTOBER 2019, Bolsonaro posted a bizarre 90-second video to his twitter account. The clip, lifted from a wildlife documentary, showed a pack of hyenas harrying a lion. Comical looking labels indicated that while the lion represented President Bolsonaro, the hyenas stood for a variety of antagonists including Brazil's Supreme Court, leftists, the Catholic Church, the media, judiciary, unions and even the president's own political party (Bolsonaro was planning to start a new one). After doggedly keeping the hyenas at bay, the tiring hero is rescued – cue cheesy music! – by the arrival of another lion tagged "Conservative Patriot". Setting Jair against society, the video rallied Bolsonaro supporters to defend their president. Prominent among the labelled attackers – TV Globo.

The following evening, on 29 October, an extraordinary development in the Marielle investigation clarified the tweet. Globo's primetime news programme, *Jornal Nacional*, reported the exclusive information that a Barra Villas *porteiro* (doorman) had identified Jair Bolsonaro as the person who granted Élcio de Queiroz access to the residence on the evening of the crime. The naming of the president in the case implied the future involvement of Brazil's Supreme Court (another hyena).

The news piece explained that detectives had discovered a photo of the Barra Villas visitors' book on Ronnie Lessa's phone. The image showed a handwritten entry noting the arrival of Élcio de Queiroz at 17.10 on 14 March 2018. However, instead of recording Élcio as visiting house 65, belonging to Ronnie Lessa, the doorman on-duty wrote down the number of a different house – number 58; Jair Bolsonaro's residence.

Twice, in statements to police given on separate occasions, the doorman explained that Élcio had asked to visit house 58.

So he had telephoned through to "Mr Jair" who had given the all clear. When he saw that the car had gone to house 65 and not 58, the doorman said he again called "Mr Jair" who had replied, "he knew where the car was going".

William Bonner, *Jornal Nacional* anchor, identified the obvious problem with the revelation. At the time a federal congressman, Bolsonaro could not have answered the internal phone at number 58 as he was in Brasília that day, more than a thousand kilometres away (although he could have answered a call to his mobile, a question not raised by Globo). The report also included an interview with Bolsonaro's lawyer who classified the claim as a "lie, fraud and farse" concocted to attack the president.[81]

Jair Bolsonaro swiftly responded from Saudi Arabia where he was on official travel. Via a live social media transmission, he rebutted the accusations. The president's outrage grew increasingly hysterical throughout the thirty-minute broadcast as he accused Globo TV of politically-motivated interference in the investigation and anti-Brazilian conspiracy. He, like his lawyer before him, laid no blame on the doorman, who must have made a "mistake".

MEET CARLOS. CARLOS BOLSONARO – Jair's second. Carlos also lived at Barra Villas, in number 36, a second house owned by his father at the condo. In 2000, at the age of 17, Carlos had contested and won a seat as the youngest ever city councillor in Rio de Janeiro. In 2016, he shared the chamber with Marielle Franco. In 2019 he was still there. Carlos had been Bolsonaro family representative at city hall for almost two decades.

Voracious on Twitter, Carlos was often credited by his father as the marketing brains behind his election success. Now, in the early hours of the morning following the Globo scoop, Carlos tweeted three times. The first, to prove he was at city hall on 14 March 2018. The Globo report had not cited him but Carlos nevertheless saw the need to defend himself. The tweet showed official records mentioning his presence at an afternoon session ending at 17.30, after the entrance of Élcio to Barra Villas.

Two subsequent tweets featured phone clips filmed by Carlos. He explains that he is showing a computer screen displaying electronic records of calls made by Barra Villas doormen to houses at the complex. Precise times, length of call and house numbers are all visible. Carlos explains that as a resident, he is entitled to access the records. Firstly, Carlos opens and broadcasts an audio file: a doorman calls house 65 at 17.13. A male voice (possibly Lessa, definitely not Jair Bolsonaro) answers and allows Élcio to proceed. Secondly, he plays two more audio recordings of calls by doormen. One is to his father's house earlier in the afternoon. Another is made to Carlos' house 36 at 17.58, which Carlos himself answers, giving the OK for an Uber to come into the villas.[82]

Two time-stretching facts revealed by Carlos immediately raise questions. Firstly, the doorman's call to Ronnie Lessa's house, 65, on behalf of Élcio, takes place at 17.13; three minutes after the handwritten visitors' book entry stating that Élcio was granted access at 17.10 to visit house number 58. What happened between 17.10 and 17.13? Secondly, Carlos reveals that he is at home at 17.58. Wasn't he supposed to have been at city hall until at least 17.30? Covering the 30km rush hour journey from central Rio to Barra in 28 minutes is physically impossible. In providing this evidence, Carlos undermined his own alibi – the time, 17.58, implies his presence at Barra Villas during the same period as Ronnie Lessa and Élcio de Queiroz.

That same day public prosecutors working on the case requested forensic examination of a CD Rom they possessed containing the Barra Villas audios. The examination, reportedly returned in a lightening two hours, found no evidence of tampering with the CD Rom. The prosecutors immediately and very publicly concluded that the porter was lying or mistaken.[83] They also said that they were only aware of the reference to Bolsonaro in October 2019, a claim subsequently proved untrue; police investigators first discovered the mention of house 58 in November 2018. This reference had been passed to the Public Prosecutor's office in March 2019.[84]

The prosecutors had not been the only individuals to be in possession of the Barra Villas audio files. Already back in Brazil, Jair Bolsonaro revealed that he too had enjoyed prior access to the material – "before the audio files could be tampered with, we took all the memory from the electronic recording machine, which has been there for years".[85] Bolsonaro later disclosed that he had been aware of the upcoming revelations before travelling to Saudi Arabia.[86] The spontaneous outrage of his live transmission from the country had been anything but! He had also known that Globo was unaware of the audio recording of the 17.13 call to house 65. By strategically allowing the *Jornal Nacional* to break the story, then using the audio to defend himself, Bolsonaro deliberately undermined the news item, successfully casting himself as the innocent victim of a media smear.

Following the presidential attack, Ali Kamel, Globo's director of journalism, issued a memorandum to staff. Kamel revealed that during October 2019, while journalists were researching the affair, a source "extremely close" to the Bolsonaro family informed the organisation that a (metaphorical) "bomb was about to go off, because the Marielle investigation had led to a person with political immunity" and that the case would now go to the Supreme Court. The same source later contacted Globo again to enquire when they would run the story.[87] Kamel's inference was clear: the Bolsonaro family had deliberately let the news story run in order to publicly attack Globo.

To add to the confusion, the professional union of forensic investigators in Rio de Janeiro issued a public statement on the day Bolsonaro admitted to possessing the sound files. The statement declared that unregistered technicians at the public prosecutor's office had conducted an invalid analysis of a copied CD, and that only forensic examination of the equipment used by the doormen at Barra Villas could identify whether someone had tampered with the recordings.[88] Despite all the uproar, investigators only seized the equipment on 7 November, more than a week after Carlos Bolsonaro tweeted about its contents.

Following these revelations about the family's interference in the investigation, opposition politicians petitioned the federal chief prosecutor to open proceedings against Jair and Carlos Bolsonaro for the obstruction of justice. The prosecutor, recently appointed by the president himself, declined. Instead, federal police were appointed to investigate the claims made by the doorman at the eye of the storm, who gave a third statement three weeks after the initial Globo broadcast. Now he retracted his previous two declarations and explained that he had made an error in writing down house number 58. He had invented the story about calling "Seu Jair" to cover his own mistake, he said.[89]

The federal police also concluded that the equipment at Barra Villas had not been tampered with. The investigation effectively cleared the Bolsonaro family.

BOLSONARO'S REACTION TO MARIELLE'S assassination was always peculiar. Despite being the leading "law and order" contender, he was the only one of 13 pre-candidates for president not to issue a public condemnation of the murder. When a journalist contacted his office for comment on 15 March 2018, an advisor said the candidate had food poisoning and was unable to comment, adding the unnecessary – but revelatory – observation that "his opinion would be too polemical" anyway.[90] The future president of Brazil's first public recognition of the crime came six days after the event – "In this case, given its symbolism, anything I might happen to say would be used and distorted against me. So at the moment, I reserve the right to remain in silence…".[91]

14

THE HORNET'S NEST

ALTHOUGH CHARGED WITH FIRING THE BULLETS that killed Marielle, former policeman Ronnie Lessa was anything but a mere gun for hire. An ambitious West Zone militia leader with sticky fingers in many pies, he operated several drinking water distribution networks across the city and reportedly planned to extend these to areas dominated by drug trafficking gangs.[92] The seizure of 117 machine guns at his friend's house exposed him as one of Rio's leading arms traffickers. He also ran illegal bingo activity in Barra. In October 2018 he was recorded negotiating the return of electronic gambling machines seized in a raid with one of Barra's highest-ranking civil policeman. As a retired policeman, Lessa also received a monthly state pension.[33]

On 27 April 2018, forty-five days after Marielle's murder, someone tried to kill him. Lessa had just parked outside his

---

33 In October 2019, Lessa's wife and four associates were arrested on suspicion of throwing several firearms, including the gun used in the assassination, into the sea.

favourite restaurant on the Barra seafront when an assailant shot and wounded him. But the attempt went awry. An associate of Lessa's fired back and injured the attacker, whom police subsequently located in hospital.

The gunman, a twenty-four year-old thief from São Paulo, was later sentenced to thirteen years in prison for robbery and attempted murder. The same homicide investigator who had attempted to pin Marielle's killing on Siciliano declared the incident a failed mugging.[93] But anonymous detectives told journalists that they believed the episode was a bungled attempt to silence Lessa. The investigation was full of inconsistencies, they said. The motorbike and weapon used in the attack were never recovered. No forensic examination of the crime scene took place. The only bullet retrieved at the scene disappeared. The gunman had no record of acting in Rio before and the inquiry did not justify his presence in the city. Above all, nothing in the trial explained why, out of all the locations available in Rio to conduct a robbery and out of all potential victims in the city, the gunman chose Ronnie Lessa as he made his way to his favourite restaurant for his habitual Friday lunch with friends.[94]

WHILE RONNIE LESSA AND ÉLCIO DE QUEIROZ waited behind bars, Adriano da Nóbrega, militia boss and founder of The Crime Office, continued on the run. While not named in public as a suspect in Marielle and Anderson's murder, investigators considered the possibility that he had played a role as a middleman. Additionally, in August 2019, an anonymous caller to a police hotline alleged that Adriano had ordered the killing of the case's chief prosecutor.[95] He might have fled the city, but Captain Adriano continued to influence events in Rio.

Adriano had vanished in January 2019, after a raid on the Rio das Pedras militia enclave. Finally, after more than a year underground, detectives located him in the north-eastern state of Bahia. They initially failed to apprehend him, however, at the well-protected luxury complex where he had rented a house with his wife. Alerted to the presence of police, he escaped across a lagoon behind the condominium and onto the beach.

In February 2020, the news that Adriano was dead shook Brazil. A massive police operation involving more than seventy members of Bahia's BOPE unit and civil police from Rio tracked him to a remote rural property, where he allegedly died in an exchange of fire with his would-be captors. Police found thirteen mobile phones and boxes of sim cards among his belongings.[96]

Suspicions rose immediately about the circumstances of Adriano's death. Once they had him cornered, why did the 75-strong force not wait for the lone gunman to give himself up? In a call to his lawyer after escaping the first attempt to capture him, the fugitive expressed fear that police were coming after him not to arrest, but to kill him. When his lawyer urged Adriano to turn himself in, the former policeman replied that doing so would not guarantee his safety. He believed he was a dead man wherever he turned.[97]

After two decades operating in the shadowy world between police and criminal activity, Adriano was a living archive of information about corruption and state delinquency in Rio. He had worked on the frontlines of the favela gang wars and provided protection for *bicheiros*. Prosecutors believed he headed the Rio das Pedras militia and had founded The Crime Office. He knew a lot about everything and everyone – including the Bolsonaro family.

FLÁVIO – *PRIMOGÉNITO* – BOLSONARO ENTERED POLITICS in 2003 at the age of 22, beginning a sixteen-year stretch in Rio's state parliament. In 2018 he won election to the national Brazilian senate, guaranteeing the family a seat in the nation's upper house until 2026. As a young Rio lawmaker, he established a role for himself as a come-what-may defender of the police. For Flávio, as for his father, any accusation that police might be involved in human rights violations was politically motivated. The family liked to label critics of the police as "defenders of criminals", a common tactic used to undermine efforts to subject Brazilian security providers to the rule of law. Flávio used his position in Rio's legislature to bestow honours upon individual police, often those accused of excesses. In October 2003, not even a full year into his political career, he issued a motion praising a military policeman called Adriano da Nóbrega.

The year 2003 saw Adriano with seven years of police service under his belt. He had made an impressive start to his career, quickly graduating to the BOPE where he was selected for specialist sniper training and received numerous commendations. Famous for the ability to assemble a machine gun in record time, he was something of a hero to his contemporaries – despite, or because of, a reputation for cruelty and violence. However, certain irregularities and a penchant for leading unofficial operations to favelas during the small hours of the night led to a fall from grace and an ignominious transfer from the elite BOPE to a regular police battalion in Rio's North Zone. Here, locals quickly nicknamed Adriano and the small group of officials he worked with as "the garrison of evil". They had a reputation for torturing and extorting money from favela residents.[98]

Flávio Bolsonaro chose this moment to propose a motion praising Nóbrega for "dedication, brilliance and gallantry". Within a month, however, Adriano had been arrested and charged with the murder of a favela resident. Even this development did not curb Flávio's zeal. In 2005 he successfully petitioned to award Adriano the state of Rio's highest honour, the Tiradentes medal, which he delivered personally to the disgraced policeman – inside prison.

Flávio was not the only Bolsonaro to go out of his way to defend Adriano. When his case came to trial in 2005, Jair Bolsonaro took time away from political duties in Brasília to attend the hearing. After Adriano's conviction, Bolsonaro returned to national congress, where he delivered a withering attack on what he perceived as a miscarriage of justice. He blamed the conviction on political pressure, saying that the Rio state government, responding to pressure from Amnesty International, was "punishing for the sake of punishing".[99] A year later, Adriano was acquitted, despite the conclusion of the military police's own internal investigations unit that he had deliberately killed Leandro da Silva for motives of revenge.

THE PERSON CREDITED with bringing together Captain Adriano and the Bolsonaro family is another military policeman called Fabrício Queiroz (no relation to Élcio). Fabrício Queiroz served as an army recruit under Jair Bolsonaro's tutelage in 1984. After leaving the army, Queiroz joined Rio's military police. He was well known and feared by residents in the City of God favela (made famous by the film of the same name). One night in 2003, he and Adriano, who worked together for a time, shot and killed a resident while on patrol. A homicide investigation into the incident remains open today.[100]

Queiroz remained firm friends with Jair Bolsonaro following his departure from the army. Numerous photographs of the pair enjoying moments of intimacy circulate on the internet: Queiroz and Bolsonaro fishing; Queiroz, Bolsonaro and sons at a barbecue and Queiroz, Flávio and Jair enjoying a meal together. In this photo, Queiroz smiles at the camera while making a pistol shape with his thumb and index finger, a pet gesture adopted by Bolsonaro during his campaign.

Queiroz worked for Flávio Bolsonaro for eleven years, between 2007 and 2018, after joining his parliamentary team on secondment from the Military Police. While his role was apparently geared towards providing protection for the young politician, Queiroz has also been described as 'chief of staff' and 'driver'. Essentially, he was Flávio's protector, fixer and right hand man for more than a decade. During these years, a number of Queiroz's friends and relatives also secured positions on the Bolsonaro payroll. These included Adriano da Nóbrega's wife (eleven years on the books – hired and fired at the same time as Queiroz) and mother. Flávio, evidently, believed in protecting Captain Adriano's interests.

The appointment of Nóbrega's immediate family came to light in 2018 when a federal government financial intelligence unit tasked with tackling money laundering, identified suspect movements of funds through both Flávio and Queiroz's accounts. The monitoring process was an extension of the giant national Car Wash corruption investigation, celebrated by the Bolsonaro family in their electoral pledges to make Brazil corruption-free. The movements of money in question included 48 separate cash deposits paid to Flávio in a one-month period totalling $30,000 and a single cheque of $8,000 made out to Jair Bolsonaro's wife.[101]

14 / THE HORNET'S NEST

The revelations triggered an inquiry by prosecutors in Rio. This uncovered compelling evidence to suggest that Bolsonaro and Queiroz operated a brazen scheme to embezzle public funds. The arrangement was absolutely simple and is not uncommon practice in Brazil. A politician hires trusted friends and family to work on his or her team. These individuals – call them ghost employees – do not actually work. They do however, pay their way, by returning a slice of their take, a 'tax', to the politician via a middleman. Evidence collected by prosecutors strongly suggested that in this case the politician was Flávio Bolsonaro, the middleman, Queiroz.

The scheme included Queiroz's daughter, Nathália, a well-known personal trainer in Rio. Nathália joined Flávio's 'team' in 2007 with her father and remained on the books until November 2016, when she signed on as a staff member of Jair Bolsonaro, then federal congressman in Brasília. A reporter writing for *The Intercept* could discover no evidence that Nathália ever even set foot in his office.[102] Like father, like son. Further digging by journalists at Rio's *O Globo* revealed that the Bolsonaro clan had employed a veritable army – more than a hundred – of their own relatives since Jair began his political career in 1991. Many of these, when questioned by reporters, denied ever having worked in public office, despite records to the contrary.[103]

In 2019, officials raided addresses linked to suspect ghost employees of Flávio Bolsonaro. These included President Bolsonaro's ex-wife and former father-in-law. They also searched premises belonging to Queiroz and a chocolate shop co-owned by Flávio Bolsonaro and located in a shopping centre in Barra. Prosecutors alleged that Flávio used the shop to launder part of the $600,000 of public funds they believe he embezzled with Queiroz's assistance.[104]

Flávio's defence was to deny everything and pass the buck to Queiroz. Jair Bolsonaro claimed the $8,000 cheque paid to his wife was part-payment for a debt. Queiroz repeatedly failed to appear for questioning, alleging ill health, and eventually withdrew from public life altogether in 2018. Shortly before disappearing he gave a TV interview, describing himself as an amateur buyer and seller of used cars. Both Bolsonaros – lions against hyenas – accused the media and judiciary of politically motivated bias. Behind the scenes, Flávio and the Bolsonaro family lawyer used every political and legal sleight of hand at their disposal to obstruct the proceedings.[34]

Two longstanding suspect ghost workers were Captain Adriano's wife and mother, who appeared to have made payments to Queiroz totalling 20 per cent of their overall wages. Before he went on the run, intercepted messages sent by Adriano to his wife indicated that he too benefited from the money. He also interfered with the investigation, advising his wife not to appear when requested to give a statement.[105] In April 2020, *The Intercept* published evidence collected by public prosecutors indicating that Flávio Bolsonaro both financed and earned profits from illegal housing built in West Zone favelas, with Adriano acting as go-between and construction manager. One such illegal building, apparently built by another militia, collapsed in 2019 – killing 24 residents.[106] A desire to obstruct these investigations reportedly motivated Jair Bolsonaro's attempts to interfere with the federal police in Rio, triggering the

---

34 On 20 April 2020, a federal court dismissed Flávio Bolsonaro's ninth attempt to halt investigations into his financial activities. The presiding judge said that available evidence strongly implicated criminal materiality and authorship on Flávio's part.

resignation of his Minister of Justice, anti-corruption crusader Sérgio Moro.

Now, however, Adriano was dead. What he knew about the Bolsonaro family would apparently have died with him. When he finally commented about the matter in public, President Bolsonaro declared that in 2005, he had insisted his son award a medal to the imprisoned captain because at the time, the policeman was "a hero". Bolsonaro then drew a perverse parallel between Marielle and Adriano, insisting that all Brazilians had the right to know who ordered both their deaths.[107]

IN JUNE 2020, police located Fabrício Queiroz hiding at a rural property belonging to the Bolsonaro family lawyer. They took him to Rio de Janeiro where he was held in custody. Prosecutors began to interview him about corruption allegations and his relationship to Flávio Bolsonaro. The Bolsonaro family lawyer reportedly claimed to hold information proving that politicians in Rio, who now wanted Queiroz dead, had ordered Adriano's killing

15

BECAUSE THE SHOW WILL GO ON

CAPTAIN ADRIANO HAD A HABIT OF making important friends. Well connected to the Bolsonaro family, for much of his life he had also been intimate with the hot-blooded Garcias. To recap, the Garcia clan are descendants of the celebrated *jogo do bicho* banker, *cúpula* member and Salgueiro samba school patron Miro Garcia. In the early years of this century, Miro and his son Maninho ran *jogo do bicho* and gambling activity across a huge swathe of Rio de Janeiro.

Their own tragedy struck the family in 2004. Unknown attackers shot and killed Maninho outside a 'Body Planet' gym in Barra. His fifteen-year-old son Mirinho, riding on the back of his father's motorbike, survived. Seventy-seven-year-old Miro died of natural causes shortly afterwards, leaving the family with no head and Salgueiro with no patron. During the ensuing power struggle, the family all but destroyed itself. The Garcia clan's devastating trajectory mirrors the legend of Salgueiro's *orixá*, Xangô, who killed his own family through misadventure before committing suicide.

15 / BECAUSE THE SHOW WILL GO ON

Adriano was close to the Garcia family most of his life. He was what is called an *agregado* (extra) in Brazil. His father lived in a rural area where Maninho Garcia owned a large ranch and bred horses. The *bicheiro*'s twin daughters, Shanna and Tamara, were accomplished horsewomen and showjumpers. As a child, Adriano spent weekends and holidays learning to ride at the ranch. The ranch administrator was a trusted friend of Maninho's called Rogério Mesquita. Mesquita was fond of Adriano, who in turn, called him *padrinho* (godfather).[108]

The split in the family arose over a disagreement between Shanna and Tamara, Maninho's twin daughters, following the death of their grandfather Miro. But rapidly shifting alliances and a high body count sometimes made it difficult to identify who was against who. To begin with, Tamara and her little brother Mirinho sided with Rogério Mesquita and their uncle Bid. Shanna, on the other hand, joined forces with and married, Zé Personal, Maninho's former sidekick.

Although Adriano was in prison when Maninho and Miro died, his godfather Mesquita sought him out. Bid needed protection. Could Adriano help? They soon reached an agreement. From his cell and for a monthly fee, Adriano organised Bid's security. He handpicked a team of fourteen active BOPE officers who would, when off duty, provide rotating protection for Bid. The agreement worked well until Adriano left prison. Then Zé Personal, Shanna's husband, convinced him to switch allegiances. Adriano now worked for his godfather's enemies.[109]

After a botched attempt had been made to kill him at the family ranch in 2008, Mesquita sought out detectives. He told them he believed Adriano was behind the attack and that he was working as killer for Shanna Garcia and Zé Personal. Shortly after, someone shot and killed Mesquita on a busy Ipanema shopping street. In 2011, police suspected that Adriano had changed sides *yet again*. This time they investigated him for killing Shanna's husband, Zé Personal. No charges were brought.

This bewildering series of assassinations confirmed one thing – to stay alive, you needed Adriano. In the meantime, he grew in stature and influence. His father occupied Mesquita's land and boasted that anyone who troubled him would have Adriano to reckon with.[110] When the police eventually fired him in 2014, Adriano found lucrative work as Rio's most expensive assassin, charging more than $60,000 per hit. He also applied himself to expanding militia activities and founded The Crime Office.

Subsequent years have not been kind to the Garcia family. Tamara and Shanna had an actual fistfight with each other in 2016. In 2017, Maninho's only son, by now 27-year-old Mirinho, was shot and killed. Homicide investigators at the time said he was the victim of kidnappers. A survivor of the attack says otherwise. In the light of revelations that *bicheiros* paid police not to investigate certain murders, following the failed cover-up of Marielle's assassination, prosecutors began to look at the murder as a possible Crime Office hit. Next on the list was Shanna. In late 2019, as she made her way to a weekly Barra beauty salon appointment, a marksman fired several bullets at her from a moving car. But the first shot failed to discharge properly, alerting her and providing time to shield herself inside her bulletproof BMW.

Shanna immediately accused her sister's ex-husband of orchestrating the assassination attempt. According to Shanna, Bernardo Bello, married to Tamara for a decade, had run the family business for years. In control of the Garcia inventory and *jogo do bicho* activities, he was supposed to pay a monthly sum to the rest of the family. But he no longer did, and had even threatened her after the 2016 altercation with Tamara. Shanna also believed that Bernardo ordered Mirinho's death and told detectives that he had an interest in seeing the "death of the whole family".[111]

Bernardo Bello was involved with Tamara at the time her father died and subsequently spent time living under the Garcia family roof. He has *jogo do bicho* pedigree – his godfather is the all-powerful Captain Guimarães, military regime torturer, patron of Vila Isabel samba school, *cúpula* member and LIESA founder. Bello was also friends with Adriano and had influence at Vila Isabel. While vice-president of the school, he granted Adriano a special 'director' pass to allow him to parade in the sambadrome.[112] Such passes carry great worth. By parading with a samba school, while deeply involved in militia and Crime Office activity, Adriano demonstrated just how adept he was at navigating the different galaxies of Rio's criminal universe. With shifting power dynamics, at a time when the surviving founder members of the *jogo do bicho cúpula* were beginning to pass their business empires over to heirs, and militias were expanding all over the city, the social status and protection provided by a samba school remained significant.

Certain members of the troubled Garcia family recognised this all too well and for this reason, were trying to return to Salgueiro. But the school was also riven by conflict. Regina Celi, Shanna's supporter and popular president of Salgueiro for more than ten years, had been ousted after a protracted, bitter judicial battle. The Garcia family was no longer welcome there. Nevertheless, at the 2020 Carnival, a few weeks after Adriano's death, Shanna's uncle Bid walked alongside Salgueiro as the school entered the sambadrome on the second night of the parade. But Bid did not wear a Salgueiro shirt, nor did he carry a pass belonging to the school. Rather, he used an official LIESA credential to get access to the procession.[113] Such accreditation is difficult to come by and meant that the *cúpula* of the *jogo do bicho*, who run LIESA, were aware of Bid's presence at Carnival. And by walking with Salgueiro without the school's authorisation, Bid was effectively joining its parade without permission.

After leaving the sambadrome, Bid arrived back at his Barra residence at 4.30am. The street replicated so many others in Rio's favourite nouveau-riche neighbourhood. It sounds crass to say they all look the same, but they often do. Impersonal luxury high-rise blocks face off over parking lots, fences and security gates. The sterile glass and steel architecture guarantees most inhabitants a sense of security.

Garcia family members are never safe, however. Bid had opened the door of his mini-van and was about to pay his driver. When a crackle of automatic weapon fire shattered Barra's early morning peace, neighbours assumed a young carnival drunk was letting off a last salvo of fireworks. They were wrong. A hooded man had crossed the road and fired more than twenty shots at Maninho's brother. Bid died on the spot, cash in hand, feet sticking ignominiously out of the vehicle. According to witnesses, two bodyguards following him in a car made no attempt to intervene.[114]

Nothing was accidental about the timing of the attack. Bid had just attended Salgueiro's parade. The murder of such a prominent Garcia family member during Carnival carried a lethal message for those remaining, especially Shanna. *Stay away from Salgueiro*. It also served to remind the city that while Adriano might have won power and influence with his talent for death, professional killers come easy in Rio. At the end of the day, Adriano was just another gun for hire.

CAPTAIN GUIMARÃES OF VILA ISABEL AND ANÍSIO OF BEIJA-FLOR also attended Carnival 2020. The two aging *bicheiros* no longer needed to worry about feigning ill-health for the authorities. Their 2012 Operation Hurricane convictions and sentences were lost, possibly forever, in a finely honed labyrinth of appeals, "ill health" and judicial chicanery. Their main concern was the future. Accordingly, both men had brought their sons on board. Anísio was grooming Gabriel David, twenty-two year old South Zone *playboy* and influencer, to take on Beija-Flor. Captain Guimarães had appointed his heir Luiz, also twenty-two, vice-president of Vila Isabel.

In 2019, Luiz informed reporters, "We are primordial (sic) for Carnival to exist in the way that it does. I, particularly, want to continue with this."[115]

Father to son, the *cúpula* of the *jogo do bicho* was guaranteeing the future. Everything was changing. Everything would stay the same.

AFTERWORD

IN 2020, JAIR BOLSONARO FLOUTED COVID-19 restrictions to attend regular demonstrations where a few hundred supporters, clad in Brazilian yellow and green, railed against democracy and called for a return to military rule. In electing this person, Brazilians chose a career politician with no proven achievements, except those of maintaining his position, establishing his sons in politics and advocating the worst excesses of the military dictatorship.

Chronic violence, insecurity and human rights abuses are entrenched by Brazil's inability to tackle these same issues. Successive national governments have palmed off responsibility for public safety onto state administrations. Powerful elements operating within, or with the support of, the security apparatus, consistently and actively undermine rule of law. Bolsonaro's rise to prominence on a pro-violence, anti-politics ticket was a logical product of these systemic faults. That Brazilians chose *en masse* to side with him, is a failure of democracy.

While Bolsonaro denied coronavirus and undermined his country's constitution, Brazilian law enforcers celebrated the April 2020 capture, in Mozambique, of a man said to be, according to headlines, "Brazil's biggest cocaine supplier".[116] Minister of Justice at the time, Sergio Moro claimed that the man, called Fuminho, was number two in the PCC, São Paulo's prison-based gang. The PCC, *Primeiro Comando da Capital* [Capital First Command], was born in the aftermath of a 1992 prison massacre when São Paulo military police slaughtered 111 unarmed detainees in their cells. Between 2000 and 2020 prison numbers in Brazil tripled, and consequently, so did the power and reach of the PCC.[35]

Whenever the international press cites the PCC as Brazil's most powerful gang, I recall a 2014 conversation with a respected member of São Paulo's state Truth Commission. Discussing law and order in the city, he informed me it was common knowledge that "whenever the PCC move guns or drugs around, they do so with a ROTA escort" – the ROTA are São Paulo's BOPE. No organised crime exists in Brazil without state support. In turn, state-entrenched organised crime needs narratives and smokescreens to hide behind.

During the same month that the Brazilian authorities trumpeted the capture of Fuminho, they granted an international travel permit to a man who, according to the country's own federal police, heads "a gigantic criminal organisation, rooted in the Brazilian state apparatus".[117] In April 2020, the Brazilian Supreme Court granted Anísio David – founding member of

---

35 With an increase from 232,755 in 2000 to 690,722 in 2018. Brazil currently has the third highest prison population in the world. *World Prison Population List* 12th Ed. (ICPR).

the *cúpula* of the *jogo do bicho*, patron of Beija-Flor, sentenced to 48 years in prison – special permission to travel to Uruguay and Argentina, countries where he is known to own shares in casinos.[118] Neither criminal convictions, nor a peaking pandemic, could contain the capo of the *jogo do bicho* within national borders. Under President Jair Bolsonaro, the eighty-two-year-old was thriving.

FURTHER READING

Readers interested in discovering more about Rio de Janeiro immediately before the 2016 Olympics can refer to *Rio de Janeiro* by Luiz Eduardo Soares. Luiz Eduardo is a respected scholar and activist, briefly in charge of Rio's police forces in the 1990s. Juliana Barbassa also captures the pre-mega-event madness in *Dancing with the Devil in the City of God*. In *Nemesis,* Misha Glenny explores Rocinha favela and the life-story of its most-wanted gang leader. For keen analysis of Rio's intersecting dynamics of crime, poverty and politics I highly recommend Enrique Desmond Arias' *Drugs and Democracy in Rio de Janeiro*. *Picture a Favela* is a beautiful graphic novel depicting Maurício Hora's life in Providência. *Can Art Change the World?* describes the story of JR's trajectory, including his work in Rio.

Duke University Press publishes some excellent books about Brazil, including *Laws of Chance* by Amy Chazkel, which helped me untangle the long tentacles of the jogo do bicho. Bryan McCann traces the arduous and difficult path of favela activism in *Hard Times in the Marvellous City*. For a comprehensive recent history of the country, look no further than *Brazil: A Biography* by Heloisa Starling and Lilia Schwarcz. I read *The Brazilian People,* Darcy Ribeiro's magnum opus in Portuguese, but luckily a translation is available.

Portuguese speakers and Brazilianists: explore the fantastic work of Valério Meinel! All his books are available on the website Estante Virtual, sourced from second-hand bookshops across Brazil. For keeping up-to-date with Marielle Franco investigations and organised crime reporting in the country, the writing of investigative journalists Vera Magalhães and Chico Otávio (*O Globo*), Rafael Soares (*Extra*) and reporting of *The Intercept Brasil* and *Piauí* magazine is indispensible. For citizen journalism directly from the favelas, *Rio On Watch* (www.rioonwatch.org) is a comprehensive online resource.

SELECT BIBLIOGRAPHY

English

Arias, Desmond Enrique. *Drugs and Democracy in Rio de Janeiro*, (University of North Carolina Press 2006).

Barbassa, Juliana. *Dancing with the Devil in the City of God* (Simon and Schuster 2016).

Chazkel, Amy. *Laws of Chance* (Duke University Press 2012).

Human Rights Watch. *Lethal Force. Police Violence and Public Security in Rio de Janeiro and São Paulo* (2009).

Diniz, André and Hora, Maurício. *Picture a Favela* (SelfMadeHero 2012).

Farris Thompson, Robert. *Flash of the Spirit* (First Vintage 1984).

Gay, Robert. *Bruno, Conversations with a Brazilian Drug Dealer* (Duke University Press 2015).

Glenny, Misha. *Nemesis* (Bodley Head 2015).

Johnson, Paul. *Secrets, Gossip and Gods* (Oxford University Press 2005).

JR. *Can Art Change the World?* (Phaidon 2019).

McCann, Bryan. *Hard Times in the Marvellous City* (Duke University Press 2014).

Ribeiro, Darcy. *The Brazilian People*. Trans: Gregory Rabassa (University of Florida Center for Latin American Studies 2000).

Rose, R.S. *The Unpast* (Ohio University Press 2005).

Saviano, Roberto. *Zero, zero, zero* (Penguin 2015).

Schwarcz, Lilia and Starling, Heloisa. *Brazil: A Biography* (Penguin 2019).

Soares, Luiz Eduardo. *Rio de Janeiro* (Penguin 2016).

Vaz, Matthew. *The Jackpot Mentality* (Colombia University 2011).

Vianna, Hermano. *The Mystery of Samba* (The University of North Carolina Press 1999).

Portuguese

Bial, Pedro. *Roberto Marinho* (Jorge Zahar Editor 2005).

Cabral, Sérgio. *Escolas de Samba do Rio de Janeiro* (Lazuli 2011).

Costallat, Benjamim. *Mistérios do Rio* (Biblioteca Carioca 1990).

DaMatta, Roberto and Soárez, Elena. *Águias, Burros e Borboletas* (Rocco 1999).

do Rio, João. *A alma encantadora das ruas* (Companhia das Letras 1997)

Gaspari, Elio. *A Ditadura Escancarada* (Companhia das Letras 2002).

Guerra, Cláudio/Netto Marcelo/Medeiros Rogério. *Memórias de uma Guerra Suja*, (Topbooks 2012).

Meinel, Valério. *Porque Claudia Lessin Vai Morrer* (2 Ed. Editora Codecri, Rio 1978).

Meinel, Valério. *Avestruz, Águia e… Cocaína* (L&PM, 1994 2nd Ed).

Otávio, Chico and Jupiara, Aloy. *Os poroēs da Contravenção* (Record 2015).

Prandi, Reginaldo. *Mitologia dos Orixás* (Companhia das Letras 2000).

Resende e Soares, *Cocaína* (Casa da Palavra, Rio de Janeiro, 2006).

Ribeiro, Darcy. *O Povo Brasileiro* (Companhia das Letras 1995).

Trinta, Joãzinho. *Psicánalise Beija-Flor* (Aoutra 1985).

Ventura, Zuenir. *Cidade Partida* (Companhia das Letras 1997).

ENDNOTES

1 *Bolsonaro diz que policial que mata '10, 15 ou 20' deve ser condecorado.* Jussara Soares in O Globo, 28 August 2018.

2 According to *The Washington Post.*

3 *Lethal Force. Police violence and public security in Rio de Janeiro and São Paulo.* (Human Rights Watch 2009) p27.

4 Achille Mbembe in *Necropolitics*, Duke University 2019.

5 *Dentro do Pesadelo.* Fernando de Barros e Silva, Piauí, May 2020.

6 *Rio elege maior bancada policial de sua história.* Lucas Vettorazzo in Folha de São Paulo, 9 October 2018.

7 Described by Maurício in the biographical graphic novel *Picture a Favela*, André Diniz and Maurício Hora (SelfMadeHero 2012).

8 Author translation from Benjamim Costallat, *Mistérios do Rio* (Biblioteca Carioca, Rio de Janeiro, 1990) p.35.

9 Author translation of Lima Barreto, *Pólvora e Cocaína*, 1915 in *Cocaína*, Resende e Soares, Casa da Palavra, Rio de Janeiro, 2006.

10 For a detailed history of the formation and rationale behind the Comando Vermelho see Gay, Robert. *Bruno, Conversations with a Brazilian Drug Dealer* (Duke University Press 2015).

11 *Dancing with the Devil* (Jon Blair 2009).

12 *Sargento da Marinha é preso com dez fuzis*. Paolla Serra in Extra, 28 November 2014.

13 *Armas roubadas ou desviadas de empresas de segurança somam 17,6 mil*, Antonio Werneck in Extra, 22 May 2016.

14 *Após defender legalização de paramilitares no passado, Bolsonaro agora se diz desinteressado no assunto.* Marco Grilo and Thiago Prado in O Globo, 8 July 2018.

15 Arias, Desmond Enrique. *Drugs and Democracy in Rio de Janeiro*, (University of North Carolina Press 2006) p.52.

16 *Policial preso diz, em depoimento, que Estado-Maior da PM recebia propina dos batalhões.* Ana Claudia Costa in O Globo, 22 September 2014.

17 *Após a instalação das UPPs, prédios voltam a abrir as janelas.* Vera Araújo in O Globo 24 March 2013.

18 Author translation from Benjamim Costallat, No Bairro da Cocaína, *Mistérios do Rio* (Biblioteca Carioca, 1990) p.22.

19 Author translation from Valério Meinel, *Porque Claudia Lessin Vai Morrer* (2 Ed. Editora Codecri, Rio 1978) p.49.

20 Author translation from Valério Meinel, *op.cit.* 1978, p.308.

21 Author translation from Benjamim Costallat, op.cit, 1990, p.22.

22 Roberto Saviano, *Zero, zero, zero,* Chapter 5 (Penguin 2015).

23 *Italian mafia's cocaine trafficking leaves trail of drug devastation among poor of Brazil*, The Guardian, 26 June 2015.

24 Alex Perry, *Cocaine Highway* (Newsweek Insights 2014).

25 Author translation from Valério Meinel, *Avestruz, Águia e... Cocaína* (L&PM, 1994 2nd Ed) p.172.

26 For further reading on the early history of the *jogo do bicho* see Amy Chazkel, *Laws of Chance* (Duke University Press 2012).

27 R.S. Rose, *The Unpast* (Ohio University Press 2005) p.233.

28 In Zuenir Ventura, *Cidade Partida* (Companhia das Letras 1997) p.48–52.

29 Matthew Vaz, *The Jackpot Mentality* (Colombia University 2011) p.210. This is a fascinating comparison of New York's numbers rackets and the *jogo do bicho*, available on line.

30 In Elio Gaspari, *A Ditadura Escancarada* (Companhia das Letras 2002).

31 Chico Otávio and Aloy Jupiara, series of articles for O Globo published in October 2013 and then in their book *Os poroēs da Contravenção* (Record 2015).

32 Interview conducted in 2013 during research for a Cambridge University Masters dissertation.

33 *Cordões* in João do Rio, *A alma encantadora das ruas* (Companhia das Letras 1997).

34 Hermano Vianna, *The Mystery of Samba* (The University of North Carolina Press 1999) p.118.

35 Paul Johnson, *Secrets Gossip and Gods* (Oxford University Press 2005).

36 Sérgio Cabral, *Escolas de Samba do Rio de Janeiro* (Lazuli 2011) p.223.

37 Sérgio Cabral, *Escolas de Samba do Rio de Janeiro* (Lazuli 2011) p.231 and p.237.

ENDNOTES

38 Simone Soares, *O Jogo do Bicho* (Bertrand Brasil 1993).

39 Author translation from Sérgio Cabral *Escolas de Samba do Rio de Janeiro* (Lazuli 2011).

40 Aloy Jupiara and Chico Otavio, *Os Porões da Contravenção* (Record 2015) p.193.

41 In Boni's autobiography. José Bonifácio de Oliveira Sobrinho, *O livro do Boni* (Casa da Palavra 2011).

42 Pedro Bial in the biography *Roberto Marinho* (Jorge Zahar Editor 2005).

43 Rio Journal; One Man's Political Views Color Brazil's TV Eye. *New York Times,* 12 January 1987.

44 Author translation from Darcy Ribeiro *O Povo Brasileiro* (Companhia das Letras 1995) (p. 207).

45 Boni in *O livro do Boni* pp.402–403. (Casa da Palavra 2011).

46 Boni in interview for GloboNews, November 2011.

47 Unsourced interview found at: A verdade emfim! Edição do debate do 1989 na Rede Globo. https://www.youtube.com/watch?v=9fDbbxMTJg8 Accessed December 2019.

48 Robert Farris Thompson, *Flash of the Spirit* (First Vintage 1984) p.85 and Prandi, Reginaldo. *Mitologia dos Orixás* (Companhia das Letras 2000).

49 *Rogério Mesquita, amigo de Maninho, é assassinado, à luz do dia, em disputa pelo espólio de bicheiro.* Marcos Nunes in Extra, 29 January 2009.

50 *Vice-presidente do Salgueiro está lúcido e orientado; ele levou três tiros ao sair de escritório de deputado estadual.* Extra, 15 January 2014.

51 As confirmed by the 2009 Federal Police investigation, Operation Gladiator.

52 Declan Hill. The Fix: Soccer and Organized Crime (McLelland & Stewart 2010) p.292.

53 Author translation from the judgement of *Operation Hurricane* 2012 pp 442–444.

54 *Operation Hurricane* 2012 p.541 and p.542.

55 Author translation from *Revista Beija-Flor de Nilópolis* No. 13 March 2014.

56 *O livro do Boni* (Casa da Palavra 2011) pp.402–403.

57 Information available on the website of the Instituto Brasileiro Giovanni Falcone (www.ibgf.org.br) and quoted in the final report of the 2004 Brazilian senate investigation into illegal gambling *Relatório Final CPI dos Bingos* (2006) p.144.

58 Judge Walter Maeirovitch in *Os Porões da Contravenção* (Record 2015) pp.134–135.

59 Author translation from Darcy Ribeiro, *O Povo Brasileiro* (Companhia das Letras 1995) p.120.

60 Guerra in *Memórias de uma Guerra Suja*, Cláudio Guerra/Marcelo Netto/Rogério Medeiros (Topbooks 2012) p.198.

61 *Delegado abriu as portas do jogo no ES para Guimarães.* Chico Otávio and Aloy Jupiara in O Globo, 7 October 2013.

62 Cláudio Guerra in statement to the National Truth Commission July 2014.

63 Author translation from *Memórias de uma Guerra Suja*, Cláudio Guerra/Marcelo Netto/Rogério Medeiros (Topbooks, 2012) p.198.

64 *O general de Temer rejeita a Comissão da Verdade.* Marco Weisheimmer in Outras Mídias, 25 May 2016.

65 Paulo Malhães in statement given to the National Truth Commission March 2014.

66 *Chefe do GSI nomeado por Temer é de ala que vê MST com preocupação*, Folha de São Paulo 30 May 2016.

67 Torturra's article can be found online https://cascadebesouro.wordpress.com/2013/06/05/o-ficaralho/. Accessed December 2019.

68 Bruno Torturra describes his experiences of the protests and the birth of Media Ninja in an extended article, *Olho da Rua,* published in Piauí magazine, December 2013.

69 Leader article published in O Globo, 6 December 2013.

70 *Jonas Tadeu: advogado ganha fama com caso de morteiro em protesto*, Sérgio Ramalho in O Globo 13 February 2014.

71 Social media post by Bruno Torturra, February 2014.

72 *The Labyrinth of the Marielle Franco Case*, Amnesty International, 11 February 2019.

73 *A Metástase, O assassinato de Marielle Franco e o avanço das milícias no Rio*, Allan de Abreu for Piauí magazine, March 2019.

74 *Exclusivo: Testemunha envolve vereador miliciano no assassinato de Marielle Franco*, Antônio Werneck for O Globo, 8 March 2018.

75 *Em carta, miliciano delatado no caso de Marielle nega acusações.* Bruna Fantti in O Dia, 10 May 2018.

76 *Caso Marielle: Grupo de matadores de aluguel formado por policiais é novo alvo das investigaçães.* Chico Otávio and Vera Araujo for O Globo, 19 August 2018.

77 *Exclusivo: miliciano acusa cúpula da Polícia Civil de acobertar assassinatos or contraventores do Rio.* Chico Otávio and Vera Araujo for O Globo, 1 November 2018.

78 *PM Ronnie Lessa, preso acusado de matar Marielle, é conhecido por ser exímio atirador e por sua frieza.* Chico Otávio, Vera Araujo and Artur Leal in O Globo, 12 March 2019.

79 *PM Ronnie Lessa, preso acusado de matar Marielle, é conhecido por ser exímio atirador e por sua frieza.* Chico Otávio, Vera Araujo and Artur Leal in O Globo, 12 March 2019.

80 *Não lembro desse cara diz Bolsonaro sobre vizinho suspeito de matar Marielle.* Leandro Colon in Folha de São Paulo, 13 March 2019.

81 *Caso Marielle: suspeito entrou em condomínio alegando ir à casa de Bolsonaro, diz porteiro.* Jornal Nacional, TV Globo, 29 October 2019. Accessible on globo.com.

82 Accessed via the Twitter feed of journalist Marlos Ápyus @apyus.

83 *Ministério Público diz que porteiro deu informação falsa ao citar Bolsonaro no caso Marielle.* Ana Luiza Albuquerque and Italo Nogueira in Estado de São Paulo, 30 October 2019.

84 *Apuração do caso Marielle levou 11 meses para expor menção à casa de Bolsonaro.* Marina Lang, Italo Nogueira and Júlia Barbon. Folha de São Paulo, 5 November 2019.

85 *Bolsonaro diz ter acessado gravação do condomínio antes que fosse adulterada.* O Antagonista, 2 November 2019.

86 *Exclusivo: O pacto é eu não interferer e eles não interferirem aqui mas eu engulo sapo.* O Antagonista, 11 November 2019.

87 *Advogado de Bolsonaro sonegou informação sobre audio, diz diretor da TV Globo.* Mônica Bergamo in Folha de São Paulo, 4 November 2019.

88 *Perícia oficial não foi acionada para examiner gravação no condomínio de Bolsonaro.* O Antagonista, 2 November 2019

89 *Caso Marielle: Porteiro volta atrás e afirma que errou ao dizer que havia falado com Seu Jair.* G1 Website, 20 November 2019.

90 *Opinião de Bolsonaro sobre morte de Marielle seria polemica demais, diz assessor.* Thais Bilenky in Folha de São Paulo, 15 March 2018.

91 *Caso Marielle: Bolsonaro revela por que não se pronuncia sobre assassinato.* Paulo Cappelli in O Dia 20 March 2018.

92 *Milícia, bingo e venda de água: os negocios do PM acusado de matar Marielle.* Flávio Costa and Sergio Ramalho for UOL, 16 September 2019.

93 *PM acusado de matar Marielle se envolveu com bicheiro.* Bonde, 13 March 2019.

94 Flávio Costa, UOL, 11 December 2019.

95 *MP do Rio recebe informação do Disque-Denúncia com plano para assassinar promotora do Caso Marielle.* Vera Araújo in O Globo, 31 January 2020.

96 Described by Globo's Fantástico programme on 16 February 2020.

97 *Adriano da Nóbrega, suspeito de envolvimento no caso Marielle, é morto em operação policial na Bahia.* Beatriz Jucá in El País Brasil, 9 February 2020.

98 *A vida e a morte de Adriano da Nóbrega.* Rafael Soares in Época, 14 February 2020.

99 Speech given by Jair Bolsonaro at congress in Brasília, 27 October 2005.

100 *Homicídio cometido por Queiroz e miliciano está há 16 anos sem solução.* Leandro Resende in Veja 16 December 2019.

101 *COAF aponta que Flávio Bolsonaro recebeu 48 depósitos suspeitos em 1 mês, no total de R$96 mil.* Arthur Guimarães e Paulo Renato Soares, Jornal Nacional.

102 *Documentos provam que Nathália Queiroz – a assessora de Jair Bolsonaro na câmara – nunca pisou lá.* Amanda Audi, 1 March 2019, The Intercept Brasil.

103 *Em 28 anos, clã Bolsonaro nomeou 102 pessoas com laços familiares.* O Globo, 4 August 2019.

104 *Flávio Bolsonaro movimentou R$2,2 milhões em imóveis e loja de chocolate; entenda.* Alice Cravo, Bernardo Mello, Juliana Castro e Juliana Del Piva in O Globo, 20 December 2019.

105 *Familia de miliciano repassou a Queiroz quase 20% do salário no gabinete de Flávio Bolsonaro, diz MP.* Bernardo Mello, Juliana Castro e Juliana Dal Piva in O Globo, 19 December 2019.

106 *"Pico do tamanho de um cometa".* Sérgio Ramalho in The Intercept Brasil, 25 April 2020.

107 *Bolsonaro diz que mandou condecorar Adriano em 2005 e afirma que, na época, o miliciano era um "heroi".* Caroline Heringer and Thais Arbet in O Globo, 15 February 2020.

108 *A vida e a morte de Adriano da Nóbrega.* Rafael Soares in Época, 14 February 2020.

109 *Ex-capitão Adriano da Nóbrega já chefiou escolta de bicheiro morto ao deixar Sapucaí.* Rafael Soares in O Globo, 1 March 2020.

110 *A vida e a morte de Adriano da Nóbrega.* Rafael Soares in Época, 14 February 2020.

111 *Shanna Garcia acusa ex-cunhado pelo assassinato de tio ao deixar a Sapucaí.* Extra 2 March 2020.

112 *Relações com Adriano da Nóbrega e saída de Sabrina Sato: as polemicas envolvendo o homem forte da Vila Isabel.* Caroline Heringer and Rafael Soares in Extra, 23 February 2020.

113 *Bicheiro assassinado desfilou no Salgueiro com credencial de liga das escolas de samba.* Caroline Heringer in O Globo, 27 February 2020.

114 *Irmão de Maninho foi morto um mês após ser testemunha em investigação de atentado contra Shanna Garcia.* Marcos Nunes and Rafael Nascimento da Silva in Extra, 26 February 2020.

115 *Filhos de patronos de escolas de samba ligados ao jogo do bicho assumem Carnaval.* Rafael Galdo and Renan Rodrigues in O Globo, 20 January 2019.

116 *Man believed to be Brazil's biggest cocaine supplier arrested in Mozambique.* AFP in The Guardian, 14 April 2020.

117 Operation Hurricane judgement, 2012 (pp442–444).

118 *STF autoriza viagem do bicheiro Anísio, presidente de honra da Beija Flor, ao Uruguai e Argentina.* Chico Otávio in O Globo, 3 April 2020.

119 In *Parting Shots* compiled by Matthew Parris and Andrew Bryson (Penguin 2011).

"*Nothing By Accident* sees Damian Platt write with empathy, wisdom and verve to unpack the chaotic soul of Rio de Janeiro, one of the world's most iconic and dangerous cities. Amidst the ferment, he reveals fascinating connections at the very heart of Carioca life in a remarkable exposé that pieces together a history of institutionalised oppression, corruption and brutality, the cocaine trade, gambling and even samba into a startling (and disturbing) portrait of a society at war with itself. Essential reading."

– Patrick Neate

"*Nothing by Accident* is a gripping account of life in Rio de Janeiro that goes deep into the experience of the city and the often poorly understood connections between the criminal underworld, political leaders, and the media and entertainment industries. This is perhaps the most complete narrative account of Rio de Janeiro in English since Alma Guillermoprieto's *Samba* three decades ago. This well written and engaging book offers much for casual readers and travellers who want to understand the city better and for specialists seeking to deepen their knowledge."

– Enrique Desmond Arias,
author of *Drugs and Democracy in Rio de Janeiro*

Printed in Great Britain
by Amazon